MW00648157

'Oppenheimer offers brilliant insights, sage advice and entertaining anecdotes. Anyone wishing to understand how financial markets behave – and misbehave – should read this book now.'

—Stephen D. King, economist and author of *Grave New World: The End of Globalisation, the Return of History.*

'Peter has always been one of the masters of dissecting financial markets performance into an understandable narrative, and in this book, he pulls together much of his great thinking and style from his career, and it should be useful for anyone trying to understand what drives markets, especially equities.'

—Lord Jim O'Neill, Chair Chatham House

'A deeply insightful analysis of market cycles and their drivers that really does add to our practical understanding of what moves markets and long-term investment returns.'

—Keith Skeoch, CEO Standard Life Aberdeen

'This book eloquently blends the author's vast experience with behavioural finance insights to document and understand financial booms and busts. The book should be a basic reading for any student of finance.'

—Elias Papaioannou, Professor of Economics, London Business School

'This is an excellent book, capturing the insights of a leading market practitioner within the structured analytical framework he has developed over many years. It offers a lively and unique perspective on how markets work and where they are headed.'

—Huw Pill, Senior Lecturer, Harvard Business School

'The Long Good Buy is an excellent introduction to understanding the cycles, trends and crises in financial markets over the past 100 years. Its purpose is to help investors assess risk and the probabilities of different outcomes. It is lucidly written in a simple logical way, requires no mathematical expertise and draws on an amazing collection of historical data and research. For me it is the best and most comprehensive introduction to the subject that exists.'

—Lord Brian Griffiths, Chairman - Centre for Enterprise, Markets and Ethics, Oxford

The Long Good Buy

The Long Good Buy

Analysing Cycles in Markets

Peter C. Oppenheimer

WILEY

This edition first published 2020

Registered office
John Wiley & Sons Ltd, The Atrium, Southern Gate, Chichester, West Sussex, PO19 8SQ, United Kingdom

For details of our global editorial offices, for customer services and for information about how to apply for permission to reuse the copyright material in this book please see our website at www.wiley.com.

Library of Congress Cataloging-in-Publication Data
Names: Oppenheimer, Peter C., author.
Title: The long good buy : analysing cycles in markets / Peter Oppenheimer.
Description: Chichester, West Sussex, United Kingdom : John Wiley & Sons, 2020. | Includes bibliographical references and index.
Identifiers: LCCN 2020001577 (print) | LCCN 2020001578 (ebook) | ISBN 9781119688976 (cloth) | ISBN 9781119688983 (adobe pdf) | ISBN 9781119689003 (epub)
Subjects: LCSH: Business cycles. | Investments. | Finance.
Classification: LCC HB3720 .O67 2020 (print) | LCC HB3720 (ebook) | DDC 338.5/42—dc23
LC record available at https://lccn.loc.gov/2020001577
LC ebook record available at https://lccn.loc.gov/2020001578

Cover Design: Wiley
Cover Image: JDawnInk/DigitalVision Vectors/Getty Images

Set in 11.5/14 STIX Two Text by SPi Global, Chennai

Printed in Great Britain by CPI Antony Rowe, UK

V411108_061120

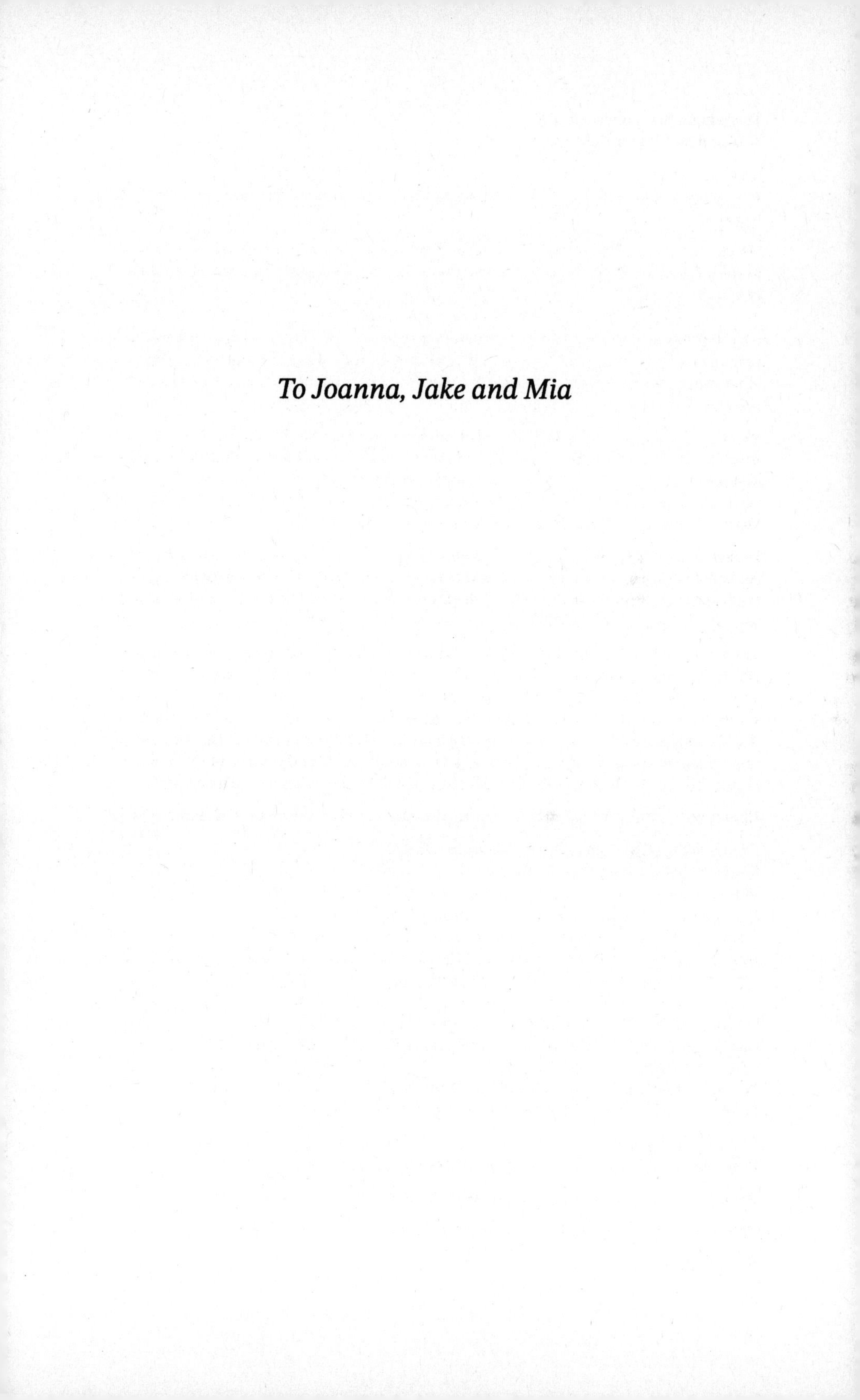

To Joanna, Jake and Mia

Contents

Acknowledgements

This book is about economic and financial market cycles and the factors that affect them.

It refers to, and reflects, much of the work that I have developed, together with my team, since the mid-1980s. I have been lucky enough to have worked with many incredible colleagues since then, and I have benefited from countless conversations with clients, all of which has helped develop my understanding of economies and markets and the factors that shape and drive them. Their influence has very much shaped the ideas and thoughts in this book.

I owe a huge debt of gratitude to all the people at Goldman Sachs who have worked closely with me in the Macro Research group. I would particularly like to thank Sharon Bell, my close colleague for 25 years; she has been instrumental to much of the work reflected in this book and it could not have been written without her. Christian Mueller-Glissmann also made a major contribution to many of the ideas and frameworks reflected in the book and in the analysis of Goldman Sachs Strategy Research over the past decade. Both have been a constant source of innovative ideas and personal support.

A number of other colleagues in my team at Goldman Sachs have worked on, and helped to develop, many of the ideas in the book. Anders Nielsen and Jessica Binder Graham coauthored our framework on Equity Risk Premia and the DDM model mentioned in the book and discussed in an article in the *Journal of Portfolio Management*.[1] I would also like to thank current members of my team – Lilia Peytavin, Guillaume Jaisson and Alessio Rizzi – for their contributions to the book and for their ideas, constant dedication and hard work; I am also very grateful to Guillaume Jaisson for preparing and developing exhibits in the book.

Thanks also go to colleagues who have read and commented on drafts of the book: Jessica Binder Graham, Paul Smith and Brian Rooney. My other long-standing colleagues in the strategy team at Goldman Sachs – David Kostin in New York, Tim Moe in Hong Kong and Kathy Matsui in Tokyo – have been a constant source of ideas and enthusiasm, as has Steve Strongin, the global head of research at Goldman Sachs, who kindly supported and encouraged me in writing this book and has been a major influence on my thinking.

I am very grateful to Loretta Sunnucks at Goldman Sachs for editing the manuscript and for her tireless patience and invaluable suggestions and input throughout the process. I would like to thank former colleagues who have read and commented on the drafts. My previous heads of research – Lord Jim O'Neil, former chief economist at Goldman Sachs and chairman of Goldman Sachs Investment Management, and Keith Skeoch, CEO at Standard Life – have both been major influences and a source of ideas. I would also like to thank Huw Pill, senior lecturer at the Harvard Business School, Elias Papaioannou, professor of economics at the London Business School, and Lord Brian Griffiths, Chairman of the Centre for

[1] Binder, J., Nielsen, A.E.B., and Oppenheimer, P. (2010). Finding fair value in global equities: Part I. *Journal of Portfolio Management*, 36(2), 80–93.

Enterprise, Markets and Ethics, for their insights. In particular, my thanks go to Stephen King, senior advisor to HSBC, for providing invaluable suggestions and for his detailed guidance and support.

Finally, I would like to thank my wonderful wife, Joanna, and my children, Jake and Mia, who are a constant source of inspiration and joy for me.

About the Author

Peter C. Oppenheimer has 35 years of experience working as a research analyst. He is chief global equity strategist and head of Macro Research in Europe for Goldman Sachs. Prior to joining Goldman Sachs he worked as managing director and chief investment strategist at HSBC and was previously head of European strategy at James Capel. Prior to that, he was chief economic strategist at Hambros Bank. Peter began his career as an economist at Greenwells in 1985. He enjoys cycling and painting.

Preface

This book is about economic and financial market cycles and the factors that affect them. The motivation for writing it has been my long-standing fascination with how repeated patterns of behaviour and market cycles seem to exist despite the enormous changes that have occurred in economies, society and technology over time.

Over the past 35 years of my career, inflation expectations have collapsed, we have entered the longest economic cycle in the US for 150 years and about a quarter of government bonds globally have a negative yield. Over the same period there have been dramatic advances in technology and changes in political conditions. Alongside this, there have been three major recessions (in most economies) and several financial crises.

Despite all the political, economic and social changes that have occurred since the mid-1980s, there have been repeated patterns in economies and financial markets. These patterns can be traced back over 100 years of market performance as financial market cycles react to, and anticipate, economic cycles. But they are also driven to some extent by changes in sentiment and psychology.

Understanding how humans process information and deal with both risks and opportunities can help to explain the existence of cycles in financial markets.

Although knowing where we are in a cycle in real time is difficult, and forecasting near-term returns is complex, there is useful information that investors can use to help them assess the risks and understand the probabilities of different outcomes.

The idea behind this book is not to present models that predict the future but rather to identify the signals and relationships between economic and financial cycles that tend to exist. I try to develop some practical tools and frameworks for assessing the risks and potential rewards as an investment cycle evolves, and highlight some of the indicators and warning signs that might point to a rising probability of an impending inflection point, either up or down, in market direction.

Finally, I try to identify ways in which some of the 'typical' relationships between economic and financial variables have changed over time and, in particular, since the financial crisis.

Recognising and understanding these changing conditions and how they affect investment opportunities can help investors to enhance their returns and, in equity markets in particular, enjoy a 'long good buy'.

The book is split into three parts:

1. **Lessons from the past:** What cycles look like and what drives them
2. **The nature and causes of bull and bear markets:** What triggers them and what to look out for
3. **Lessons for the future:** A focus on the post-financial-crisis era; what has changed and what it means for investors

Part I starts with a description of some of the major changes that have taken place in economic conditions, politics and technology since the 1980s.

Chapter 1 describes how, despite these changes, bear markets, financial crises and crashes, bull markets and bubbles have come and gone and familiar patterns have repeated themselves despite significantly varying circumstances. The chapter discusses the reasons for these cycles, including the impact of human sentiment and psychology.

Chapter 2 documents the longer-term returns that have been achieved in different asset classes and through specific holding periods, and examines the reward for taking risk. It describes the power of dividends in the total return for equities and also the key factors that tend to affect returns for investors.

Chapter 3 focuses on the tendency for equity bull and bear markets to be split into four phases – despair, hope, growth and optimism – and shows how each is driven by different factors with varying returns.

Chapter 4 looks at the pattern of returns across competing asset classes through a typical investment cycle.

Chapter 5 focuses on how equity investment styles or factors tend to evolve through the cycle.

Part II is a deeper dive into the nature, causes and implications of both bull and bear markets in equities.

Chapter 6 describes the different types of bear markets: cyclical, event-driven and structural, as well as the factors that can be used to identify bear market risks.

Chapter 7 describes the different types of bull markets and, in particular, the difference between secular rising bull markets and those that are more cyclical in nature – and why these differ.

Chapter 8 focuses specifically on bubbles and their characteristics, as well as identifying the common signposts that identify a developing speculative bubble.

Part III looks at how many of the fundamental factors and characteristics of the cycle have changed since the financial crisis of 2008/2009.

Chapter 9 focuses on the secular slowdown in profitability, as well as in inflation and interest rates. It discusses some of the lessons that can be learned from Japan and its post-1980s bubble experience.

Chapter 10 describes the impact and consequences of zero, or even negative, bond yields on returns and the cycle.
Chapter 11 is about the extraordinary shift in technology in recent years, its historical parallels and its impact on equity markets and the cycle.

Introduction

My first job as a trainee research analyst started at the end of 1985. Since then, many things in economies and society have changed beyond recognition. The world has become more interconnected; the Cold War ended and the Soviet Empire unravelled, heralding an era of 'globalisation'. When I began my career, the UK had only recently, in 1979, removed restrictions on foreign exchange controls (for the first time in 90 years), while France and Italy still had them in place, only abolishing them in 1990.[1] Economic conditions have also transformed, and several key fundamental macro drivers have shifted dramatically: over the past three decades, inflation has fallen persistently and interest rates have collapsed; 10-year government bond yields in the United States have come down from over 11% to 2%, Fed funds rates have fallen from over 8% to 1.5% and currently one-quarter of all government

[1] Under European Community guidelines, France and Italy were required to end all exchange controls by 1 July 1990 but France implemented these six months earlier in order to show its commitment to the principles of free movement of goods, capital and people in Europe.

bonds globally have a negative yield. Inflation expectations have become well anchored and economic volatility has declined.

Meanwhile, technological innovations have also altered how we work and communicate, and computing power has revolutionised the ability to process and analyse data. The most powerful supercomputer (the Cray-2) in 1985 had a similar processing ability to an iPhone 4.[2] The scale of the digital revolution and the quantity of available data since then would have been unimaginable at the time, and this seems to be accelerating. Microsoft's president Brad Smith recently signalled that 'this decade will end with almost 25 times as much digital data as when it began'.[3]

Over the same period, there have been three major recessions (in most economies) and several financial crises, including the US Savings & Loan crisis of 1986, the Black Monday stock market crash of 1987, the Japanese asset bubble and collapse between 1986 and 1992, the Mexican crisis of 1984, the Emerging Market crises of the 1990s (Asia in 1997, Russia in 1998 and Argentina in 1998–2002), the ERM currency crisis of 1992, the technology collapse in 2000 and, of course, the most recent global financial crisis, starting with the subprime mortgage and US housing declines of 2007, and the European sovereign debt crisis of 2010/2011.

Despite the huge changes in economic conditions and technology over the past three decades, and occasional financial and economic crises, there has been a tendency for similar patterns to repeat themselves in financial markets, and for cycles to emerge, albeit in slightly different forms. In a 2019 paper, authors Filardo, Lombardi and Raczo noted that, over the past 120 years, the US has gone through the Gold Standard period, when inflation was low, and the 1970s, when inflation was high and volatile, and that over this long historical period the price stability credentials of central banks has shifted and fiscal and regulatory policies have

[2] Stone, M. (2015). The trillion fold increase in computing power, visualized. Gizmodo [online]. Available at `https://gizmodo.com/the-trillion-fold-increase-in-computing-power-visualiz-1706676799`

[3] Smith, B., and Browne, C. A. (2019). *Tools and weapons: The promise and the peril of the digital age*. New York, NY: Penguin Press.

varied considerably, but that 'through all of this, the financial cycle dynamics have remained a constant feature of the economy'.[4]

It is these cycles, and the factors that drive them, that this book explores. Its purpose is to show that, despite significant changes in circumstances and environments, there still appear to be repeated patterns of performance and behaviour in economies and financial markets over time.

But, although acknowledging the changes, and trying to assess how much of the change we observe is cyclical and how much is structural, the main body of this book aims to examine what there is about financial markets that is predictable, or at least probable.

Interest in economic cycles, and their impact on financial markets and prices, has a long history and there are many theories on how they function. The Kitchin cycle, after Joseph Kitchin (1861–1932), is based on a 40-month duration, driven by commodities and inventories. The Juglar cycle is used to predict capital investment (Clement Juglar, 1819–1905) and has a duration of 7–11 years, whereas the Kuznets cycle for predicting incomes (Simon Kuznets, 1901–1985) has a duration of 15–25 years and the Kondratiev cycle (Nikolai Kondratiev, 1892–1938) has a duration of 50–60 years, driven by major technological innovations. There are, clearly, problems with all of them and the fact that there are so many different descriptions of cycles points to the fact that there are many different drivers. Several of them, such as the very long Kondratiev cycle, are difficult to test statistically given the existence of so few observations.

Although the traditional focus on cycles has related mainly to the economy, the focus in this book is on financial cycles, their drivers and different phases – a topic discussed in detail in chapter 3. The idea that there are cycles in financial markets in general, and in equity markets in particular, has been with us for a very long time. Fisher (1933) and Keynes (1936) both examined the interaction between the real economy and the financial sector in the Great

[4] Filardo, A., Lombardi, M., and Raczko, M. (2019). Measuring financial cycle time. *Bank of England Staff Working Paper No. 776* [online]. Available at `https://www.bankofengland.co.uk/working-paper/2019/measuring-financial-cycle-time`

Depression. Burns and Mitchell found evidence of the business cycle in 1946 and later academics argued that the financial cycle was a part of the business cycle, and that financial conditions and private sector balance sheet health are both important triggers of the cycle and factors that can amplify cycles (Eckstein and Sinai 1986). Other research has demonstrated that waves of global liquidity can interact with domestic financial cycles, thereby creating excessive financial conditions in some cases (Bruno and Shin 2015).[5]

More recent studies suggest that measures of slack in the economy (or output gaps – the growth rate versus potential output) can be explained partly by financial factors (Boria, Piti and Juselius 2013) that play a large part in explaining fluctuations in economic output and potential growth, as well as 'determining which output trajectories are sustainable and which are not',[6] thereby implying a close link and feedback loop between financial and economic cycles.

That said, although interest in economic and financial cycles has a long history, views on whether they can be predicted are widely contested. One set of ideas about the inability to anticipate future price movements in markets stems from the efficient market hypothesis (Fama 1970), which argues that the price of a stock, or the value of a market, reflects all of the information available about that stock or market at any given time; the market is efficient in pricing and so is always correctly priced unless or until something changes. Following on from this idea is the argument that an investor cannot really predict the market, or how a company will perform. This is because no individual will have more information than is already reflected in the market at any time, because the market is always efficient and prices change in fundamental factors (such as economic events) immediately.

But theory is one thing and practice is another. Nobel Laureate Robert Shiller, for example, showed that while stock prices are

[5] Bruno, V., and Shin, H. S. (2015). Cross-border banking and global liquidity. *Review of Economic Studies*, 82(2), 535–564.

[6] Borio, C., Disyatat, P., and Rungcharoenkitkul, P. (2019). What anchors for the natural rate of interest? *BIS Working Papers No 777* [online]. Available at `https://www.bis.org/publ/work777.html`

extremely volatile over the short term, their valuation, or price/earnings ratio, provides information which makes them somewhat predictable over long periods (Shiller 1980), suggesting that valuation at least provides something of a guide to future returns. Others have argued that the returns one can expect from financial assets are linked to economic conditions and therefore the probability of certain outcomes can be assessed even if accurate forecasts are not particularly reliable.

Although there are relationships between financial cycles and economic cycles, mainly because bonds are affected by inflation expectations and equities by growth, there are some patterns of human behaviour that reflect and sometimes amplify expected economic conditions. It is the way in which economic and corporate fundamentals (expected growth, profit, inflation and interest rates, for example) are perceived by investors that is the crucial mix. Academic work has increasingly shown that risk-taking appetite has been a key channel through which supportive policy (for example, low interest rates) can affect cycles (Borio 2013).[7] Willingness to take risk and periods of excessive caution (often after a period of weak returns) are factors that tend to amplify the impact of economic fundamentals on financial markets and contribute to cycles and repeated patterns.

The emotions of fear and greed, of optimism and despair, and the power of crowd behaviour and consensus can transcend specific periods of time or events, supporting the tendency for patterns to be repeated in financial markets even under very different circumstances and conditions. There is also a tendency for errors to be repeated when investors fail to heed some of the important warning signals of overheating and excess that can develop when conditions are supportive and there is a powerful narrative. I discuss this topic in chapter 8, which looks at the role of sentiment in developing speculative excesses and financial bubbles.

---

[7] Borio, C. (2013). On time, stocks and flows: Understanding the global macroeconomic challenges. *National Institute of Economic and Social Research*, 225(1), 3–13.

Of course, although there are repeated patterns in markets over time, there are also events and economic conditions that are unique to each cycle or circumstance. In reality, no two periods are ever precisely the same; even faced with fairly similar conditions, the precise permutations of factors are unlikely to be repeated in the same way. Structural changes in industries and in economic factors, such as inflation and the cost of capital, can shift relationships between variables over time. For example, the behaviour and performance of a stock market cycle in an era of high inflation and interest rates could well be rather different from a cycle in a period of very low inflation and interest rates, and the way in which companies, investors and policymakers react to a given impulse may change over time as they adapt to the experiences of the past.

It is also important to recognise that when we look for relationships between factors and variables in history we are enjoying the benefit of hindsight. We can recognise patterns after they exist, whereas in real time this can be a great deal more difficult. This is, in part, what makes consensus and crowd behaviour so important in driving fluctuations in asset prices. For example, when economic data are expected to slow and stock prices weaken, it is unlikely to be obvious at the time whether this represented a 'mid-cycle' slowdown and a correction, or whether this was the start of a much more serious bear market and recession; this can only be known for sure in retrospect. Certainly, it is not uncommon for financial markets to 'overprice' an expected shift in future economic conditions, and this is one reason why market cycles and inflection points in particular can be so sharp. But the greater swings that tend to exist in financial markets, relative to economies, do not weaken the relationships between them. The fact that links exist between stock returns and prospective growth can at least help us to understand the typical leads and lags, varying strengths of relationships between variables and the signals to look for.

Understanding the dynamics of cycles, and what variables may have changed, may help us to make more informed investment decisions and make risk management more effective. As Howard Marks, the co-chairman and cofounder of Oaktree Capital Management, notes in his book *Mastering the Market Cycle*,[8] 'Economics and markets have never moved in a straight line in the past, and neither will they do so in the future. And that means investors with the ability to understand cycles will find opportunities for profit.'

Over the long run, even accepting the fluctuations caused by cycles, investing can be extremely profitable. Different assets tend to perform best at different times, and returns will depend on the risk tolerance of the investor. But for equity investors in particular, history suggests that, if they can hold their investments for at least five years and, especially, if they can recognise the signs of bubbles and of inflection points in the cycle, they can benefit from the 'long good buy'.

---

[8] See Marks, H. (2018). *Mastering the cycle: Getting the odds on your side* (p. 293). Boston, MA: Houghton Mifflin Harcourt.

Part I

Lessons from the Past: What Cycles Look Like and What Drives Them

Chapter 1
Riding the Cycle under Very Different Conditions

In 1985, when I started as a graduate trainee at Greenwells & Co, a stockbroking firm in the City of London, I spent a short period on the floor of the London Stock Exchange, along with the other new graduate recruits. At that time, many of the practices were probably much as they had been for many decades. The government Gilt brokers still wore top hats, and it was just 12 years since the first women had been elected as members of the exchange. One of my classmates was jeered for turning up in brown shoes and was sent home to change. So-called blue buttons – the juniors, or clerks – would walk around the various stalls of 'jobbers' (market-makers) asking for quotes on stocks, write the prices down on paper, and then take them to the back office behind the trading floor, where they would be written on a large board. When a salesperson in the brokerage office had an order, the 'blue buttons' on the floor would be able to give a fairly up-to-date estimate of the price to buy or sell.

After my initial training, I joined the economics team in the research department at Greenwells. One of the tasks of the juniors was to collect the latest data releases after they were published. This involved physically going to the Bank of England on Threadneedle Street, a few blocks away from our office. When handed the release at the Bank, the analysts would then rush to the large bank of telephone boxes outside of the stock exchange (in the adjacent block) to communicate the details to the economists, who would interpret them and write a data comment, which was then photocopied and distributed to the sales team.

This rather cumbersome system was about to change. Our senior partner and economist decided to invest in a new time-saving technology – a mobile telephone (a rather large device in a box) – that enabled the junior economist to telephone through the information directly to the office as soon as it was released, thereby saving the time and effort of having to put coins into a telephone box. Even then, small improvements in time could be critical in winning business (by the new millennium, speeds would accelerate dramatically as average trade execution times would go from multiples of a second to millionths of a second[1]).

But this was just one small innovation in a wider environment of rapid change and disruption that was about to revolutionise financial markets. The City of London was on the brink of the 'Big Bang' deregulation of 1986. For the first time, face-to-face transactions were replaced by computers and telephones, resulting in an explosion of volumes. The old way of doing business was under threat. Barriers to entry were blown apart and gave way to a new wave of entrants, many from overseas.

Technology was fast changing the landscape of business and society more generally. Personal computing also saw major innovations at this time. In 1985, Microsoft Corporation released Windows 1.0, the first version of its computer operating system that would come to dominate the PC market. The first dotcom domain name, symbolics.com, was also registered in 1985 by the Symbolics Corporation, adding a commercial domain to the then dominant .edu domains used by educational institutions. At the time, of course, this was probably not well known, nor were the implications and far-reaching changes that would result from the commercial

[1] Lovell, H. (2013). Battle of the quants. *The Hedge Fund Journal*, p. 87.

application of the internet and the speculative bubble that emerged because of the dotcoms in the late 1990s.

In 1986, IBM introduced the first laptop computer and Intel launched the 386 series of microprocessor. This was also the year when the Internet Message Access Protocol (IMAP) was developed, which was to become the first standard protocol used to enable people to retrieve email from a mail server and manage an email box.

Other far-reaching innovations – which may have seemed less significant at the time but would be the start of significant changes to come – were unfolding as well. In 1986, for example, a group of British scientists discovered a hole in the earth's ozone layer, a finding that led just two years later to the Montreal Protocol, the first international agreement to protect the ozone layer and the first United Nations treaty to achieve universal ratification. The discovery raised awareness of environmental risks,[2] and climate change became an important political issue for the first time. This issue has since taken on far greater dominance and is becoming central to policy and politics, particularly in Europe, where legal commitments to decarbonisation may, in part, change the nature and structure of our economies in the years to come.

The wave of new technologies in this period facilitated many other social changes in the mid-1980s when I entered the workforce. In July 1985, just before my first job started, the Live Aid concert had taken place, staged both in London's Wembley stadium and the JFK stadium in Philadelphia. New communications technology meant that, for the first time, a concert could be beamed around the world in real time. Using 13 satellites, the live concert reached a global audience of over one billion people in 110 countries; it was a triumph of both organisation and technology.[3]

---

[2] Cawley, L. (2015). Ozone layer hole: How its discovery changed our lives. BBC [online]. Available at https://www.bbc.co.uk/news/uk-england-cambridgeshire-31602871

[3] In fact, this wasn't the first global live event. This had already been achieved in 1967 with Our World, which had used satellites to beam to a global audience of 400,000 to 700,000 people, the biggest ever at the time, and included appearances and performances from Pablo Picasso, Maria Callas, and the famous UK entry, The Beatles, who performed 'All You Need Is Love' for the first time.

There were, of course, strong elements of the past that featured in the concert: when Bob Dylan sang 'Blowin' in the Wind' together with Rolling Stones members Keith Richards and Ronnie Wood, it could have been Woodstock 16 years earlier, but the sheer technological scale of this endeavour made it feel like a new world; perhaps Dylan's 'The Times They Are a Changin'' might have been more appropriate.

These changes were felt in the world of politics, too, where there were stirrings of major reforms that would change the shape of the global political and economic system in the years that followed. The supply-side reforms of UK prime minister Margaret Thatcher and US president Ronald Reagan were in full swing, and the divisive miners' strike in the UK had just ended with the closure of most of the nation's coal mines. The US introduced the Tax Reform Act of 1986, designed to simplify the federal income tax code and broaden the tax base. Meanwhile, international events were also in flux. Mikhail Gorbachev had just (in March 1985) become leader of the Soviet Union following the death of former leader Konstantin Chernenko. During a speech in Leningrad in May 1985, President Gorbachev admitted to the problems in the economy and poor living standards; he was the first Soviet leader to do so. This was followed by a series of policy initiatives, which included *Glasnost* – allowing more freedom of information – and *Perestroika* – political and economic reform; these were to prove seminal and more influential than seemed obvious at the time. The shift in approach by the Soviet Union paved the way for the resumption of talks with the United States and the signing of three important treaties in 1987, 1990 and 1991, which resulted in a significant reduction in military spending and, eventually, the mutual reduction of strategic nuclear weapons.

Although these reforms were aimed at reversing the bureaucratic structure that had become a major constraint to economic progress, now they are often seen as important catalysts in the eventual collapse of the Soviet Union in 1989 and, as such, the end of the Cold War and the start of the modern era of globalisation.

In the summer of 1989, just a few months before the collapse of the Berlin Wall, as the pressures on the Eastern European communist states intensified, Francis Fukuyama, a US State Department official, wrote a paper titled 'The End of History' where he argued, 'What we may be witnessing is not just the end of the Cold War, or the passing of a particular period of postwar history, but the end of history as such: that is, the end point of mankind's ideological evolution and the universalization of Western liberal democracy as the final form of human government.'[4] The paper seemed to capture the zeitgeist.

In parallel, about this time China was also beginning to open up its economy and embark on reforms. Following the landmark 1978 Chinese reforms that started the 'household responsibility system' in the countryside, giving some farmers ownership of their products for the first time, the first 'special economic zone' was formed in Shenzhen in 1980. This concept allowed for the introduction and experimentation of more flexible market policies. Although the reforms were slow and not without controversy, by 1984 it became permissible to form individual enterprises with fewer than eight people and, by 1990, a year after the fall of the Berlin Wall, the first stock markets were opened in Shenzhen and Shanghai. The broadening reach of market capitalism seemed assured.

The changes of the times brought with them many investment opportunities and a more interconnected world, sparking an optimism that infected stock markets. In 1985, during my first year at work, the Dow Jones stock index in the US rallied by just over 27%, the strongest single year since 1975 (the year of recovery from the crash that followed the oil crisis and deep recession of 1973/1974). Rising prices reflected both improving fundamentals and a fall in uncertainty and geopolitical risk. Low inflation and interest rates led to a growing belief that, after a period of strong growth, the major economies could achieve a 'soft landing' – avoiding a recession and enjoying an extended economic expansion. The fall of

[4] See Fukuyama, F. (1989). The end of history? *The National Interest*, 16, 3–18.

communism and the 'peace dividend' that followed, together with the expansion of liberal capitalism, enabled risk premia to fall.

This optimism and strong market rises continued throughout 1986 and, in the first 10 months of 1987, the Dow Jones appreciated by an astonishing 44%. Then, quite suddenly, on 18 October, everything changed. The Dow collapsed by 22.6% in a single day. That day became known as Black Monday, in reference to Black Monday, Tuesday and Thursday in 1929, almost exactly 58 years earlier, when the stock market had dropped by 13% (with much sharper falls to follow). Despite all of the changes that had taken place, and a time span of nearly 60 years, panic ensued and a there was a sense that we had seen it all before. All of a sudden, there was a gnawing anxiety that the optimism driven by falling interest rates and lower inflation had been unjustified.

Indeed, the parallels to the 1929 crash were also clear to policymakers. In an attempt to avoid repeating the mistakes of the past, they responded swiftly and decisively. The Federal Reserve in the United States immediately acted to provide liquidity to the financial system and Chairman Alan Greenspan issued a statement on the following day in which he affirmed '[the Fed's] readiness to serve as a source of liquidity to support the economic and financial system'. The next day the Fed cut the funds rate to about 7%, from over 7.5% on the Monday before the crash. It worked. Although it took nearly 25 years for the stock market in the US to fully recover from the losses from the 1929 crash, the recovery took less than two years following the crash of 1987.

It wasn't too long before there was another crisis. In 1992, I moved to a new role at James Capel & Co, a leading UK stockbroking company, as European strategist within the economics department. This was the year of the so-called Black Wednesday, when Sterling collapsed out of the exchange rate mechanism (the ERM) after it failed to remain stable within the lower limits of the band mandated by the system.[5] Pressure was building on the weaker

[5] http://news.bbc.co.uk/onthisday/hi/dates/stories/september/16/newsid_2519000/2519013.stm

currencies in the system (the UK and Italy both had large deficits) following a rejection of the Maastricht Treaty[6] in a Danish referendum in spring 1992 and the announcement that France would also hold a referendum. The collapse of sterling came just three days before the French referendum, which narrowly passed with 51%. The crisis forced the Bank of England to raise rates consistently in order to protect the value of sterling. On September 16, it hiked interest rates initially from 10% to 12%, and then, as sterling continued to weaken, to 15%. I, like many of my friends, had recently taken out a mortgage on my first flat – we were terrified given that most mortgages were floating rate at that time in the UK. The resolution came in the swift easing of policy as interest rates were cut again.

The power of central banks has been wielded many times since, not least in the current cycle, with the introduction of quantitative easing (QE) and, at times, similarly powerful guidance to instil confidence. This was, perhaps, most famously demonstrated in 2012 in the midst of the European sovereign debt crisis, when ECB president Mario Draghi said 'the ECB is ready to do whatever it takes to preserve the euro. And, believe me, it will be enough.'

Since the 1980s, therefore, there have been many shocks and crises, quite often knocking economies off course and triggering sharp corrections in markets. Despite these, however, there tend to be repeated patterns of cycles in economies and financial markets.

Although cycles exist in very different economic circumstances, many of these can be very difficult to predict. As the renowned investor Warren Buffett said, 'We've long felt that the only value of stock forecasters is to make fortune tellers look good. Even now, Charlie [Munger] and I continue to believe that short-term market forecasts are poison and should be kept locked up in a safe place,

---

[6] The Maastricht Treaty, officially known as the Treaty on European Union, marked the beginning of 'a new stage in the process of creating an ever closer union among the peoples of Europe'. It laid the foundations for the euro single currency and also expanded cooperation between countries in several areas. For details, see Five things you need to know about the Maastricht Treaty. (2017). ECB [online]. Available at https://www.ecb.europa.eu/explainers/tell-me-more/html/25_years_maastricht.en.html

away from children and also from grown-ups who behave in the market like children' (letter to shareholders 1992).

The difficulty of forecasting, of course, does not mean that there is little value in trying to understand potential risks and assess unfolding opportunities. Although precise point forecasts may not be very accurate when it comes to economic and financial markets, it is easier, and in many ways more important, to recognise the signals that point to a greater probability of an important turning point in financial markets. It is these inflection points that are so important because, as we will see in later chapters, avoiding sharp corrections, and participating in the early stages of a market recovery, are the times that can make the most difference to an investor's returns. Very often it is the behaviour of investors and their changing sentiment that are often overlooked in traditional forecasting models, and this partly explains why turning points in the economic and financial cycle are not well anticipated.

The difficulty of forecasting is not limited to the social sciences; even forecasting the weather, based on physical sciences, can prove challenging as the influences and variables on which the models rely can be fast-changing. This was an even greater challenge before the introduction of the most recent computer-based models. Ironically, one of the most glaring examples of failure to predict a major weather event coincided with the similarly unpredicted collapse in the stock markets in 1987, two years into my first job. The night before the crash, a violent storm hit England, causing immense damage. According to many estimates, this was the most severe storm to hit urban areas in the UK since 1706. Over 15 million trees fell on 17 October, including six of the famous seven ancient oak trees of Sevenoaks in Kent, an area in the commuter belt of London where many senior stockbrokers lived at the time.

The transport disruption was so widespread that the majority of those who were able to make it into the offices in central London were the most junior staff, myself included, who lived in the (then) less expensive areas closer by (before the wave of gentrification and the trend for families to move back into more central city locations).

As there was no internet at that time, or even instant pricing systems on terminals on every desk, information was slower to arrive and less reliable than today. When reports of the US stock market collapse started to come through as the New York market opened, we were bemused and unsure at first whether this was genuine or just an error caused by the storm on the one electronic pricing system we shared.

But it was the forecasting, or lack of it, that people focused on. On 15 October 1987, the BBC's lead weatherman, Michael Fish, reported that 'earlier on today, apparently, a woman rang the BBC and said she'd heard there was a hurricane on the way. Well, if you're watching, don't worry, there isn't.'[7] Arguably, part of the difficulty in forecasting is a function of data availability and current techniques. Modern computers should be able to deal with multiple inputs to a model more effectively than in the past.

This appears to be true for weather forecasting, where short-term five-day forecasts are nearly as accurate as two-day projections were as recently as 1980.[8] Hurricane predictions today are off by an average of 161 km (100 miles), down from 563 km (350 miles) 25 years ago.[9] But the same does not appear to be true of economic or market forecasts. When speaking to an audience at the Institute for Government in London, the Bank of England's chief economist Andy Haldane likened the failure to predict the financial crisis as a 'Michael Fish' moment for economists.[10]

The events surrounding the 2008 financial crisis and the failure to predict it resulted in widespread reflection about the ability of models to anticipate and predict economic and financial events. At

---

[7] Michael Fish subsequently argued that these comments related to Florida and were linked to a news bulletin before the weather forecast, but the severity of the storm was not generally anticipated.

[8] `https://phys.org/news/2019-01-geoscientists-insist-weather-accurate.html`

[9] Why weather forecasts are so often wrong. (2016) *The Economist explains.*

[10] See BBC news website: Crash was economists' 'Michael Fish' moment, says Andy Haldane, 6 January 2017, where they quote 'Remember that? Michael Fish getting up: "There's no hurricane coming but it will be very windy in Spain". Very similar to the sort of reports central banks – naming no names – issued pre-crisis: "There is no hurricane coming but it might be very windy in the sub-prime sector" '.

a gathering of academics in November 2008 at the London School of Economics, the Queen famously asked why people had not seen the crisis coming. It was a good question. An International Monetary Fund (IMF) study into more than 60 recessions around the world between 2008 and 2009 showed that none of them had been predicted by the consensus of professional economists. Moreover, of the 88 recessions that occurred between 2008 and 2012, economists had expected just 11. The royal question prompted the British Academy to convene a group of leading academics, politicians, journalists, civil servants and economics practitioners for a discussion to address this question and provide a written reply to the Queen. The letter, written by Tim Beasley, an LSE professor and member of the Bank of England's Monetary Policy Committee, and professor Peter Hennessey, a political historian, explained that '. . . the psychology of herding and the mantra of financial and policy gurus, lead to a dangerous recipe. Individual risks may rightly have been viewed as small, but the risk to the system as a whole was vast. So in summary, Your Majesty, the failure to foresee the timing, extent and severity of the crisis and to head it off, while it had many causes, was principally a failure of the collective imagination of many bright people, both in this country and internationally, to understand the risks to the system as a whole.'[11]

It is often when broader risks in the economy and financial market valuations become excessive that failure to predict turning points in cycles become most obvious. But even in more normal times, it is the extent of the moves at inflection points that models tend to be poor at picking up. In a study examining the accuracy of GDP forecasts covering 63 countries for the years 1992 to 2014, it was found that 'while forecasters are generally aware that recession years will be different from other years, they miss the magnitude of the recession by a wide margin until the year is almost over'.[12] As

[11] https://wwwf.imperial.ac.uk/~bin06/M3A22/queen-lse.pdf

[12] An, A., Jalles, J. T., and Loungani, P. (2018). How well do economists forecast recessions? *IMF Working Paper No. 18/39* [online]. Available at https://www.imf.org/en/Publications/WP/Issues/2018/03/05/How-Well-Do-Economists-Forecast-Recessions-45672

IMF researcher Prakash Loungani put it, 'The record of failure to predict recessions is virtually unblemished.'

The problem for investors is that forecasting markets, and the economic variables that influence them, is not a very precise science, and many of the traditional approaches and models have fallen short because of an overreliance on models and an insufficient understanding of the broader systemic risks and the impact of human psychology on behaviour.

That said, there were, it should be stressed, some people who did recognise and warned of the risks – particularly in relation to excess risk-taking and valuations. These people were very much more focused on the systemic consequences of heightened risk-taking and expectations than on standard economic models.[13]

The weaknesses of economic forecasting models in understanding or taking account of human sentiment, especially in periods of extreme optimism or pessimism, is not a new finding. In his 1841 book, *Extraordinary Popular Delusions and the Madness of Crowds*, Charles Mackay argues that 'men . . . think in herds; it has been seen that they go mad in herds, while they only recover their senses slowly, one by one'.

Even outside of bubble periods, or in the depths of a crisis, individuals do not, as the traditional economic theories suggest, always act in 'rational', predictable ways. As George Loewenstein, a prominent economist and psychologist points out, 'whereas psychologists tend to view humans as fallible and sometimes even self-destructive, economists tend to view people as efficient maximisers

[13] There were those who did warn about the risks of downturn and the papers written by these people are useful guides to the signals that they had identified. Nouriel Roubini gave a speech warning about the collapse in the US housing market and its implications in September 2006 to the IMF (see Roubini, N. (2007). *The risk of a U.S. hard landing and implications for the global economy and financial markets*. New York: New York University [online]. Available at `https://www.imf.org/External/NP/EXR/Seminars/2007/091307.htm`). Raghu Rajan gave a speech in 2005 warning of the excessive risks in financial markets risks: Rajan, R. J. (2005). Financial markets, financial fragility, and central banking. *The Greenspan era: Lessons for the future*, sponsored by the Federal Reserve Bank of Kansas City, Jackson Hole, WY. The Bank of International Settlements (BIS) warned in its July 2007 annual report that there were significant risks to the global economy.

of self-interest who make mistakes only when imperfectly informed about the consequences of their actions'. It is partly the understanding of how humans process information and deal with risks and opportunities that helps explain the existence of cycles in financial markets.[14]

In fact, the notion that individuals are rational and always use available information efficiently was not always the convention in economics. Keynes asserted that instability in financial markets was a function of psychological forces that can become dominant in times of uncertainty. According to Keynes, it is waves of optimism and pessimism that affect markets and animal spirits that drive desire to take risk.[15] Other economists, such as Minsky (1975), have also analysed these effects.[16]

This 'human' complication in forecasting was also featured in work on cycles by Charles P. Kindleberger,[17] who argued that there was a tendency to herding in markets when investors coordinate on buying assets when it would not normally be rational to do so, ultimately with the risk that financial bubbles develop (a subject covered in chapter 8). He and other economists advanced the ideas that psychological and sociological behaviour triggered emotional contagion and euphoria that can spread through crowds during booms while also driving pessimism and extreme risk aversion that can cause, and worsen, a bust.[18]

A significant impact on the understanding of psychology in social sciences came from two psychologists, Kahneman and Tversky, whose 'partnership was extraordinary in terms of scientific

---

[14] Loewenstein, G., Scott, R., and Cohen J. D. (2008). Neuroeconomics. *Annual Review of Psychology*, 59, 647–672.

[15] Keynes also argued that investors are affected, particularly in uncertain times, by what other people do.

[16] A good summary of the literature on behavioural finance and markets can be found in Shiller, R. J. (2003). From efficient markets theory to behavioral finance. *Journal of Economic Perspectives*, 17(1), 83–104.

[17] Kindleberger, C. (1996). *Manias, panics, and crashes* (3rd ed.). New York, NY: Basic Books.

[18] For a detailed discussion of some of the literature, see Baddeley, M. (2010). Herding, social influence and economic decision-making: Socio-psychological and neuroscientific analyses. *Philosophical Traditions of The Royal Society* [online]. Available at https://doi.org/10.1098/rstb.2009.0169

impact – they are the Lennon and McCartney of social science' (*The New Yorker Magazine*).[19] Their work on prospect theory (first presented in 1979 and developed by them in 1992) describes how investors behave when faced with choices that involve probability. They argue that individuals make decisions based on expectations of loss or gains from their current position. So, given a choice of equal probability, most investors would choose to protect their existing wealth rather than risk the chance to increase wealth.[20] But this tendency to protect what you have rather than risk a lot for future gains seems to disappear in extreme situations when markets increase a great deal and a fear of missing out becomes a dominant driver of behaviour.

Since the financial crisis, the interest in behavioural explanations and the psychology of markets has increased, and this information helps to better understand how and why financial cycles develop and can often significantly exaggerate the developments of economic and financial variables on which they are driven. Nobel Prize winners George A. Akerlof and Robert J. Shiller wrote that 'the crisis was not foreseen, and is still not fully understood . . . because there have been no principles in conventional economic theories regarding animal spirits'.[21] It is the impact of human behaviour and the way in which information is processed by humans that makes the forecasting of markets so much more complicated than forecasting physical systems such as the weather.

In this sense, forecasting physical science, such as weather forecasts, is different because these forecasts are not affected by how inputs change the behaviour of people. A storm that causes people to stay indoors, for example, does not change the path or severity of the storm. In the case of economies and financial markets, there

---

[19] See Sunstein, C. R., and Thaler, R. (2016). The two friends who changed how we think about how we think. *The New Yorker* [online]. Available at https://www.newyorker.com/books/page-turner/the-two-friends-who-changed-how-we-think-about-how-we-think

[20] Kahneman, D., and Tversky, A. (1979). Prospect theory: An analysis of decision under risk. *Econometrica*, 47(2), 263–292.

[21] Akerlof, G., and Shiller, R. J. (2010). *Animal spirits: How human psychology drives the economy, and why it matters for global capitalism*. Princeton, NJ: Princeton University Press.

are significant feedback loops, or what George Soros describes as 'reflexivity',[22] a concept that has its roots in the social sciences but has strong effects in financial markets. A stock market that falls in anticipation of a recession, for example, might itself lead to a collapse in business confidence that alters the decisions of companies in terms of investment, thereby making the risks of a recession that much greater.

An additional complication is that the response of individuals to particular inputs, such as changes in interest rates, can vary over time even when faced with similar conditions. In recent research, Malmendier and Nagel (2016)[23] argued that investors overweight their personal experiences when they form judgements about their expectations over time. For example, perceptions about inflation may vary according to the conditions that you have been used to, and this might influence your decisions about the future more than would be suggested by relying on long-term historical relationships. This may explain why there are differences in inflation expectations among people of different age groups; rather than being rational and responding to a particular policy or trigger in a consistent and predictable way, investors may act quite differently depending on their own experience and psychology.[24]

Neuroeconomics, a relatively new field, provides further evidence of these types of varying reactions. This approach looks at how decision-making takes place in the brain and also provides some insight into how individuals face choices that involve risk. Academics (such as George Loewenstein, Scott Rick and Jonathan D. Cohen) argue that people react to risks in two ways: a dispassionate way and an emotional way. This approach argues that we overreact to new risks that may be low probability events but underreact to risks that are known to us, even though these are much more

---

[22] https://ritholtz.com/2004/04/the-theory-of-reflexivity-by-george-soros/

[23] Malmendier, U., and Nagel, S. (2016). Learning from inflation experiences. *The Quarterly Journal of Economics*, 131(1), 53–87.

[24] Filardo, A., Lombardi, M., and Raczko, M. (2019). Measuring financial cycle time. *Bank of England Staff Working Paper No. 776* [online]. Available at https://www.bankofengland.co.uk/working-paper/2019/measuring-financial-cycle-time

likely to occur. In this way, for example, a collapse in equities may make people very cautious of investing because they have faced a new risk, despite the fact that a new bear market is unlikely. At the same time, investors may be happy to buy equities towards the top of the markets, despite regular warnings about higher valuations, because they have seen recent price rises and feel more confident to take the risks.

This would seem to be consistent with investor behaviour in the run-up to and following the recent financial crisis, as well as countless other booms and busts in history. Persistent rising returns in financial markets lead to optimism and the belief that the trend can continue. The required risk premium falls and investors are lured into markets with the belief that risks are low and prospective returns will continue to be as strong as they have been in the past. By contrast, the proximity to large losses has pushed up the required risk premium – the expected future return that investors require to take on risk. In particular, the way in which companies and markets have responded to sharp interest rate cuts has been different in the period after the financial crisis relative to the period before it. Having faced the experience of the financial crisis and recession that followed, people collectively seem to have responded with greater caution than might have been the case previously. It is these swings in sentiment and confidence, partly informed by recent history, that also drive financial market cycles.

The policy world has also focused increasingly on the feedback loops and on how expectations in financial markets can affect the economic cycle – and in particular 'financial conditions', which are measures of the impact of monetary policy on the economy that are broader than simply the central bank's policy rate – in an attempt to take into account the impact of investor expectations and confidence. These typically include credit spreads, equity prices and the real exchange rate.

The problem for policymakers, therefore, is that it is hard to know how to respond to violent market moves given that these may, or may not, be accurately implying a fundamental move in economic activity. As former US Federal Reserve vice chairman Roger Ferguson wrote, ‘Detecting a bubble appears to require judgment based on scant evidence. It entails asserting knowledge of the fundamental value of the assets in question. Unsurprisingly, central bankers are not comfortable making such a judgment call. Inevitably, a central bank claiming to detect a bubble would be asked to explain why it was willing to trust its own judgment over that of investors with perhaps many billions of dollars on the line.’[25]

Of course, the impact of a change in policy will depend on the availability of credit and how easy it is.[26] But, it also seems to be dependent on how the action is received by financial market participants (which can, in turn, affect its success), and it is therefore ultimately down to human psychology and crowd behaviour. As one recent study put it, ‘there is increasing evidence that psychology plays a big role in economic developments. Results indicate that the economy is highly driven by human psychologies, a result which is in conformity with the prediction of Keynes (1930) and Akerlof and Shiller (2010).’[27] The renewed focus on psychology in understanding responses to and behaviour regarding decisions is also increasingly used in public policy. In 2008, Richard H. Thaler and Cass R. Sunstein published *Nudge: Improving Decisions about Health, Wealth, and Happiness*, which focused on behavioural economics. The book became a bestseller and has had a widespread impact on policy. Mr Thaler went on to win the Nobel Prize for Economics in 2017 for his work in the field.

So, despite all the political, economic and social changes that have occurred since the 1980s, and notwithstanding the extreme events and difficulty of predicting human sentiment and responses

[25] Ferguson, R. W. (2005). Recessions and recoveries associated with asset-price movements: What do we know? *Stanford Institute for Economic Policy Research*, Stanford, CA.

[26] Aikman, D., Lehnert, A., Liang, N., and Modugno, M. (2017). Credit, financial conditions, and monetary policy transmission. *Hutchins Center Working Paper #39* [online]. Available at https://www.brookings.edu/research/credit-financial-conditions-and-monetary-policy-transmission

[27] Dhaoui, A., Bourouis, S., and Boyacioglu, M. A. (2013). The impact of investor psychology on stock markets: Evidence from France. *Journal of Academic Research in Economics*, 5(1), 35–59.

to conditions, there have been repeated patterns in economies and financial markets. Although knowing where we are in a cycle in real time is difficult, and forecasting near-term returns is complex, there is useful information that investors can look at to help assess the risks and understand the probabilities of outcomes. Recognising the signs of excess (either pessimism or optimism) and the prospects of important inflection points can help to generate higher returns.

Chapter 2
Returns over the Long Run

A starting point in any long-term study of cycles is to ask what kind of returns an investor can expect in the various competing asset classes. This may seem a simple question, but part of the challenge in answering it is that different investors have very different time horizons. Holding periods change and the willingness (or even regulatory ability) to take mark-to-market losses can vary considerably across investor types.

Most investors would expect a higher return for taking risk, and the long-run historical data do bear this out. Starting with very-long-run data series, and using the US – the world's biggest stock market – as an example, the total return for US equities since 1860 has averaged about 10%, over anything from a 1-year to a 20-year time horizon, as shown in exhibit 2.1.

For 10-year US government bonds, often viewed as a 'risk-free' asset (because the debt is backed by a government that does not default on its debt), returns have averaged between 5% and 6% over the same holding periods.

In his famous book *Stocks for the Long Run*, Jeremy J. Siegel (1994) argued that real returns (nominal returns adjusted for inflation) in equities had been remarkably stable over many different periods and different economic regimes: 'over all major sub periods:

Exhibit 2.1 Average annualised total returns for different holding periods (since 1860)

	1 year	5 years	10 years	20 years
S&P 500	11%	12%	10%	10%
US 10y bond	5%	6%	5%	5%

SOURCE: Goldman Sachs Global Investment Research.

7.0 percent per year from 1802 through 1870, 6.6 percent from 1871 through 1925, and 7.2 percent per year since 1926'.

Although the long-run returns for equity holders are therefore reassuring, risk and volatility are much higher than for less-risky assets, such as government bonds (which have a guaranteed nominal return). Over 1-year holding periods, for example, equity volatility (the variance or spread of returns near the average) is roughly three times as high as it is for government bonds. This means that if you want to be confident of your return, particularly over shorter time horizons, bonds are a more attractive asset, as you are more certain of the likely return ex ante. However, the advantage of being offered this security fades somewhat over longer holding time horizons. Looking at 20-year holding periods, for example, reveals that the volatility of equities falls sharply (exhibit 2.2).

Simply put, an investor faces a simple trade-off between expected return and volatility. Over long-term periods, equities offer roughly twice the return of government bonds but with about twice the risk and volatility. The longer an investor can hold an investment, the more attractive equities become. As exhibit 2.3 shows, over 1-year holding periods equities have fallen 28% of the time, compared with 18% for US Government bonds, but this falls to 11% of the time for

Exhibit 2.2 Average 1-year standard deviations of total annualised returns for different holding periods (since 1860)

	1 year	5 years	10 years	20 years
S&P 500	10%	2%	1%	1%
US 10y bond	3%	1%	0%	0%

SOURCE: Goldman Sachs Global Investment Research.

Exhibit 2.3 Percentage of years with negative returns for different holding periods (since 1871)

	1 year	5 years	10 years	20 years
S&P 500	28%	11%	3%	0%
US 10y bond	18%	1%	0%	0%

SOURCE: Goldman Sachs Global Investment Research.

equities over 5 years, and 1% for bonds. Over 10-year holding periods, the occurrences of negative returns in equities fall dramatically to 3%. So, for an investor who can take mark-to-market risk (who does not need to take losses as they occur) and can afford to take a long-term investment horizon (at least 5 years), then equities tend to make a good long-term return even with the ups and downs of a typical cycle. Such conditions can be described as providing the best opportunity for investors to achieve a 'long good buy'.

Returns over Different Holding Periods

However, looking at averages over the long-run data histories masks the fact that returns do not just vary from year to year; they also tend to move in cycles.

As we shall see in later chapters, the returns for an equity investor tend to vary over the course of a cycle largely as a function of what is happening to economic fundamentals, such as interest rates and growth expectations. But it is also the case that returns for investors vary across cycles. Some offer much better returns than others. A number of factors determine these trends, but they are a function typically either of structural shifts in fundamentals, such as sales growth and corporate margins, or a result of changes in valuations. Understanding these factors, and their influence on markets, can have a significant impact on returns, and, at the very least, help investors to avoid the periods of greatest risks. It is also important to stress that using the US as a guide to long-term returns may be misleading. After all, the returns in the Japanese equity market since its financial crisis in 1989/1990 have been significantly lower. There are good reasons for this: slower nominal GDP over the past quarter of a century in Japan is certainly one reason, but an excessive starting point in valuation is another. I discuss in chapter 9 some of the similarities between Japan over the past couple of decades and other markets since the more recent global financial crisis.

A useful guide to the long-term patterns in returns, and how they have changed over time, is to look at returns over specific holding periods. Exhibit 2.4 plots, for example, US equity market returns in specific 10-year holding periods over time (each bar in the chart shows the annualised return on equities after inflation from the date shown, over the following decade).

Looking at aggregate returns over long periods can mask significant differences over time by showing the rolling average total return in real terms (adjusted for inflation). An investor might have expected that if she had held equities for a medium-term period,

Exhibit 2.4 S&P 500 (10-year rolling annualised real returns)

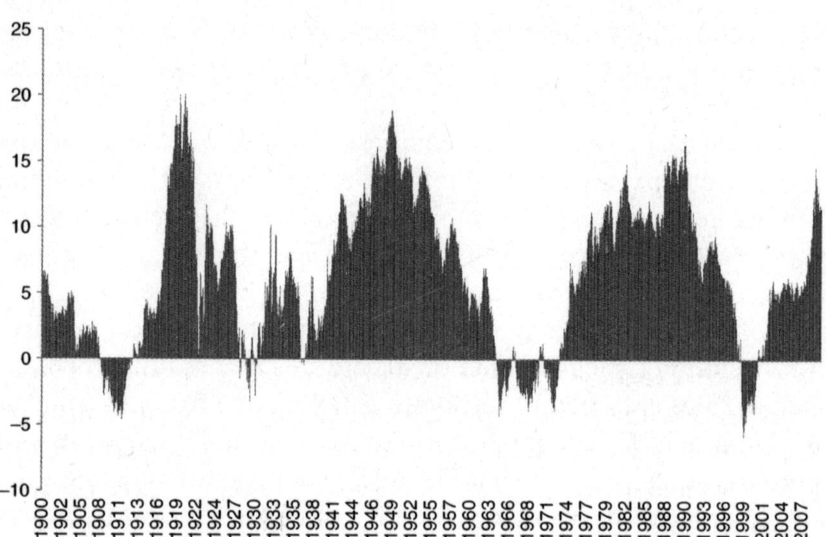

SOURCE: Goldman Sachs Global Investment Research.

then her returns would likely be similar to those of other periods of an equivalent length. But in practice that is not necessarily true. For example, returns on equities that were purchased at the start of major conflicts (the First and Second World Wars) have been negative for long periods, because it took a great deal of time to recover from the initial losses. Equities bought at the peak of the bull market in the late 1960s, before the spike in global inflation and interest rates that was to occur over the life of the bond, also saw very negative returns.

In an historical context, the period of the technology bubble and its collapse at the end of the 1990s is particularly striking. Equities bought at the top of the technology bubble in 2000 – and even through to 2003 – achieved over the subsequent decade some of the lowest real returns in US equities (along with the 1970s) in over 100 years. Equities bought during the period that followed have resulted in much stronger returns – in line with long-run averages. Meanwhile, investors who entered the stock market following the financial crisis in 2007/2008 (the final reading in the chart) have enjoyed strong returns.

The 10-year holding periods with the highest returns typically occur in periods of strong economic growth; the booms of the 1920s and post-war reconstruction of the 1950s are good examples. Others are periods of very low or falling interest rates, such as in the 1980s and 1990s, and periods following large bear markets, when valuations reached low levels.

But although equities have performed better over the longer-term holding periods, and have performed very well post the financial crisis in particular, it is the real returns in the bond market since the 1980s that have been truly remarkable compared with most periods in history (exhibit 2.5). US Treasuries bought in the early 1980s, at the peak of the inflation cycle, have annualised real returns of over 10% for 10 years (and over 7% for 20 years). This means that if an investor had invested $1,000 in US government bonds in 1980, in real terms (adjusted for inflation) her investment would be worth about $6,000 at the time of writing.

Exhibit 2.5 US 10-year bond (10-year rolling annualised real returns)

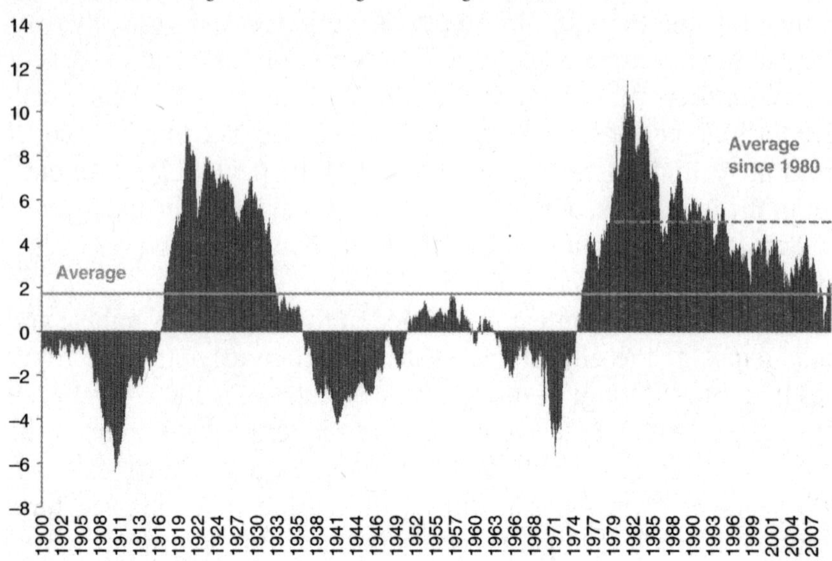

SOURCE: Goldman Sachs Global Investment Research.

Even bonds bought in the early 1990s have annualised real returns of about 5% for 20 years – the kind of real returns that investors used to hope for in equities. These extraordinary returns suggest that investors had not fully priced in at the outset the likely fall in inflation and interest rates, and they emphasise the critical part that expectations play in the eventual returns that are achieved.

As bond yields are now much lower, together with inflation expectations, one would expect much lower long-run returns in future. In the current environment, a remarkable one-quarter of global government bonds have a negative yield – suggesting a very low, if not negative, future rate of return. Austria recently launched a 100-year bond that has a yield of just over 1.1%.[1] These are not ordinary times, which suggests that we are in a particularly unusual environment for picking assets, a topic dealt with in chapter 9.

[1] Ainger, J. (2019). 100-year bond yielding just over 1% shows investors' desperation. *Bloomberg* [online]. Available at `https://www.bloomberg.com/news/articles/2019-06-25/austria-weighs-another-century-bond-for-yield-starved-investors`

The Reward for Risk and the Equity Risk Premium

Comparing returns on bonds and equities enables us to look retrospectively at the reward for taking risk (investing in the unknown future return on equities compared with the fixed nominal return on bonds).

Equities are on the riskier side of the investment range because equity investors have the last claim over a company's profits (after bond holders and other creditors). Equity therefore has an uncertain future return. It is possible for a company to lose money and the price of the stock can fall, or, worse still, the company can go bankrupt. For investors in fixed income assets (the income is known in nominal terms at the time of purchase), the risk is one of government or corporate default; lending to governments is generally much safer than lending to companies because it is more likely that a company will lose money or collapse entirely than a government default on its debt (although it is typically seen as riskier in emerging economies where there is often a history of default). For equity investors, the downside risks are higher than for many other investments, but so too are the upside potential returns.

The achieved return in equities compared with bonds is often referred to as the ex post equity risk premium (ERP), or the actual reward over time that investors achieve by investing in equities relative to safe government bonds. This is different from the required equity risk premium, which is more a measure of likely relative future returns, or the expected premium of risk assets versus safe assets that an investor would require at any point in time to put her marginal investment into equities and not into bonds. When she is uncertain about the future, that required future return will rise, and, by contrast, if the environment is seen to be positive and stable, that required extra return for taking risk will fall.

A large body of literature has focused on calculating and interpreting the ERP over time. In 1985 an article published in the

Journal of Monetary Economics by Mehra and Prescott[2] argued that the actual returns achieved in equities were too high relative to standard economic models. Specifically, they found that between 1889 and 1978 the average real return on stocks was approximately 7% per year (in the US), and the rate of return on government bonds was just below 1%. Subtracting the return on bonds from the return on stocks left a so-called equity risk premium of over 6% per year, which could only be explained by a high degree of risk aversion. They went on to argue that other trade-offs between risk and reward in the economy suggest that investors did not require nearly as large a risk premium as they had been getting in practice, and that measures of risk aversion in other areas of financial behaviour are much lower, consistent with an ERP of 1% or less. They called this conundrum *the equity risk premium puzzle*.

Since then, much of the research has found that the equity risk premium has varied over time. Bernstein (1997), for example, suggested that because equity valuations have changed over time, this could distort the required return. As an example, if you were to start the long-run sample period in 1926 at a price-to-earnings (P/E) ratio of about 10 times and end the period at a P/E of about 20 times (for example, in the 1990s), the actual return on equities would be higher than investors expected or required at the outset, so that the actual historical achieved rate of return (the ex post risk premium) overstates the future expected return (the ex ante risk premium). This finding was strengthened by the work of Fama and French (2002), which used a discounted dividend model (the DDM) to show that investors from 1926 onwards had an expected equity risk premium that averaged about 3%.

Others have emphasised that spot valuations can also distort the expectations for returns. In particular, Robert Shiller in his book *Irrational Exuberance* (2000) argued that stocks can become overextended, so that returns can be above normal and then below normal for extended periods. He introduced the valuation measure called

---

[2] Mehra, R., and Prescott, E. C. (1985). The equity premium: A puzzle. *Journal of Monetary Economics*, 15(2), 145–161.

Exhibit 2.6 S&P vs. US 10y BY (10-year rolling annualised) = ex post ERP

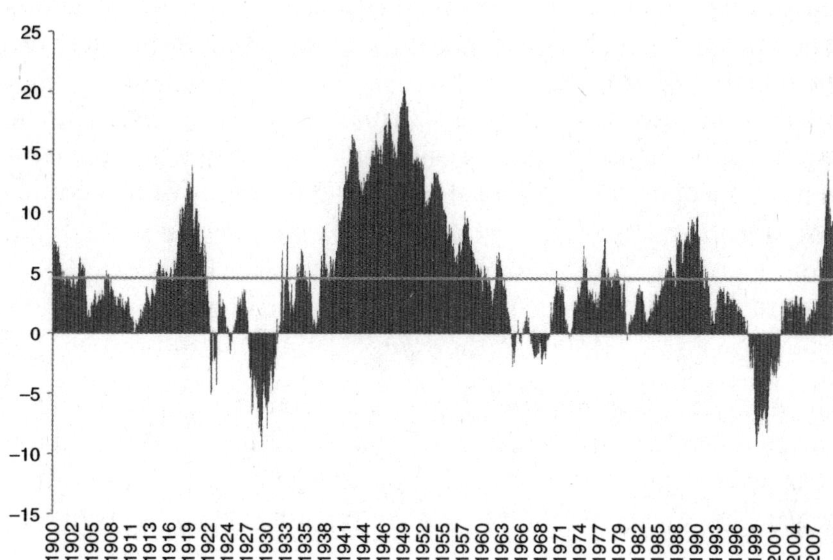

SOURCE: Goldman Sachs Global Investment Research.

CAPE (cyclically adjusted price-to-earnings ratio), which uses 10 years of trailing earnings data in the denominator rather than just 1 year of forward expected earnings, as in the standard valuation tool of the P/E ratio. This adjustment, he argued, can be better at predicting returns.

Whatever the risk premium is, however, it does seem to vary over different periods, the duration of which seems to be largely dependent on the valuation at the starting point. The annualised excess returns in equities compared with government bonds were very negative after the equity market bubble burst in the late 1920s, but they were extraordinarily high in the post-war years of the 1950s and 1960s (coming from low valuations post-war and supported by strong economic growth), as exhibit 2.6 illustrates.

The technology bubble of the 1990s created a valuation-led collapse in stock prices, which resulted in a negative ex post (or achieved) ERP for several years. Equities bought at the height of the stock market before the financial crisis also generated very low achieved risk premia over the following decade. By contrast, the collapse in equity prices in 2008 – and the aggressive policy stimulus that followed – resulted in strong returns over the decade following the March 2009 trough.

This suggests that, although returns over the long run tend to be higher in riskier assets, the prevailing macro conditions can have a major impact on both the absolute and relative returns on equities over time.

The Power of Dividends

The power of dividends over time can be seen in exhibit 2.7, which breaks down the total return performance of the S&P 500 into the price index appreciation (what people usually look at) and dividends (and dividends reinvested). Reinvesting dividends is one of

Exhibit 2.7 Don't forget the power of dividends (S&P 500 total return since 1973)

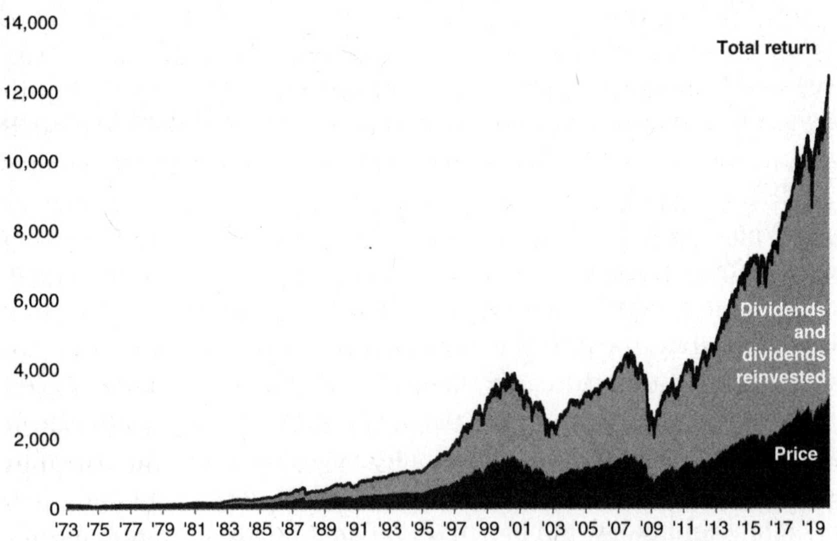

SOURCE: Goldman Sachs Global Investment Research.

the most powerful and reliable ways to grow wealth over the long term. Since the early 1970s, roughly 75% of the total return of the S&P 500 can be attributed to reinvested dividends and the power of compounding.

From 1880 to 1980, the dividend payout ratio in the US equity market has averaged 78% of earnings and the resulting dividend yield averaged 4.8%. Buybacks were typically not a major part of the cash returns to investors and, in the US, were only explicitly permitted by the SEC following the passage of Rule 10b-18 in 1982. This means that in recent years the rapid growth in share repurchases has come at the expense of common dividends. Since 2000, the dividend yield averaged 1.9% and the buyback yield 2.0%. Compounded, a 4.0% annual return coming from dividends (or buybacks) implies that an investor can potentially double her investment in less than 18 years even without any price appreciation.

In some markets, industries are more mature and the need to reinvest for future growth is less important. As a result, the payout ratios are higher and the proportion of returns coming from dividends can be greater. For example, in Europe, the stock market (the STOXX Europe 600 index) is, at the time of writing, still not significantly higher than levels reached in 2000, 2007 or 2015. But in terms of total returns, including dividends, results have been much better for investors. In these markets, where the equity index has a high proportion of companies in very mature industries, such as oil, banks, utilities and telecoms, the proportion of returns coming from dividends can be about 80% based on a 20-year rolling average.

Although the US equity market has significantly outperformed Europe and Japan in the years since the financial crisis, the gap between Europe and the US begins to close when we look at total returns (exhibits 2.8 and 2.9). Japan, on this basis, has really lagged behind. Similar to Europe, Japan has suffered from low earnings growth in recent years but, unlike Europe, it has not paid out much in dividends. Being aware of these differences is important for investors when choosing between markets.

Exhibit 2.8 Europe and Japan are similar in price performance terms . . . (price returns: equity market)

SOURCE: Goldman Sachs Global Investment Research.

Exhibit 2.9 . . . but Europe has outperformed Japan in total return terms (total returns: equity market)

SOURCE: Goldman Sachs Global Investment Research.

Factors That Affect Returns for Investors

In general, we can say that equity markets perform best when economic conditions have been weak, valuations are low, but there is an improvement in the second derivative of growth – that is to say, the rate of change stops deteriorating.

And equity markets suffer when valuations are high and/or concerns over growth start to be priced late in the cycle when the second derivative of growth starts to deteriorate.

Low volatility of macro variables also supports returns (it makes conditions easier to predict and therefore reduces perceived risks), whereas high macro volatility is generally a hindrance.

But other factors have an impact on returns to investors.

The historical pattern of returns in asset markets depends on two key factors, which are often linked:

- The timing of the investment (the conditions when they are bought).
- The valuation at the time of investment.

Market Timing

When it comes to investing, timing the best entry point is probably the most difficult factor involved, particularly in the short term. But the outcome for investors can vary significantly. For example, if we look at the period since the beginning of 2009 (shortly before the trough reached after the financial crisis), which has been rewarding for investors in general, an investor who bought and held onto an index fund would have seen the price of the fund rise by about 250% in the US (annualising at over 12%).

In the real world, although no investor would have been astute, or lucky, enough to avoid all of the worst days, timing still matters a great deal even as we extend the timing phases. An investor who avoided the best month per year would have generated approximately 2% on average in equities since 1900, whereas an investor who managed to avoid the worst month would have generated nearly 18% annual returns – close to 80% higher than an investor who stayed fully invested the whole time. Although these results demonstrate the impact of avoiding sharp drawdowns, they also show that missing the best months can be very painful indeed.

The timing issue extends to all financial markets. A benchmark 'multi-asset' portfolio – for example, one that is always made up of 60% equities and 40% bonds – would have achieved roughly a 2% annual return by missing the best months and over 12% by avoiding the worst months.

Although all this shows how important timing can be, it is not particularly realistic because most investors cannot focus on daily or even monthly moves in the market. That said, being able to avoid the worst periods and being invested in the better ones might be more feasible when we take 1-year horizons. As exhibit 2.10 shows, the worst years for the equity market have seen falls of between 20% and 40%, and the best years have seen rises of between 40% and 60%. Because most of the worst years occur near economic stress periods, such as recessions or sharply rising interest rates, and the best years occur in periods of stronger or recovering economic activity, lower perceived risks and interest rates and/or periods of lower valuations, we can begin to see why cycles in markets are so important.

For bond markets, the variance is less stark but only because the worst years are not as dramatic. The best years, however, have

Exhibit 2.10 S&P 500 best and worst years in total returns

Best yearly performance		Worst yearly performance	
1862	67%	**1931**	-44%
1933	53%	**2008**	-37%
1954	52%	**1937**	-35%
1879	50%	**1907**	-30%
1863	48%	**1974**	-27%
1935	47%	**1930**	-25%
1908	45%	**1917**	-25%
1958	43%	**2002**	-22%
1928	43%	**1920**	-20%
1995	38%	**1893**	-16%

SOURCE: Goldman Sachs Global Investment Research.

Exhibit 2.11 US 10-year bonds best and worst years in total returns

Best yearly performance		Worst yearly performance	
1982	39%	**1931**	-13%
1985	30%	**2009**	-10%
1995	26%	**2013**	-9%
1986	21%	**1999**	-8%
1863	20%	**1994**	-7%
2008	20%	**1907**	-6%
1970	19%	**1969**	-6%
1921	19%	**1920**	-4%
1991	19%	**1967**	-3%
1989	18%	**1956**	-3%

SOURCE: Goldman Sachs Global Investment Research.

generated returns in line with, if not higher than, the average returns over time in equities (exhibit 2.11).

Valuations and Returns of Equities versus Bonds

Most analysts and investors focus their attention, understandably, on the 'fundamental' drivers of returns: the prospects for economic growth, profit growth, rates of return on capital, margins and so on. But the economic climate and stage of the business cycle are not the only factors that can fully explain the returns to shareholders over specific periods of time.

For example, the end of the final decade of the last century (when the technology bubble burst) was one of unusually strong economic and profit growth in most regions. Inflation was generally low and stable and, in the US and Europe, profit shares of GDP and return on equity (ROE) rose to record highs. Despite all of this, if an investor had bought equities towards the height of the boom, when investors were at their most confident, she would have received very poor returns over the subsequent decade. By contrast, these fundamentals were much poorer during much of the 1980s, but equity returns were much higher. How, then, can we explain this apparent paradox?

Much of the explanation comes down to valuations. Understandably, great valuation peaks (1929, 1968, 1999) tend to be followed by very poor returns on a risk-adjusted basis, and very low returns, at market troughs (1931, 1974, 2008) tend to be followed by strong returns.

Higher valuations imply either greater risk of a correction/bear market or a sustained period of low returns in the future. The read-across from valuation to future returns varies from one measure to another and is also a greater predictor of medium-term returns than those in the short term. For example, once again based on US data, the R-squared between the Shiller (CAPE) P/E (real price/10-year average real earnings) and 10-year future equity returns is very high (roughly 0.70). Meanwhile, the R^2 is 0.20 for the 2-year returns, 0.40 for 5 years and 0.60 for 20 years (see exhibit 2.12).

The message from valuation is clearer when it is at a relative extreme (either very low or very high). But there is a distribution for this because other factors also have an impact on returns.

Exhibit 2.12 Correlation between cyclically adjusted P/E and forward returns (over 10 years) (S&P 500 since 1950)

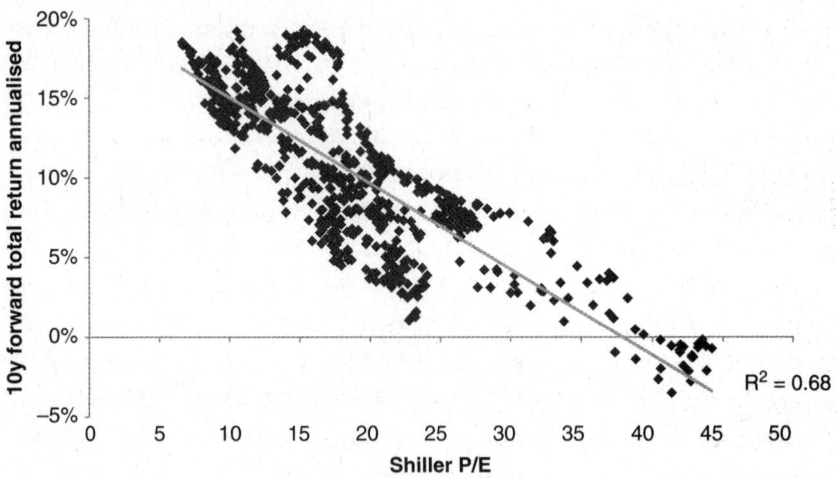

SOURCE: Goldman Sachs Global Investment Research.

The read-across from valuation for future returns is evident when comparing returns between asset classes and within an asset class. In a comparison across asset classes, there are various ways of demonstrating the likely future relative return. One simple way is to use the real yield gap in the US (the difference between the dividend yield and the real bond yield) as a proxy.

When comparing the progression of valuation with the relative performance 5 years later, a reasonable relationship can be seen. Higher relative valuations for equities at the outset imply lower equity returns on a relative basis in the future, and vice versa. The main period when this relationship broke down was in the mid-1990s. At the time, equities did not look particularly cheap versus bonds, but over the following 5 years they significantly outperformed bonds, although this reflected the onset of the technology bubble. Although valuation is clearly not the only factor driving relative returns, it is nonetheless significant.

The Impact of Diversification on the Cycle

Because equities and bonds can move in different directions (although they do not always do so), or at least have different risk and volatility profiles, it is often considered wise to combine these two major asset classes when building a portfolio. In this way, the volatility can be reduced by reducing the impact of sharp corrections in equities (even if bond prices fall when equity prices do, they are likely to do so by a smaller degree) but typically aggregate returns would be lower. By the same token, this may reduce the upside returns in a portfolio. Over time, and through many different cycles, combining equities with government bonds (with, say, a 60/40 mix, respectively) can result in cycles of varying length and strength. Using US equities and government bonds as a reference, exhibit 2.13 shows the length and strength of each cycle.

Exhibit 2.13 We are in the longest 60/40 bull market without a 10% total return drawdown (60/40 bull and bear markets [real total return drawdown of more than 10%])

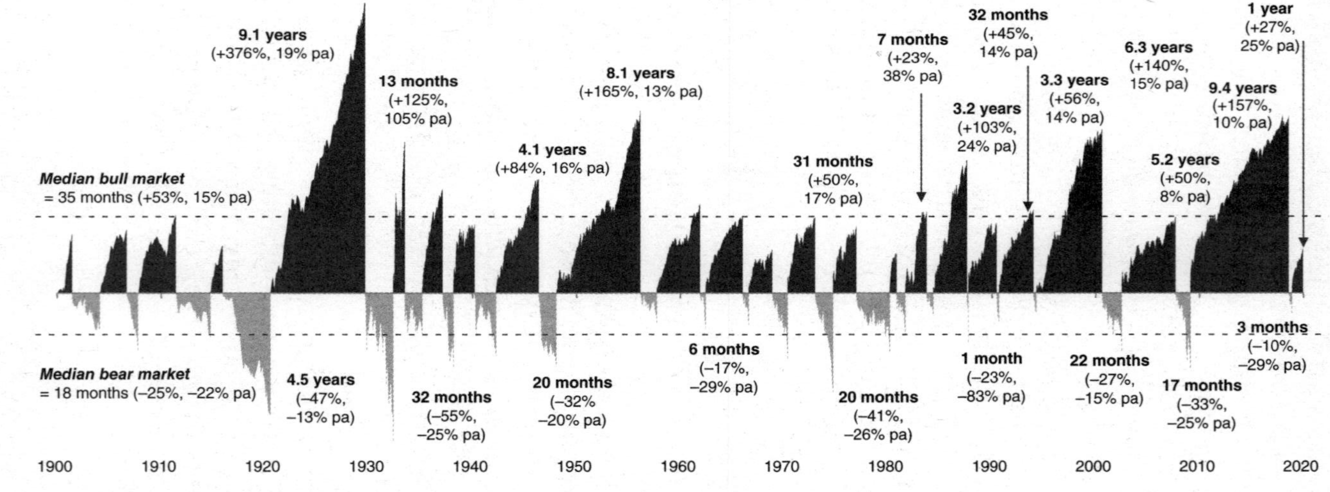

SOURCE: Goldman Sachs Global Investment Research.

That said, combining the two asset classes can often provide a very good return while also diversifying the risk. Using data back to 1900 shows that the median bull market lasts roughly 3 years, generating total real (inflation-adjusted) returns of 50%, or 15% annualised. The median bear market has lasted 1.5 years, with total real losses of 25%, or 22% annualised. The strongest balanced portfolio period was in the 1920s, with total real returns of over 360%, annualising at close to 20% for 9 years. The period since the financial crisis has actually produced the longest balanced bull market, lasting over 9 years and achieving annualised returns in real terms of about 10%. Of course, both of these periods were exceptional. The average bull market of a multi-asset (60/40) benchmark index in the US has been 81% (22% annualised) over 3.5 years.

Chapter 3
The Equities Cycle: Identifying the Phases

Although there are long-term shifts in the return profile of equities that depend on prevailing macroeconomic conditions (in particular, the trade-off between growth and interest rates), most equity markets show a tendency to move in cycles that relate to some degree to business cycles. Because equity markets move in anticipation of future fundamentals, expectations for growth and inflation tend to be reflected in prices today. These changes can also affect valuation; if investors start to expect a recovery in future profits from a recession, for example, the valuation of the equity market will rise in the period before the improvement actually emerges.

Across an investment cycle, there is typically both a bear market (a period when prices are falling) and a bull market (a period when stock prices are generally rising or are relatively stable in price returns). The nature, shape and differences in these are discussed in more detail later in the book. This chapter focuses more specifically on the profile, shape and drivers of the entire investment cycle – the whole period from a market low through to its eventual peak. These cycles vary in length, but for the US equity markets have generally averaged about 8 years in the past.

Of course, in real time it is much more difficult to know which part of this cycle you may be in; this is only really possible to know in retrospect. But even recognising that these patterns exist through time can be helpful in alerting the investor to the possible shifts in returns and the signs to look for.

Looking at data from the early 1970s, these cyclical patterns seem to repeat themselves, albeit somewhat differently each time, and in most of these cycles returns can be split into four distinct phases, each driven by distinct factors (for example, expectations of changes in future growth rates or in changes in valuations).

The Four Phases of the Equity Cycle

The division of the cycle into phases is simplified and illustrated in exhibit 3.1. This is very much a stylised version of reality but it mirrors the tendency for markets to move in cycles, and it shows how distinct phases reflect the extent to which the index price performance is driven by actual profit growth when it emerges and/or by expectations of future profit growth, which we can measure as changes in the P/E multiple (valuations rise as investors anticipate future improvements in profit growth and decline when they

Exhibit 3.1 The four phases of the equity cycle

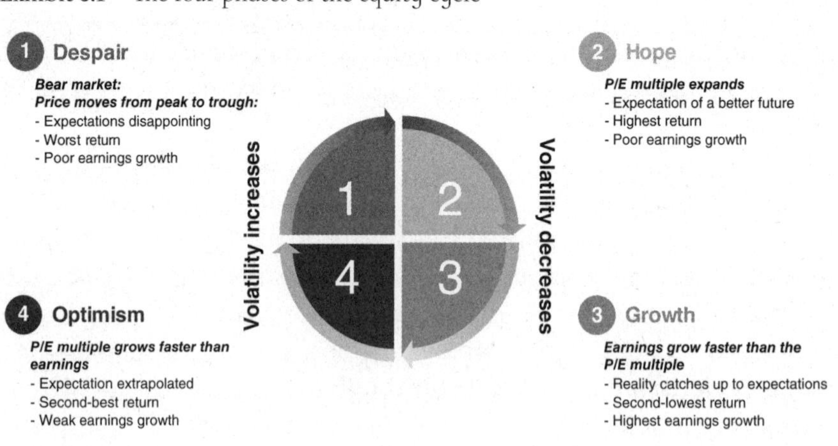

SOURCE: Goldman Sachs Global Investment Research.

anticipate weaker growth). For simplicity, the four phases can be described as follows:

1. **The despair phase.** The period when the market moves from its peak to its trough, also known as the bear market. This correction is mainly driven by falling valuations, such as P/E multiple contraction, as the market anticipates and reacts to a deteriorating macroeconomic environment and its implications in terms of lower expected earnings.
2. **The hope phase.** This is typically a short period (on average 9 months in the US), when the market rebounds from its trough valuation, or P/E multiple expansion. This occurs in anticipation of a forthcoming trough in the economic cycle, as well as future profit growth, and leads to a rise in the trailing P/E multiple. Generally speaking, the end of the hope phase roughly coincides with the peak of the trailing P/E multiple (maximum positive sentiment about future growth). This phase is critical for investors because it is usually when the highest returns in the cycle are achieved. However, it tends to start when the actual macro data and profit results of the corporate sector remain depressed. Crucially, the main driver here is expectations: although the hope phase often coincides with weak data, it occurs when the second derivative (the rate of change) in the data starts to improve. So the best time to buy into the equity market is usually when economic conditions are weak and after the equity market has fallen, but when the first signs start to emerge that economic conditions are no longer deteriorating at a faster pace.
3. **The growth phase.** This is usually the longest period (on average 49 months in the US), when earnings growth is generated and drives returns.
4. **The optimism phase.** This is the final part of the cycle, when investors become increasingly confident, or perhaps even complacent, and where valuations tend to rise again and outstrip earnings growth, thereby setting the stage for the next market correction.

This framework demonstrates that the relationship between earnings growth and price performance changes systematically over the cycle. Although earnings growth is what fuels equity market performance over the very long run, most of the earnings growth is not paid for when it occurs but rather when it is correctly anticipated by investors in the hope phase and when investors become overly optimistic about the potential for future growth during the optimism phase.

Exhibit 3.2 illustrates this for the US using data since 1973. For each phase, it indicates the average length of the phase, the average price return, and how that is distributed between multiple expansion and earnings growth. Although the growth phase sees most of the growth in earnings, the price return mainly occurs in the hope and optimism phases.

The phases are clearly linked to the economy. This allows for a clearer interpretation of the phases and helps to identify when we are moving from one phase to the next.

GDP, or economic activity, tends to contract during the despair and hope phases as output falls behind potential. The trough occurs

Exhibit 3.2 Decomposition of returns during US equity phases (return [%], data since 1973)

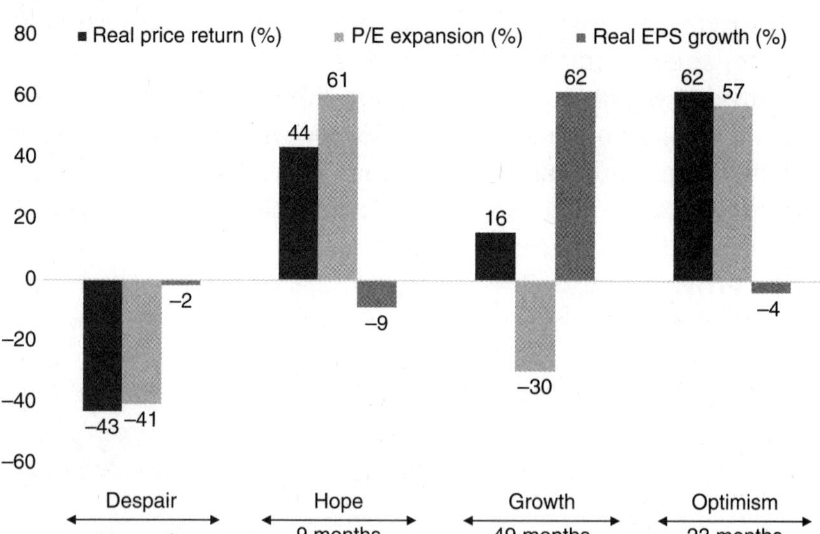

SOURCE: Goldman Sachs Global Investment Research.

between the middle and the end of the hope phase. In the growth phase, economic activity tends to expand and, eventually, output growth outpaces potential growth.

There is also a link between the cycle and valuations. Using simple valuation metrics such as the P/E ratio, valuations tend to fall in the despair phase and rise sharply in the hope phase as expectations about a future profit recovery push up prices in anticipation of the recovery actually materialising.

Using this simple framework, investors' forward-looking return requirements across the phases evolve as follows:

- **During the despair phase**, investors become increasingly concerned about the prospects for future returns and therefore require an increasingly high future expected return for holding equities. This reaction typically occurs against a backdrop of an increase in volatility, an increase in spare capacity (often described as the output gap)[1] and, typically, the start of a recession during this phase. This leads to lower equity valuations (P/E multiples) and a falling market. Taking data since 1973, this phase has lasted on average 16 months in the US. It is a phase when earnings are still rising (modestly) but prices fall sharply, on average by over 40%, with valuations contracting by a similar amount.
- **In the hope phase**, investors start to anticipate the end of recession or crisis as the rate of deterioration in data slows (things are still bad but are not deteriorating), and this visibility caps the potential downside risk. Investors respond to the lower tail risk by increasingly accepting lower future expected returns (and higher valuations); the equity risk premium declines and valuations rise as the 'fear of missing out' often drives investor sentiment. Although volatility is still high, it tends to fall towards the end of the hope phase as activity data start to stabilise, even at a low rate. In this phase, investors essentially prepay for the expected recovery in earnings during the growth phase. Although

[1] The output gap is usually described as the amount by which the actual output of an economy falls short of its potential output.

the hope phase typically is the shortest of the phases (on average about 9 months), it tends to be the strongest part of the cycle, with average returns of 40% and valuations rising by even more because earnings are usually still in contraction at this stage of the cycle.

- **In the beginning of the growth phase**, investors have already been paid for expected future earnings growth during the hope phase, but the growth has yet to materialise. The output gap typically peaks some time during the hope phase alongside unemployment, but remains very high at the beginning of the growth phase. Investors often pause, questioning long-run growth expectations very much in a wait-and-see frame of mind. The result is that value in terms of expected future returns is rebuilt during the growth phase as earnings growth outpaces returns and volatility declines. On average, this phase of the cycle in the US has lasted for 49 months, generating average returns of 16% backed by an increase in earnings of 60%. As a consequence, P/E multiples tend to contract by about 30% over this period.

Another likely driver of the higher real return requirements in the equity market that are built up during this phase is the increase in the real yield typically seen in bond markets.

- **Eventually, in the optimism phase**, the built-up value becomes large enough to attract more investors who fear missing out; returns outpace earnings and expected future returns consequently decline. Towards the end of the phase, volatility picks up as the sustainability of the high returns is tested by the market. This phase lasts an average of 23 months but once again experiences strong price appreciation and multiple expansion (both over 50%) and very little profit growth.

Some conclusions from these patterns are as follows:

- **The highest annualised returns** (the average return that an investor would have achieved over a specific period of time if the return were compounded at an annual rate) **occur during the hope phase. In the case of the US and Europe, the return in this phase has averaged between 40% and 50% (with**

total price appreciation in real terms annualising at over 60% in the case of the US). This is followed by the optimism phase (in both cases above 30% on an annualised basis in the US and Europe), while little is achieved during the growth phase. In both the US and Europe, the losses in the despair phase annualise at about 45%.

- **Actual profit growth and returns are surprisingly unsynchronised.** Almost the entire earnings growth for each region occurs during the growth phase; for example, in the case of the US, real earnings growth (adjusted for inflation) has increased on average by roughly 60% (40% in Europe), whereas in both cases profits are still falling during the hope phase, when much of the return in the market is actually realised. This emphasises the key point that investors tend to pay forward for expected growth in the future at a time when valuations are low.
- **Valuations expand most during both the hope and optimism phases (exhibits 3.3 and 3.4).**

This discussion is, of course, about averages over many decades and so provides a useful framework. But, in reality, each cycle is slightly different: inflation dynamics may change from one period to another, or there could be stronger economic growth than in the past. It also appears that over time each cycle seems to be dominated by one or another particular factor.

Exhibit 3.3 Valuations expand most during both the hope and optimism phases

S&P 500				
	Despair	Hope	Growth	Optimism
Length (m)	16	9	49	23
Cumulative				
Real price return (%)	-43	44	16	62
Real EPS growth (%)	-2	-9	62	-4
P/E expansion (pts.)	-9	6	-5	7
Proportion of return	-	*36%*	*13%*	*51%*
Annualised				
Real price return (%)	-45	64	-1	31
Real EPS growth (%)	4	-5	19	-4

SOURCE: Goldman Sachs Global Investment Research.

Exhibit 3.4 The pattern of valuation expansions is the same outside the US

STOXX Europe 600				
	Despair	Hope	Growth	Optimism
Length (m)	13	13	27	14
Cumulative				
Real price return (%)	-39	43	13	32
Real EPS growth (%)	-2	-8	40	0
P/E expansion (pts.)	-7	6	-3	5
Proportion of return	-	*49%*	*15%*	*37%*
Annualised				
Real price return (%)	-49	74	2	42
Real EPS growth (%)	-4	-6	18	4

SOURCE: Goldman Sachs Global Investment Research.

The main cycles we have seen since the early 1970s are as follows:

The 1970s. The 1970s has a reputation for having produced some bad fashion, but it was also very bad for financial assets. The peak for the US Dow Jones index in 1972 was not surpassed again until November 1982. Of course, this turned out to be a structural bear market (see chapter 6 for more details). Rising inflation, in particular, was a key factor behind the poor returns, which pushed up both interest rates and bond yields, overpowering earnings growth and pushing down valuations. The P/E multiple contractions over the cycle were significant, ranging from 42% in the UK to 52% in the US. The poor market performance reflected the large supply-side shock from higher oil prices, which became embedded in wage inflation and resulted in inflation expectations getting out of control.

Generally, cycles in which the initial setback is driven by structural problems tend to have longer growth phases than other cycles, because it takes longer for investors to regain the confidence that makes them willing to pay more for earnings and therefore move the market into the optimism phase. This is particularly pronounced in the US, where the growth phase in the 1970s was one of the longest on record. The end of the cycle includes the first part of the double-dip recession in the early 1980s for the US.

The early 1980s. The strong cycle in the early 1980s (as explained previously) was driven by the combination of falling inflation expectations and interest rates, together with a meaningful decline in the equity risk premium, which triggered substantial P/E multiples expansion. This increase in valuations was marked and prompted by significant shifts downwards in bond yields and central bank interest rates as inflation started to fall.

The 1990s. This cycle was very strong. The economic backdrop was one of solid growth but with low inflation and interest rates, frequently described as the 'Great Moderation'. The combined effect of globalisation, partly in the wake of the collapse of the Soviet Union and the opening up of China, was also crucial. In November 1995, China formally requested to accede to the WTO (although it did not become a full member until 11 December 2001). The move towards independence of central banks was also an important contributing factor to the perceived stability of the economic cycle.

2000–2007. This was one of the best cycles in terms of earnings growth for all the major equity markets but it offered some of the lowest returns for investors. The problem was that much of the strong profit growth in this cycle was partly driven by very strong earnings in the financial sector, which, driven by increased leverage, became illusory in the aftermath of the US sub-prime housing crisis.

2008–now. This is the post-financial crisis cycle and the longest so far (discussed in more detail in chapter 9), but it is rather different from other cycles for several reasons. First, the phases of the cycle, particularly outside of the US, were heavily distorted by the rolling nature of the global financial crisis and its subsequent waves following the initial problems in the US housing market in 2007/2008. In particular, following the US-led leg of the crisis, the sovereign debt crisis in Europe became a major focal point of risk for financial markets in 2010/2011 and, just as fears around Europe began to subside, the emerging market and commodity price falls resulted in sharp drawdowns in 2015/2016.

Second, this cycle has been different from others in that it has been marked by unconventional policy easing (and the start of quantitative easing), together with historically low inflation and bond yields.

Relatively weak profit growth has been another particular feature of this cycle, but alongside rising valuations. It has also been a cycle of significant dispersion between relative winners and losers. This has been reflected in the US equity market's substantial outperformance relative to Europe and emerging markets, and in technology generating much higher profits and returns than the rest of the market (which also partly explains the differences between regional stock returns).

Mini/High-Frequency Cycles within the Investment Cycle

In practice, we can find evidence of different types of cycles in history. As described, the length of historical investment cycles tends to vary, particularly during the longest growth phase. Partly, this also reflects the fact that these major cycles are also punctuated by shorter-lived cycles near periods of slowing and expanding economic activity. Often these reflect changes in inventory cycles and policy, and these shorter cycles can be repeated several times within a longer investment cycle. So, in addition to measuring investment cycles spanning the entire period between one bear market and the next, it is also common for there to be more than one, and sometimes several, mini cycles of slowing and accelerating economic activity within an entire investment cycle. These periods often occur within growth phases in particular, as in the case of the recent cycle, which has become elongated and supported by a long period of low and stable interest rates. Typically, these mini cycles do not involve recessions but merely pauses or slowdowns within a longer economic expansion.

It is sometimes difficult to identify these mini cycles with infrequent data points such as GDP releases, which are published quarterly and are often subsequently revised. Market participants tend to place quite a lot of emphasis on higher-frequency data points, many of which rely on surveys of business confidence or order books rather than 'hard' data points. Commonly used measures in places such as China and Europe are the so-called purchasing managers' index (or PMI) and, in the US, the widely observed Institute of Supply Management index (usually referred to as the ISM). These are widely followed by investors because they correlate closely with GDP but have the advantage of being monthly, and therefore of higher frequency than the quarterly reports of GDP.

If we look at the ISM in the US, for example, we find that there are many more of these shorter cycles than there are entire investment cycles. So, for example, in the current investment cycle, which started in 2009, there have been three mini industrial cycles, during which the economy had slowed and then accelerated, according to the companies surveyed (exhibit 3.5). But each of these cycles evolved without generating a broader economic recession.

As we find with the broader and typically longer investment cycles, there is a relationship between the performance of the equity market and other asset classes and these mini cycles.

Exhibit 3.5 The manufacturing cycle: Several mini cycles in the last growth phase

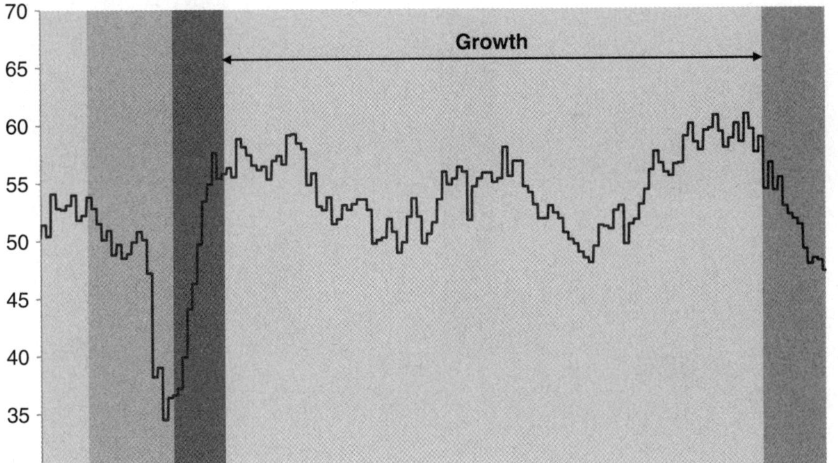

SOURCE: Goldman Sachs Global Investment Research.

As exhibit 3.6 shows for the S&P 500 index in the US (based on averages since the 1950s), the best period for equities tends to be when the ISM is in negative territory (with a reading of below 50) – usually consistent with recession or weak economic activity – but when it reaches a positive inflection point. This is shown in exhibit 3.6 as the recovery phase. The important point about this is that the best returns usually do not come when the data are strongest, but rather when they are at their weakest point and starting to inflect. This second derivative, a period of weak but improving activity, is the point at which animal spirits tend to kick in and investors buy into equity markets in anticipation of a future recovery. Just as we find with the hope phase in the main investment cycle, it is during this part of the cycle that returns tend to be strongest. Similarly, the worst phase for the market is when the PMI is below 50 and contracting. Again, this tends to be pretty clear-cut: things are bad and getting worse. This often coincides with the despair phase of the investment cycle.

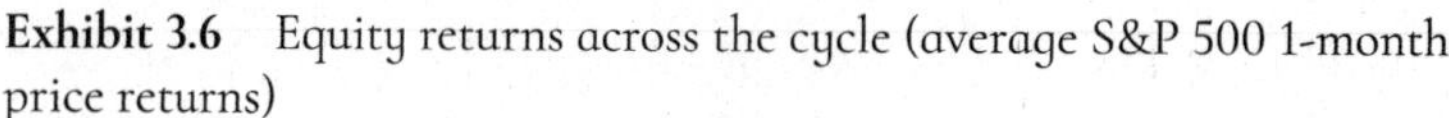
Exhibit 3.6 Equity returns across the cycle (average S&P 500 1-month price returns)

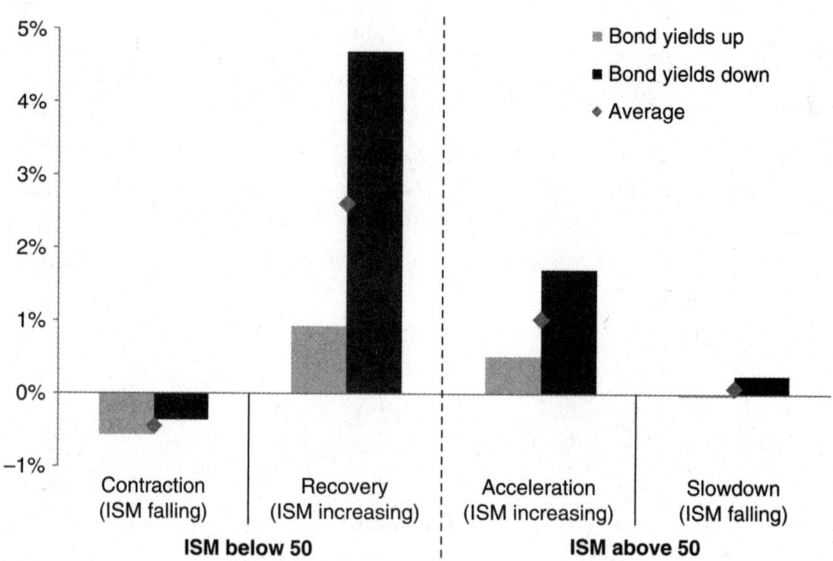

SOURCE: Goldman Sachs Global Investment Research.

The acceleration period when growth rates improve is generally the next best period – closely aligned to the growth phase of the investment cycle. The next weakest period after the contraction, on average, is the 'slowdown', when the ISM is positive but deteriorating. This is not as bad as the contraction itself but still generally associated with lacklustre or flattish returns in the equity market.

The Interplay between the Cycle and Bond Yields

Another feature of this pattern is that the returns in the equity and bond markets are dependent on the interplay between growth expectations and bond yields. The average performance in the equity market varies over the cycle depending on whether bond yields are rising or falling. This is because the bond market reflects the stance of central bank monetary policy and interest rates, as well as expectations of future inflation. When we add bond yields into the mix, we find there are more complex permutations that help explain returns. These combinations are illustrated in exhibit 3.6, where the diamond represents the average return and the bars show the average returns in each phase depending on whether bond yields are falling or rising.

Although the average returns in the recovery phase are highest (when the ISM is below 50 but increasing), there is quite a large difference in returns depending on whether bond yields are rising or falling at the same time. Generally speaking, returns are higher if bond yields are falling, and this is the case in all phases of the industrial cycle.

But, as we will see in the next chapter, the relationship between the equity market and bond yields is a complex one. In general, over long periods of time, falling bond yields do tend to be more positive for returns than periods when bond yields and inflation are structurally rising; the 1980s, for example, generated higher returns for investors than the 1970s, when inflation continued to rise and bond yields increased. But, over short-term periods, the moves in bond yields – and indeed the general shape of the yield curve (whether bond yields are higher or lower than short-term interest rates) – matters a great deal. Depending on what is happening to inflation expectations, it is possible that improving growth prospects coupled with rising rates are associated with the strongest returns in equity markets. This is particularly true – as in the recent cycle – when the starting level of interest rates is very low as rising bond yields, alongside growth expectations, may reflect more confidence that policy is working and that recessionary risks are fading. By the same token, a steepening yield curve (long-term bond yields rising above the levels of short-term interest rates) would generally imply a supportive central bank monetary policy, and an inverted yield curve, when bond yields are below short-term, policy-driven interest rates, would tend to reflect a restrictive monetary stance.

Chapter 4
Asset Returns through the Cycle

Chapter 3 looks at how the equity market tends to deliver different returns across the phases of the cycle. It is also possible to illustrate a tendency for equities to vary their pattern of relative returns in comparison to other asset classes through the cycle, and for different asset classes to respond to both growth and inflation in different ways. These characteristics help to make diversification across assets such a useful tool in seeking to reduce risks in an investment portfolio over time.

Assets across the Economic Cycle

For example, one simple way of thinking about the relative performance of assets as an economic cycle matures is to look at their average monthly real returns in early and late phases of both an economic expansion and contraction (these are shown for the US in exhibit 4.1 in total real terms, adjusted for inflation). In the later period of a recession, when economic activity is most depressed, there tends to be an outperformance of very defensive assets, including gold and long-term bond yields (which benefit from lower policy

Exhibit 4.1 Equity vs. bond performance is closely linked to the business cycle; commodities tend to lag in a recession (average monthly, real total returns (since 1950))

Note: We use US NBER recessions. We further divide expansions and recessions if growth is positive or negative. Usually late expansion with positive growth is the longest phase in the cycle. Pre-1973 oil prices were regulated by the Texas Railroad Commission and gold prices were fixed by Bretton Woods until 1968.

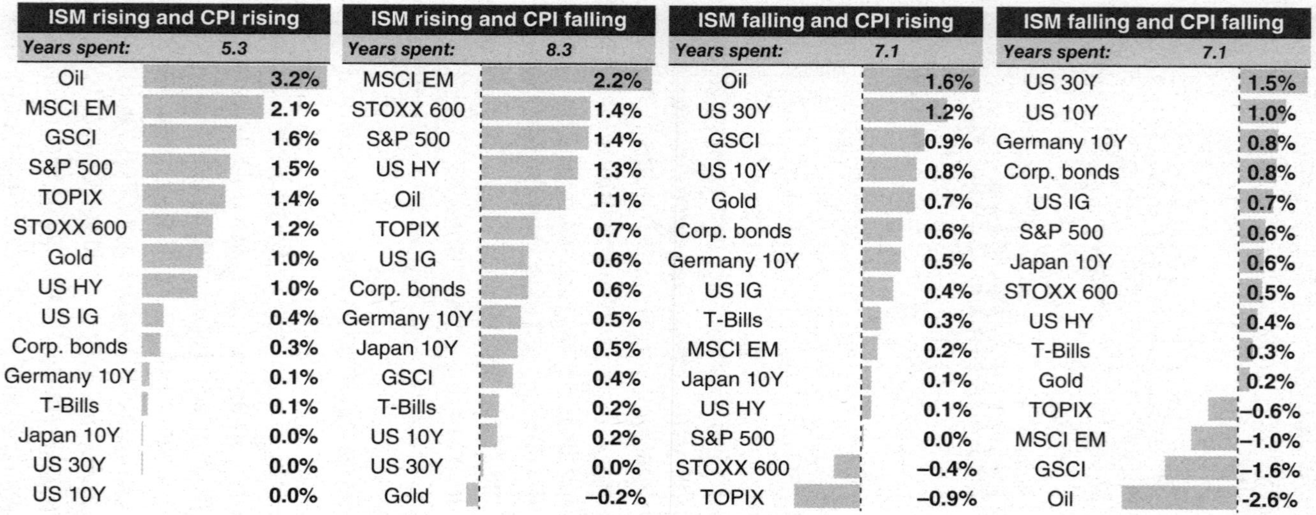

ISM rising and CPI rising		ISM rising and CPI falling		ISM falling and CPI rising		ISM falling and CPI falling	
Years spent:	5.3	*Years spent:*	8.3	*Years spent:*	7.1	*Years spent:*	7.1
Oil	3.2%	MSCI EM	2.2%	Oil	1.6%	US 30Y	1.5%
MSCI EM	2.1%	STOXX 600	1.4%	US 30Y	1.2%	US 10Y	1.0%
GSCI	1.6%	S&P 500	1.4%	GSCI	0.9%	Germany 10Y	0.8%
S&P 500	1.5%	US HY	1.3%	US 10Y	0.8%	Corp. bonds	0.8%
TOPIX	1.4%	Oil	1.1%	Gold	0.7%	US IG	0.7%
STOXX 600	1.2%	TOPIX	0.7%	Corp. bonds	0.6%	S&P 500	0.6%
Gold	1.0%	US IG	0.6%	Germany 10Y	0.5%	Japan 10Y	0.6%
US HY	1.0%	Corp. bonds	0.6%	US IG	0.4%	STOXX 600	0.5%
US IG	0.4%	Germany 10Y	0.5%	T-Bills	0.3%	US HY	0.4%
Corp. bonds	0.3%	Japan 10Y	0.5%	MSCI EM	0.2%	T-Bills	0.3%
Germany 10Y	0.1%	GSCI	0.4%	Japan 10Y	0.1%	Gold	0.2%
T-Bills	0.1%	T-Bills	0.2%	US HY	0.1%	TOPIX	–0.6%
Japan 10Y	0.0%	US 10Y	0.2%	S&P 500	0.0%	MSCI EM	–1.0%
US 30Y	0.0%	US 30Y	0.0%	STOXX 600	–0.4%	GSCI	–1.6%
US 10Y	0.0%	Gold	–0.2%	TOPIX	–0.9%	Oil	-2.6%

SOURCE: Goldman Sachs Global Investment Research.

rates and typically falling inflation expectations). As the cycle moves into the early phase of recovery, when growth is still negative but the second derivative is improving (the rate of deterioration slows), equities tend to rebound sharply, with gold and bonds the worst performers. Financial assets that are priced off future expectations understandably do better than 'real' assets, whose performance is more a reflection of the current balance of supply and demand, and tend to perform the worst.

In the later phases of expansion, the best-performing assets remain equities, but these are dominated by equities with a higher beta, or those that tend to amplify movements in underlying fundamentals to a greater degree, such as EM equities. Commodities tend to be more neutral in this phase, and fixed income assets tend to underperform as a consequence of a higher investor tolerance for risk and, in most cases, higher inflation. In the early part of a recession, defensive assets start to outperform but oil tends to continue to do well as growth levels are still positive (albeit decelerating). In this phase, risky assets and most cyclical and high-beta equities tend to underperform most. Corporate debt has generally been a hybrid between a fixed income and equity asset, and generally does best in the latter part of the recessionary phase as bond yields fall and forward growth risks start to moderate.

The response to inflation across assets is less straightforward than the relationship with growth, because asset performances vary materially depending on both levels of and changes in inflation. High and rising inflation is good for neither equities nor bonds. Rising inflation (and inflation volatility) tends to put upward pressure on bond yields, owing to monetary policy tightening and rising term premia (the premium demanded by investors for investing in assets with a longer maturity). Rising inflation at high levels can also weigh on equities, particularly if growth is not strong enough to compensate for the rise in inflation and the likely associated rise in interest rates. This can also be a problem if rising inflation results in profit margins coming under pressure, perhaps because of higher material input or labour costs. That said, rising inflation from low levels often signals the end of a recession and thus can be positive for equities. Since the 1990s, inflation has been low and stable for most of the time, and consequently it has been a less important driver and generally supportive for equities and bond markets alike. In the 1970s and 1980s, when inflation was generally high (>3%), changes in inflation drove large rotations between equities and bonds to real assets.

During late-cycle periods that are accompanied by rising inflation, bonds are usually less good diversifiers for risky assets, and equity/bond correlations have often increased alongside rising oil prices. An extreme example of this was during the 1970s stagflation, when equities and bonds declined together. Commodities can be an important diversifier in such a scenario, because they are among the best diversifier in inflation, both headline and core, in particular during periods of rising inflation volatility.

Assets across the Investment Cycle

We can extend this analysis by looking at how the different asset classes perform across the phases of the typical investment cycle. Exhibit 4.2 shows the annualised real total returns for US equities, bonds and the S&P GSCI Commodity Index® for each of the phases in all of the five cycles from 1973 to 2019.

It is not surprising that equities are the poorest performer in the despair phase, because this is the point in the cycle when investors anticipate a downturn in profits. What is perhaps more surprising is quite how large the potential is for outperformance by diversifying into other asset classes at this point in the cycle. It is this difference that strengthens the case for diversifying or for active asset allocation strategies as the cycle matures so that investors may increase or decrease exposures in different assets at the same time to maximise the likely risk and volatility.

In the hope phase, equities tend to offer by far the best returns, with a clear ranking of the asset classes. In all six cycles, equities have outperformed bonds, and in four of the six cycles, bonds have outperformed commodities. Equities enjoy a strong price boost as

Exhibit 4.2 Performance of asset classes for each phase, annualised, real, total return

S&P 500

	Despair	Hope	Growth	Optimism
1973–1980	-35	69	-3	63
1980–1987	-19	86	-13	31
1987–1990	-77	96	1	20
1990–2000	-61	31	9	27
2000–2007	-24	48	10	-
2007–2019	-44	86	9	102
Average	**-44**	**69**	**2**	**48**
Median	**-40**	**77**	**5**	**31**

US 10y Treasuries

	Despair	Hope	Growth	Optimism
1973–1980	-7	1	-6	3
1980–1987	2	30	-6	15
1987–1990	-1	21	-4	7
1990–2000	-10	15	4	5
2000–2007	11	7	-1	-
2007–2019	12	-6	1	13
Average	**1**	**11**	**-2**	**9**
Median	**0**	**11**	**-2**	**7**

GSCI Commodities

	Despair	Hope	Growth	Optimism
1973–1980	53	-27	2	34
1980–1987	-19	6	1	7
1987–1990	10	-1	26	20
1990–2000	362	-18	3	-2
2000–2007	2	18	10	-
2007–2019	-38	36	-10	80
Average	**62**	**2**	**5**	**28**
Median	**6**	**2**	**2**	**20**

SOURCE: Goldman Sachs Global Investment Research.

investors start to anticipate, and price in, a future rebound in corporate profits, and is the asset class most geared to such a shift in economic and profit potential.

In the growth phase, commodities tend to lead the relative performance. Commodities have outperformed both bonds and equities in this phase in four of the six cycles. Both equities and bonds tend to perform poorly in this phase, with the relative ranking somewhat unstable. This pattern makes sense. Bonds and equities, which are more forward-looking assets, see a larger part of their returns during the hope phase, whereas commodities (which are driven by the supply and demand balance rather than expectations) are the first to perform well when the earnings growth is realised and actual growth (rather than anticipated growth) is reflected in stronger demand.

In the optimism phase, equities outperform again. In this phase equities outperformed commodities and bonds in most of the cycles. The relative performance of bonds and commodities was mixed.

The Impact of Changes in Bond Yields on Equities

In practice, many investors cannot diversify with commodities, and there tends to be much more focus on balanced portfolios that combine equities and government bonds in varying proportions over time. Ideally, the weight between equities and bonds in a portfolio should adjust across the cycle depending on the way in which bonds and equities perform together.

There is a complex but clear relationship between economic activity and financial markets. Equities are making a claim on future nominal growth – and so are referred to as a 'real asset' – and, over time, profits should rise with inflation and with economic activity. The current value should be the present value of future discounted earnings or dividends. This is why equity markets are affected so much by the discount rate (the risk-free interest rate) as well as by future expected growth.

This relationship is encapsulated in the simple one-stage DDM or Gordon growth model, which states that

$$\text{Dividend yield} + \text{growth} = \text{Risk-free Rate} + \text{ERP}.$$

If bond yields fall, all else being equal, the dividend yield should fall (and the price of equities rise). But if lower bond yields are matched by a change in long-term growth expectations, then there should be no positive impact on the current valuation from lower yields. Indeed, the uncertainty about future cash flows may increase the ERP, forcing the dividend yield up (or the price down).

Fixed income assets, by contrast, provide a fixed nominal return over a defined period. The future returns are known in advance in nominal terms but not in real terms (because investors are not protected against surprises in future inflation). The ultimate return will depend on the current level of interest rates and a risk premium (an extra return) to compensate for the risk of default.

The varying relationship between bonds and equities, which is affected by both the cycle and longer-term inflation expectations, can be viewed through the correlation between these two asset markets. Theoretically, when bond prices rise (and their yields, or the level of interest rates, fall), equity prices tend to rise (often buoyed by higher valuations). By contrast, rising interest rates or bond yields (and falling bond prices) tend to be negative for equities because the rate at which future cash flows can be discounted would be increasing (therefore reducing the net present value of equity cash flows). So, there is usually a positive correlation between equity and bond prices (or a negative correlation between bond yields and equity prices).

For much of the history, the positive correlation between bond and equity prices has generally been the norm. After the technology bubble burst in the late 1990s, however, the reverse occurred. Growth expectations collapsed and easier monetary policy pushed down bond yields. But equities were at such high valuations to start with that they derated sharply despite lower bond yields, such that the price correlation turned negative.

Conditions started to normalise from about 2002 as confidence began to recover and growth expectations improved. But this was a brief respite. Before long, the collapse of the US housing bubble (which was partly fuelled by the lower interest rates that followed the end of the technology bubble) heralded the start of the global financial crisis. Easier monetary policy in the wake of the crisis resulted in lower bond yields and inflation amid new worries about growth. The move to a negative correlation between bond and equity prices has proved to be more sustained than ever, as lower bond yields are viewed as a reflection of lower structural growth and potential deflation (as per Japan).

Inflation is the biggest risk for investors in fixed income securities because, although government bonds offer a fixed nominal return over a specific maturity, they offer no protection against surprises in inflation. For equities, their cash flows are linked to inflation and therefore offer some protection in the event of rising prices. Of course, the opposite is the case in periods of deflation. In these circumstances, a fixed nominal return is highly prized, whereas equities – whose cash flows and dividends would fall in line with inflation – are more exposed and require a higher prospective return (lower valuation or higher ERP) to compensate for the risk. This is why in economies that are more prone to deflation, such as Japan and (more recently) Europe, rising interest rates and bond yields have often been seen as positive for equity investors. This seems to be one of the main reasons why the ERP in many markets appears so high currently relative to the past. Another way to think about this is that future returns are more certain for bond investors (there is less perceived risk that inflation will eat away at the fixed nominal returns) and so equities need a higher relative yield to continue to attract investors.

To summarise, there is a constant tug of war between the bond yield and growth expectations that influences the relationship between bond and equity returns. As the long-run relationship (for the US) shows in exhibit 4.3, the main periods when the correlation

Exhibit 4.3 Correlation between equities and bonds has been less negative in recent years owing to QE (equity prices and bond returns)

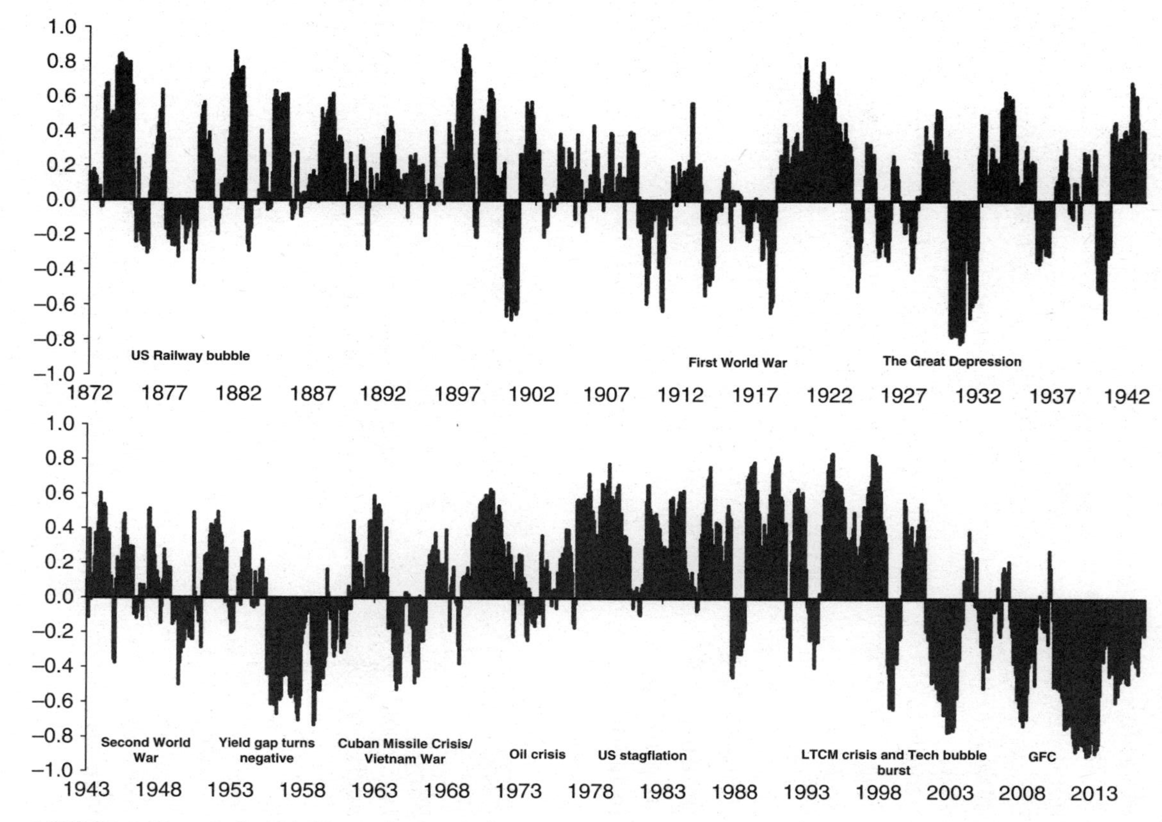

SOURCE: Goldman Sachs Global Investment Research.

turned negative were when there was a growth shock and a deep recession, or a major political event such as a war that pushed up the uncertainty levels, and therefore the required risk premium for equities.

It is not always the case, then, that rising bond yields (or falling bond prices) are negative for equity markets. The impact on equities when bond yields rise differs markedly depending on a number of factors:

- The point of the cycle. Equities tend to be more immune earlier in the cycle.
- The speed of adjustment. Slower is better for equities.
- The level of yields at the time. Historically, UST 10-year yields at 5% or more have been definitively 'bad' for equities, but the crossing point is likely earlier in this cycle.
- The valuation of equities. This relates to the cycle, and clearly equities are less vulnerable when they are cheap.
- The drivers of the yield rise. Real or nominal, inflation-led rises are often easier for equities to digest.

Exhibit 4.4 shows the performance of the S&P 500 during periods when US bond yields have risen. The main observation is that the relationship is not clear or consistent over time. Occasionally equities do well, as in the 1998–2000 period when, although US 10-year Treasury yields rose from 4.2% to 6.8%, the US market rose 46%, with a 29% rise in P/E (the European market was up 72%). But, at other times, most notably in 1994, equities fell as bond yields increased, despite reasonably good earnings growth at the time. There are several factors to consider when analysing this crucial relationship.

The Point of the Cycle: Earlier is Better

The reason why it is tricky to foresee the impact of higher bond yields on equities is that higher yields can happen at different points in the equity cycle – and for different reasons. Quite often,

Exhibit 4.4 US equity performance during periods of rising US 10-year bond yields

US 10y BY						**S&P 500**		
Date		**Level**		**Change**	**Length**	**Change**		
Trough	**Peak**	**Start**	**End**	**(bp)**	**(m)**	**Price**	**NTM PE**	**NTM EPS**
Dec-91	Mar-92	7	8	98	2	-3%	-3%	1%
Oct-93	Nov-94	5	8	288	13	-1%	-14%	12%
Jan-96	Jul-96	6	7	153	6	7%	4%	3%
Nov-96	Apr-97	6	7	93	4	-2%	-5%	3%
Oct-98	Jan-00	4	7	262	16	46%	29%	17%
Nov-01	Apr-02	4	5	124	5	3%	-1%	4%
Jun-03	Sep-03	3	5	149	3	3%	0%	4%
Mar-04	Jun-04	4	5	119	3	1%	-6%	7%
Jun-05	Jun-06	4	5	136	13	4%	-10%	14%
Dec-06	Jun-07	4	5	86	6	6%	2%	4%
Dec-08	Jun-09	2	4	188	5	5%	22%	-16%
Oct-09	Apr-10	3	4	81	6	15%	-3%	19%
Oct-10	Feb-11	2	4	135	4	14%	7%	7%
Jul-12	Sep-13	1	3	161	13	24%	15%	8%
Jul-16	Mar-17	1	3	124	8	11%	6%	6%
Sep-17	Nov-18	2	3	117	14	14%	-8%	22%
Average		**4**	**5**	**145**	**8**	**9%**	**2%**	**7%**

SOURCE: Goldman Sachs Global Investment Research.

the sharpest rise in bond yields is from the trough of the economic cycle. This is typically a constructive time for equity investment and it is usually when equities have a cheap starting point as well. Some of these periods when bond yields have increased were early cycle: 1991, 2001–2003, 2008 and 2012. Others have been later in the cycle.

Generally, the early-cycle rises in bond yields are accompanied by sharp rises in valuation, and earnings growth in the corporate sector is not the main driver of returns – indeed, profits are oftentimes still falling in this phase. These are very different from mid- and later-cycle rises in bond yields, when there may be more worries about inflation, and yields are starting from a higher point and equity valuations are already stretched.

The Speed of Adjustment: Slower Is Better

The speed of bond yield rises is another important factor in explaining the relationship between equities and bonds through the cycle. For example, since the global financial crisis when US 10-year yields increased by more than two standard deviations in a 3-month period, equities have sold off alongside bonds.[1] When rates rise too quickly, they can weigh on growth expectations and valuations for risky assets, and rate volatility can spill over to equity volatility (exhibit 4.5).

The Level of Yields: Lower is Better

In most of the past 15 years, equities have been negatively correlated with bond prices; falling bond prices (rising bond yields) have coincided with strong equity performance. This has been especially

Exhibit 4.5 Sharp bond yield moves have coincided with negative equity returns (average SXXE returns depending on absolute moves in US 10-year Treasury yields [weekly changes])

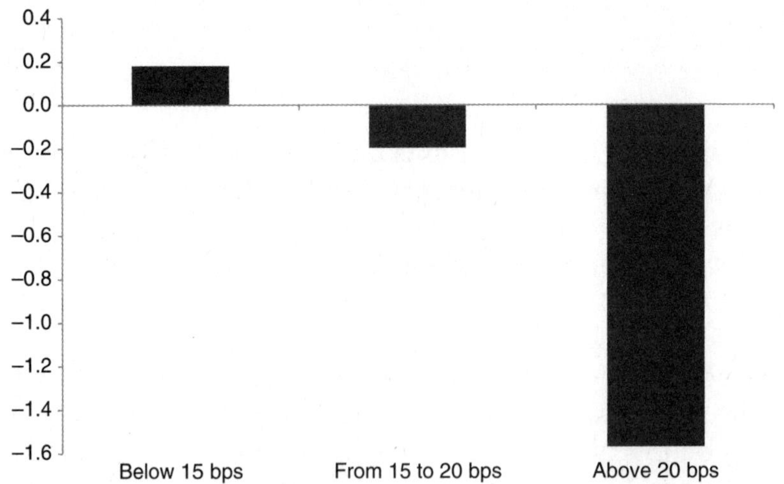

SOURCE: Goldman Sachs Global Investment Research.

[1] Mueller-Glissmann, C., Wright, I., Oppenheimer, P., and Rizzi, A. (2016). *Reflation, equity/bond correlation and diversification desperation.* London, UK: Goldman Sachs Global Investment Research.

helpful for balanced and multi-asset investors, for whom not only have returns over time been strong for both equities and bonds but also the negative correlation has enabled reduced overall risk and volatility in balanced portfolios.

For most equity markets, the correlation of equities with bond yields is loosely dependent on the level of yields. If yields are very low – as they have been in recent years – then equities will tend to be negatively correlated with bond prices. Equities do well as bond yields rise from low levels. Similarly, they will perform poorly as bond yields fall. For example, the period when investors worried about persistent deflation risks in early 2016 was not a good time for equities. By contrast, once bond yields started to rise in mid-2016, equities enjoyed stellar performance. This is also shown in exhibit 4.4.

One way to observe the impact of the level of interest rates on the relationship between equities and bonds is to look at how the correlation between the two varies. The scatterplot in exhibit 4.6 shows that when yields are above 4%–5%, the monthly correlation between equity and bond prices tends to be positive. This means

Exhibit 4.6 Equity/bond correlation can turn positive with higher yields (12m rolling US equity correlation with US 10-year bonds since 1981, weekly)

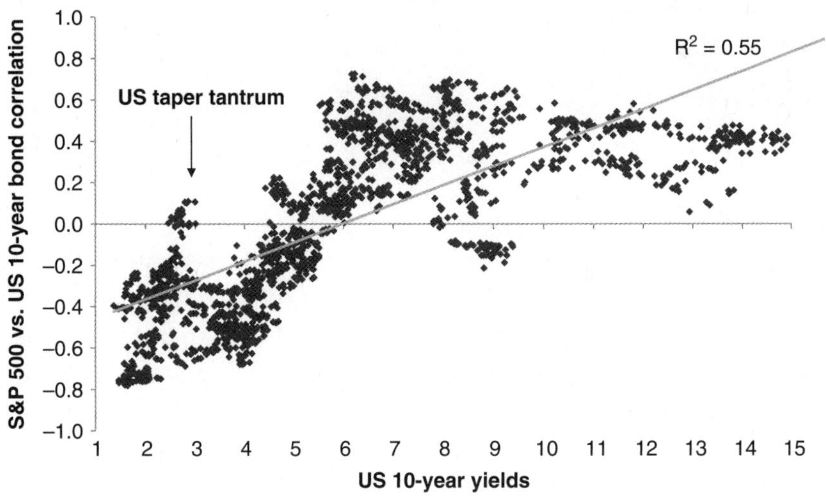

SOURCE: Goldman Sachs Global Investment Research.

that for fairly 'normal' levels of interest rates (perhaps when long-term bond yields are quite similar to long-term expected nominal GDP trend growth), rising bond prices (falling bond yields) are good for equities; equities underperform when yields rise, because this is a signal of inflationary problems and it raises the discount rate for equities. But this relationship typically flips the other way when bond yields fall below 4%–5%; at these lower levels, rising bond prices (falling interest rates) are actually associated with weaker equity returns because the much lower than normal yields for bonds reflect the growing risk of recession or even deflation – which would hit corporate cash flows and earnings. In this way, countries that have experienced very low levels of interest rates, as we have seen in recent years, often tend to see equity prices rise most as bond yields rise (or bond prices fall). This is seen as a reflection of increased confidence in growth and inflation, which helps to reduce perceived risks in the equity market.

Hence, while there is a cycle in equity and equity valuations, and part of this reflects the interplay between growth expectations and the bond yield (the 'risk-free rate'), cycles can be complicated by the changing relationships between bond yields (prices) and equities over time that might be affected by structural factors, such as the prevailing inflationary environment and the level of interest rates.

Structural Shifts in the Value of Equities and Bonds

Although this chapter has focused mainly on the cyclical drivers that determine the relationship between bond and equity performance, the shifts in correlation that have occurred since the end of the 20th century, and in particular since the financial crisis, also demonstrate some of the secular or structural changes in the relationship. Over long periods of time equities have often been seen as a risk asset that requires a much higher yield (dividend yield) than the yield on a much less risky asset, such as a government bond. After all, the yield or valuation is one way of illustrating the expected or required return that an investor demands for putting money into a risky relative to a risk-free asset (or the risk premium).

One of the famous discussions about this relationship, and its implications for investors and asset allocation, followed a controversial speech given by George Ross Goobey, general manager of the Imperial Tobacco pension fund in the UK in 1956 to the Association of Superannuation and Pension Funds (ASPF).[2] He argued the merits of investing in equities to generate inflation-linked growth for pension funds. He became famous for allocating the entirety of the pension fund's investments to equities, a move that is often associated with the start of the so-called cult of the equity.

Prior to this, equities were largely seen as volatile or risky assets that achieved lower risk-adjusted returns than government bonds and, consequently, required a higher yield (and therefore lower valuation). As more institutions warmed to the idea of shifting funds into equities to protect against inflation, the yield on equities declined and the so-called reverse yield gap was born. This refers to the fall in dividend yields to below government bond yields: a pattern that continued, in most developed economies, until the collapse of the technology bubble in the late 1990s.

In his speech to the ASPF, Ross Goobey presented the long-run historical evidence that the ex post equity risk premium (the return investors achieved in equities versus bonds) was positive in real terms, and that investors ignored this at their own peril. The long-run performance of equities was much greater than for bonds after adjusting for inflation. As Ross Goobey said, 'I know that people will say: "Well, things are never going to be the same again", but . . . it has happened again, and again. I say to you that my views are that it is still going to happen yet again even though it may not be the steep rises which we have had in the past.'

Over the 50 years that followed Ross Goobey's pitch, his predictions proved very successful. The annualised real total return to US equities (as a proxy) between 1956 and 2000 was 7%.

[2] Goobey, G.H.R. (1956). Speech to the Association of Superannuation and Pension Funds. The pensions archive [online]. Available at http://www.pensionsarchive.org.uk/27/

Conditions, and forward expectations, began to change from the start of this century in the aftermath of the collapse in equity markets following the end of the technology bubble. In this post-bubble world, equity valuations fell from unrealistically high levels. The onset of the credit crunch, and the deleveraging of balance sheets in many developed economies that followed this, have punctured the confidence that once surrounded equities, and the pre-1960s scepticism about equity returns came back. Dividend yields once again rose above bond yields, and both historical and expected future returns have collapsed.

An illustration of the secular shift in the bond versus equity valuation can be seen in exhibit 4.7 for the US, which compares the 10-year government bond yield with an estimated cash yield to shareholders in the equity market (taken here as the combination of the dividend yield and the buyback yield). Back in the early 1990s investors were being offered a cash return of about 4.5% in

Exhibit 4.7 Equities have remained attractively valued over recent years despite falls in bond yields (US 10-year Treasury yield and cash yield [dividend yield and buyback yield])

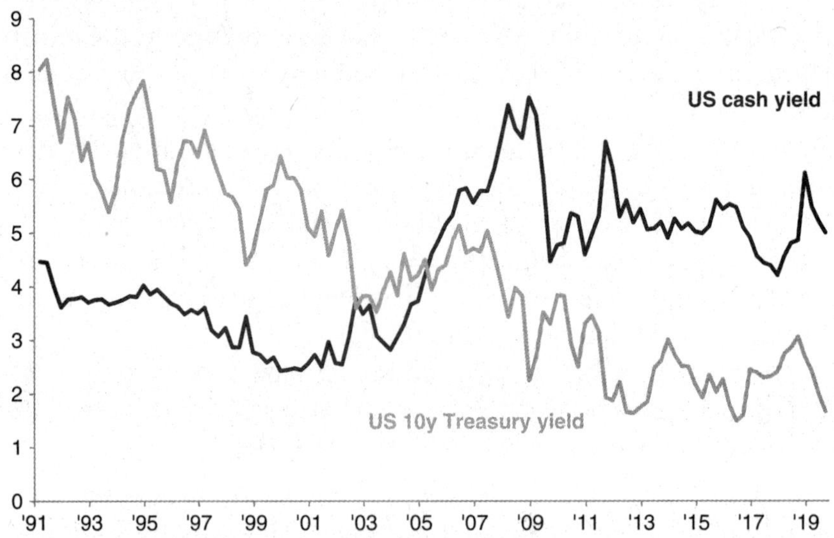

SOURCE: Goldman Sachs Global Investment Research.

the equity market at a time when they were offered an 8% yield by lending to the US government for a 10-year period. Ten years after the financial crisis, investors are being offered a total cash return of over 5% on equities, relative to less than 2% on government bonds. This change reflects many things, of course, but generally it implies a significant relative derating of equities because of greater uncertainty and lower expectations about future growth. Aligned to this, the falls in inflation to much lower levels have reduced the risks for an investor in government bonds (who is offered a fixed nominal return) but equally has reduced the attraction of holding a real asset, such as equity, which may offer some protection over time for higher inflation (because revenues and profits will move alongside inflation).

In low-inflation countries that also have weak long-term expected economic growth, the gap between bond yields and equity cash yields is even higher. Germany, for example, whose equity index also has a disproportionally high weight in mature industries (such as banks and autos) has, at the time of writing, a dividend yield plus buy back yield above 4% compared with a 10-year bond yield below 0%.

Chapter 5
Investment Styles over the Cycle

Looking at investment styles across past cycles shows that generalising at this level can often be misleading. The more you examine the equity market at a micro level (that is, the more you look at individual companies or groups of companies rather than the broad equity market index), the more likely it is that returns will be affected by idiosyncratic issues, such as the specifics of a company or industry, the regulatory environment, issues related to competition, such as mergers and acquisitions, and so on. Patterns that might be evident in one or more cycles – for example, when comparing the performance of large cap companies with that of smaller companies – are not always evident or consistent in other cycles. This makes it difficult, and sometimes risky, to overgeneralise when it comes to forecasting returns.

This issue of consistency is even more evident when it comes to looking at the performance of sectors within the market, or patterns of performance across industries. Although some sectors or industry groups within the stock market are often affected by their relationship with the economic or interest rate cycles, they can also be influenced by a whole host of other issues. Equally, their sensitivity to economic conditions can change over time. For example, historically the chemical industry has been considered cyclical, in that its revenues are highly influenced by the economic cycle. This is because chemical companies have generally produced bulk chemicals, which are similar to commodities. When the economy and demand are strong, these companies see profits rise, and when the economy and demand slow, then, understandably, their profits will often weaken. This sort of company is also often described by analysts as 'operationally levered' – that is to say, they have high fixed costs of production. This means that when demand is weak, their margins can fall dramatically and can result in large losses (it is harder to cover the fixed costs). For the same reason, however, when demand is strong, their profit margins can rise sharply and profits can rise strongly.

This example would be very different for a company in the food production industry, for example. Typically, such companies would face a more stable and predictable end market, irrespective of whether the broader economy is strong or weak; most customers continue to eat the same amount when times are good or bad.

But the examples above cannot be always relied on. For instance, large parts of the chemical industry have changed their business mix in recent years to higher value products such as coatings, adhesives, cleaning materials and agrichemicals (fertilisers and pesticides), for which final demand is likely to be more stable. There has also been a transition of some business models into the production of flavours and fragrances, which are categorised as food or personal care products. Similar changes have occurred in the past in the technology industry, which combines very cyclical commodity products such as semiconductors with generally less cyclical companies producing software. Over time, the market capitalisation, or weighting, of the cyclical component of the industry has fallen relative to the size of the more stable or defensive part.

Similarly, the food producer selling branded food products may have found its end demand becoming more cyclical over time as competition from supermarkets' own-branded goods has meant that the premium customers are prepared to pay for the branded product may be more cyclical than it has been in the past.

The point of these examples is not to say that there are no discernible patterns over time but merely that an investor should recognise that relationships between parts of the stock market and macro factors are subject to change over time as the drivers and competitive developments within and across industries can also change.

Sectors and the Cycle

Notwithstanding these difficulties, broader generalisations can be made about sector returns in relation to the economic cycle. Sectors are often viewed through a lens of sensitivities or beta to economic variables, for example, in relation to how much their valuation and performance is affected by changes in economic growth, inflation and bond yields. I find it quite useful to place industries and sectors of the stock market into four groups according to sensitivity *and* valuation.

As exhibit 5.1 shows, the more economically sensitive industries, or cyclical ones, can be broadly split into those that are cyclical

Exhibit 5.1 Industries and sectors can be divided in four groups according to sensitivity and valuation

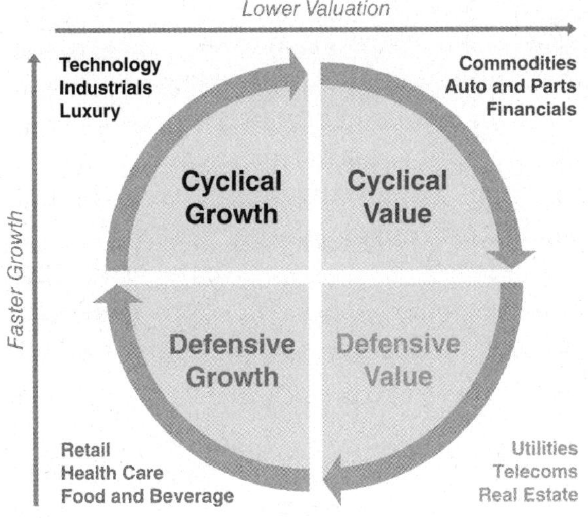

SOURCE: Goldman Sachs Global Investment Research.

but fast-growing, let's say technology, and those that are cyclical but mature (and typically low valuation) such as autos. Similarly, the more defensive, less economically sensitive industries can be grouped into those that are fast-growing, say health care, and those that are defensive but mature, and cheaper, for example, telecom companies. As a broad guide, some of these sectors are then placed in a quadrant that relates to how they tend to perform on a relative basis under different economic conditions.

The best environment for cyclical value is when growth is accelerating alongside rising inflation and interest rates. Stronger growth is a benefit to cyclicals in general, but the mature sectors – where fixed costs (both wages and assets) are often a higher proportion of revenues than in younger, faster-growing sectors – have higher leverage to inflation. This is often described as high 'operational leverage'. When inflation and interest rates rise, their revenue growth tends to increase and margins improve, resulting in a larger than average boost to earnings. Meanwhile, defensive growth, at the other end of the spectrum, tends to perform better on a relative basis when growth is generally weaker and more scarce. Lower inflation and interest rates also tend to benefit these companies because they have very long-term expected cash flows, and lower interest rates mean lower discount rates for these cash flows and, as a result, higher valuations.

Of course, specific industries may also, at any time, be affected by specific stock issues (particularly if the industry is dominated by one or two large companies), and can be affected by regulation and changes in the competitive landscape, including possible consolidation or new entrants, along with a whole host of other factors.

As a result of these complications, investors often group companies or industries together into styles. To the extent that generalisations can be useful, some relationships across styles of investment and sector or industry sensitivity are particularly relevant:

- The relationship between cyclical and defensive companies.
- The relationship between value and growth companies.

These two broad groupings are useful to investors because they tend to have a clear relationship with investment and economic cycles over time.

Cyclical versus Defensive Companies

Notwithstanding the points mentioned previously about changes to the composition and business mix of companies over time, it is possible to describe industries as cyclical when they have a high sensitivity, or beta, to the economic cycle. Similarly, those that have a low sensitivity can be reasonably described as relatively defensive. Exhibit 5.2 shows the sensitivity or beta of expected (consensus 12 months forward) earnings growth by industry to GDP in the global stock market.

The results are fairly intuitive. Auto companies, resources and technology have been the most sensitive to the economic cycle, and utilities, telecoms and food and beverages the least.

Exhibit 5.2 Beta of forward EPS growth to World GDP growth

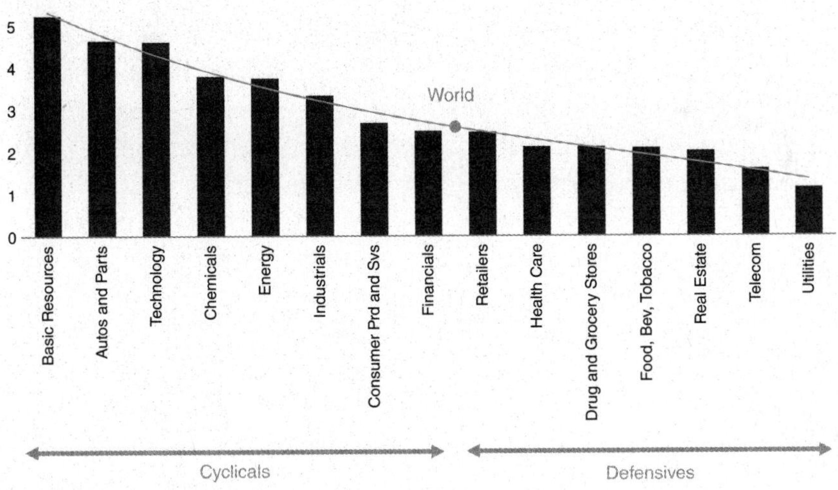

SOURCE: Goldman Sachs Global Investment Research.

Exhibit 5.3 US Cyclical/Defensive annualised performance; The despair phase is by far the worst period for cyclicals and the hope phase is the best period

	Despair	Hope	Growth	Optimism
1973–1980	-6%	1%	9%	10%
1980–1987	-31%	34%	-18%	-7%
1987–1990	-14%	6%	-4%	-12%
1990–2000	-17%	7%	17%	70%
2000–2007	-47%	16%	9%	-
2007–2019	-37%	30%	0%	9%
Average	**-25%**	**16%**	**2%**	**14%**
Median	**-24%**	**12%**	**4%**	**9%**

SOURCE: Goldman Sachs Global Investment Research.

Because of the relationship of these styles with the economic cycle, one can find a pattern of performance that fits with the 'typical cycle' phases noted in chapter 3. Exhibit 5.3 shows the annualised performance of cyclicals versus defensives for the US stock market (S&P 500). The patterns here are reasonably clear. The despair phase is by far the worst period for cyclical companies relative to defensive ones. This is intuitive: it is during this phase that investors are anticipating recession, a prospect that is bad for equity markets in general and for those that are most sensitive to the cycle in particular. Defensive companies at least provide some relative haven during this phase and, on average, have in the past generated close to a 30% relative outperformance during these phases. The hope phase, as expected, is the best period for cyclical companies relative to defensive ones, with a median outperformance of 25%. The growth phase is the longest phase and it produces the most ambiguous outcomes. Partly, this is because during this phase there may be several mini cycles when higher-frequency survey data such as the PMI or ISM improve (see chapter 3). The optimism phase is generally also one in which the more cyclical companies outperform and tolerance for rising valuations in the market tends to increase.

These patterns are also evident when we compare the relative performance of cyclical and defensive companies across a standard industrial cycle. One easy way to do this is by looking at the cycles in survey data, such as the so-called PMI or, in the US, the widely observed ISM index. These are widely followed by investors because they correlate closely with GDP but have the advantage of being monthly, and therefore of higher frequency than the quarterly reports of GDP.

The PMI and ISM index are calibrated to show expansion or contraction; typically, below a level of 50 they are consistent with contraction and above 50 with expansion.

By splitting industries into cyclical and defensive groups, based on their GDP sensitivity, we can see that there is a close relationship over time between the relative performance of the two groups and the level of these indices. Generally speaking, if there is a rise in these surveys, it is likely to be a time when more cyclical industries outperform, whereas in a period of falling or slowing cycle data, more defensive sectors tend to do better (see exhibit 5.4).

Exhibit 5.4 Global Cyclicals versus defensive across industrial cycles

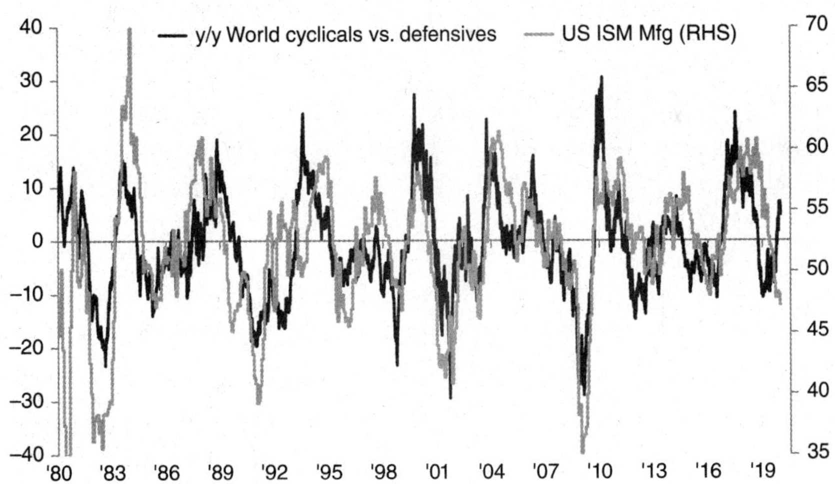

SOURCE: Goldman Sachs Global Investment Research.

Another driver of the relative return between cyclical versus defensive company performance is bond yields. As exhibit 5.5 shows, lower bond yields, which are usually consistent with weaker growth prospects, tend to result in cyclical companies underperforming, while rising bond yields are supportive for cyclical companies on a relative basis. There are two logical reasons for this. First, bond yields tend to rise when growth is stronger, thereby boosting revenues more for economically sensitive companies than for those with stable cash flows. Second, cyclical companies generally have a high proportion of their costs that are fixed, such as labour or the cost of materials, as well as production costs and depreciation of capital (factories and equipment). In this way, inflation (and the high bond yields associated with it) is generally helpful because it reduces a company's fixed costs relative to sales (which will rise with inflation). The opposite is also true. But, generally, if you own a depreciating asset, then inflation (up to a point) is actually rather beneficial. This may be why cyclicals, unusually, did well in the 1973–1980 despair phase, when inflation was high.

Exhibit 5.5 Lower bond yields tend to result in cyclical companies underperforming

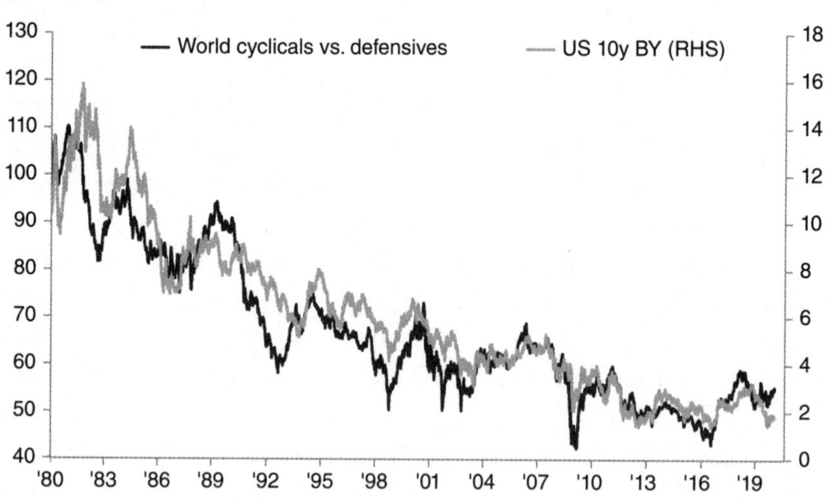

SOURCE: Goldman Sachs Global Investment Research.

However, investors are sensitive not just to the *level* of these indicators but also to the *rate of change*; is the index below 50 but inflecting upwards, indicating an improvement in the so-called second derivative, or is it perhaps above 50 but slowing?

To make things more complex, the interplay between the rate of change in the cycle and what is happening to bond yields becomes particularly important. Specifically, when the economy is growing (when the PMI is above 50) but at a slower pace, this will generally result in a different sector and/or style leadership if accompanied by rising or falling bond yields.

In reality, therefore, there is a complex interplay between the cycle measured as the level of growth and its direction of travel (is it improving or deteriorating?), and between whether bond yields are increasing or decreasing. There are many permutations. When it comes to cyclical versus defensive sector performance, the least favourable combination is during a contraction – when the PMIs are below 50 (contracting) and getting worse, and bond yields are also falling (typically consistent with expectations of a further deterioration in inflation and growth).

The best combination, as shown for the market as a whole in chapter 3, is during a recovery – when the economy is still in recession, but the rate of growth is inflecting upwards, or starting to look less weak. This is when animal spirits tend to kick in and investors begin to anticipate better times ahead. If this is accompanied by rising bond yields (an expression of confidence in future growth), then the more economically sensitive companies, or those that are most cyclical, will tend to outperform the more defensive companies, which are less leveraged to the cycle.

A simple way of summarising these permutations is shown in exhibit 5.6 for the US market cycle. It illustrates one extreme in the permutations mentioned previously: in this case, the PMI is above 50 (consistent with a growing economy) and starting to fall from a peak level just as bond yields are falling. This shows quite clearly that average returns have been higher in the more defensive industries of the market, and the worst performers have been those that are most at risk from an economic downturn, such as banks,

Exhibit 5.6 US Cyclical versus defensives monthly performance (since 1973)

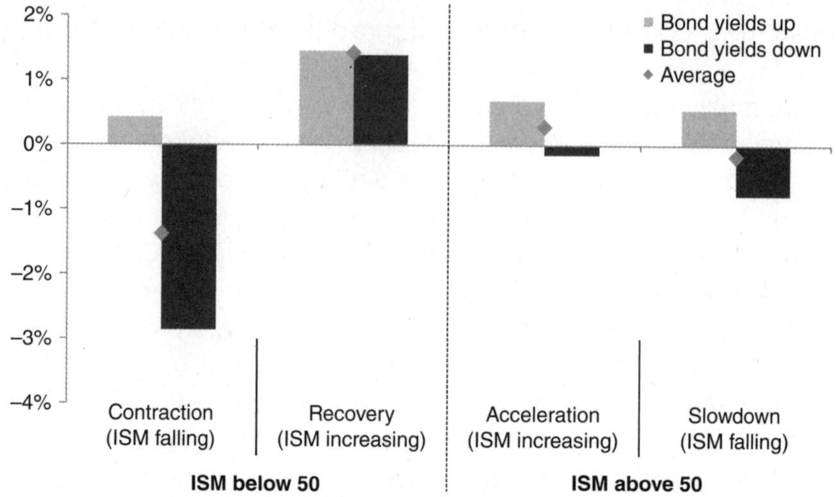

SOURCE: Goldman Sachs Global Investment Research.

construction, media and technology – all sectors where demand is discretionary and where orders can be easily delayed.

At the other extreme – where the PMI is below 50 (the economy is probably in recession) but rising from a trough level just as bond yields are rising – the pattern of leadership in the market reverses.

Value versus Growth Companies

Although the relative performance of cyclicals versus defensives is fairly easy to understand, the relationship between so-called value and growth companies is somewhat less straightforward because these definitions tend to cut across companies in different industries. In general, growth refers to companies that enjoy more stable or higher growth in revenues over time and that tend to trade at higher valuations. Value companies are usually defined as those that trade on a cheaper valuation, such as a lower price/earnings ratio, than the average company.

The MSCI indices based on growth and value, for example, include the following definitions:[1]

MSCI growth segmentation is based on five variables:

- Long-term forward EPS growth rate.
- Short-term forward EPS growth rate.
- Current internal growth rate.
- Long-term historical EPS growth trend.
- Long-term historical sales per share growth trend.

MSCI value segmentation is based on three variables:

- Book value to price.
- 12-month forward earnings to price.
- Dividend yield.

There tends to be some crossover between these factors and the cyclical versus defensive axis. Typically, value companies are more cyclical and defensive ones can overlap with growth to some degree.

A simple correlation between value relative to growth and industrial production (a measure of growth in the real economy) shows a positive, albeit not very strong, relationship. Stronger economic growth is usually associated with better performance of value (cheap) stocks because these are often more cyclical in terms of sensitivity. But it is more complicated than this cyclical/defensive axis because the relationship between value and growth has changed over time and, in particular, since the global financial crisis of 2008.

When comparing value versus growth with the average of the phases of the cycle (exhibit 5.7), a much less clear pattern emerges than in a comparison of cyclicals and defensives. The only clear picture – at least on average – is the underperformance of value in the optimism phase. In this final part of the investment cycle, when investors tend to be most confident, they allow valuations to increase in equity markets even as profit growth slows. It is this environment where growth stocks typically have their strongest relative returns.

---

[1] Full definitions are available at https://www.msci.com/eqb/methodology/meth_docs/MSCI_Dec07_GIMIVGMethod.pdf

Exhibit 5.7 The relationship between US value and growth companies is less straightforward

	Despair	Hope	Growth	Optimism
1973–1980	-	-	46%	-5%
1980–1987	16%	1%	5%	-2%
1987–1990	3%	3%	5%	-17%
1990–2000	2%	-14%	14%	-37%
2000–2007	39%	12%	18%	-
2007–2019	-17%	4%	-18%	-11%
Average	**9%**	**1%**	**12%**	**-15%**
Median	**3%**	**3%**	**10%**	**-11%**

SOURCE: Goldman Sachs Global Investment Research.

Value, Growth and Duration

Although exhibit 5.7 shows average returns through different phases, a clearer pattern becomes visible when we look at the relative performance over time, which tends to show a fairly persistent longer-term trend of value outperforming. This is consistent with the evidence documented in academic studies. According to the so-called value premium, first identified by Graham and Dodd (1934),[2] shares with a high book-to-market ratio of equity value or low P/E ratio (generally referred to as value stocks) provide, on average, higher returns than shares with a low book-to-market ratio (growth stocks). This has been widely corroborated in the academic literature, perhaps most famously by Eugene F. Fama and Kenneth R. French,[3] who showed that in the period from 1975 to 1995 the difference between average returns on global portfolios of high and low valuation stocks (using price-to-book value) was 7.68% per year and that value had outperformed growth in 12 of the 13 markets they examined.

A more important driver of the relative performance between value and growth is their respective relationship with interest rates

[2] Graham, B., and Dodd, D. L. (1934). *Security analysis*. New York, NY: McGraw-Hill.

[3] Fama, E., and French, K. (1998). Value versus growth: The international evidence. *Journal of Finance*, 53(6), 1975–1999.

and bond yields, typically described as their 'duration'. The definition of equity duration closely follows the definition of bond duration (identified by Macaulay [1938]).[4] Similar to bond duration, equity duration relates to the length of time until investors expect to receive future cash flows from their investment in a company's shares; hence, in this sense, duration is a measure of the company's cash-flow maturity and, therefore, interest rate sensitivity. If a company is expected to pay a large fraction of cash flows in the distant future, then it is considered a long-duration stock. A good example is a technology company, or the whole technology sector, where companies are investing rapidly for future growth and likely pay no dividends as they do so. By contrast, stocks of mature companies exhibiting high dividend-to-price ratios (such as utility companies) are short-duration stocks. Long-duration stocks will see their net present value rise more for any given fall in interest rates than a shorter-duration company, and vice versa.

There has been a significant change in the relationship between bond yields and the relative performance of growth and value over time. As exhibit 5.8 shows, from 1980 to 2007 there was generally a negative relationship between the two. During the 1980s and 1990s, falling bond yields were associated with generally strong growth and lower risks – an environment that was conducive to value companies. Then, in the period running up to the technology bubble in the late 1990s, there was a sharp rotation in favour of growth stocks when low interest rates were seen as beneficial to growth companies that enjoyed long duration. Also, technology companies (and at the time telecom and media stocks) were seen as 'new economy' companies that would benefit from much higher future growth than those in traditional industries (often referred to at the time as 'old economy') where demand was mature.

In the wake of the collapse of the technology bubble, many of these growth stocks (and technology stocks in particular) experienced the biggest falls in valuations. Indeed, at the time, the gap

[4] Macaulay, F. R. (1938). *Some theoretical problems suggested by the movements of interest rates, bond yields, and stock prices in the United States Since 1856*. Cambridge, MA: National Bureau of Economic Research.

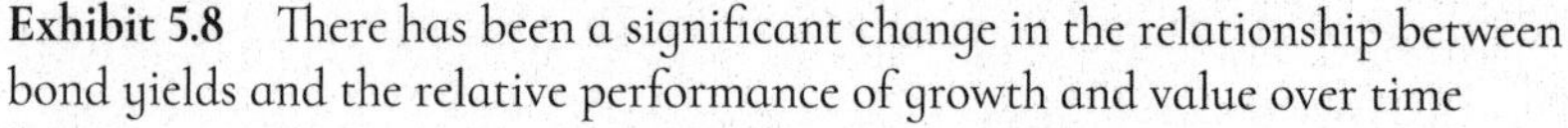
Exhibit 5.8 There has been a significant change in the relationship between bond yields and the relative performance of growth and value over time

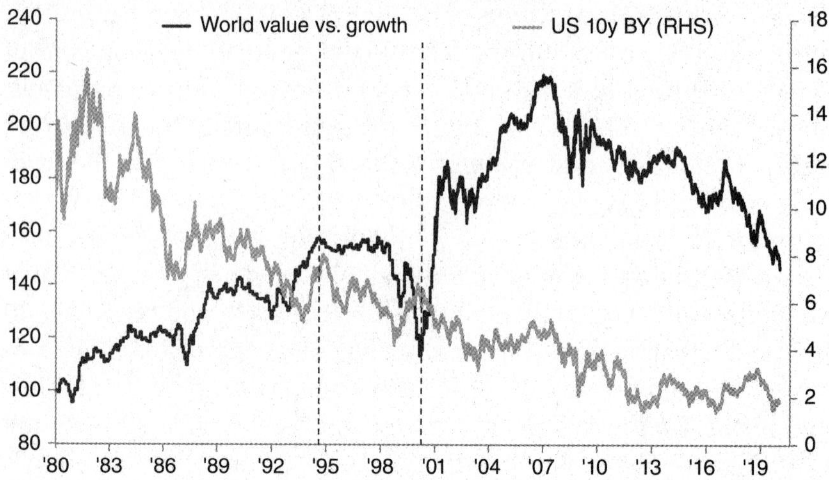

SOURCE: Goldman Sachs Global Investment Research.

in valuations between growth and value stocks had reached record highs, leaving them exposed to a reversal as confidence in the long-term growth opportunities for these stocks, and the value that had been attributable to them, started to fade.

The period between 2000 and the start of the financial crisis in 2007 was one in which the value premium reasserted itself. Investors generally reassessed the value in the 'old economy' and many companies in these mature industries also restructured to improve their competitive and growth credentials. Meanwhile, the fashion for growth had been dealt a heavy blow as investors were left with huge losses in overvalued growth stocks whose stock prices had collapsed.

Since the global financial crisis of 2007, the relationship seems to have reversed once again, with lower bond yields associated with weaker performance in value stocks relative to growth stocks. The underperformance of value relative to growth has been one of the most notable shifts that has taken place in stock market relationships since the financial crisis in 2007/2008, and this topic is discussed in more detail in chapter 9.

In general, there have been four drivers of the style relationships in the most recent investment cycle.

- Technology companies have generally seen much better growth in earnings than the rest of the equity market, and this has benefited the growth style (which tends to include more technology companies). At the same time, in the wake of the financial crisis, banks have suffered poor returns. This has partly been a function of lower economic activity in general and partly the environment of very low (and in many cases negative) interest rates, which hamper the ability of banks to generate margins on their loans.
- Even if we look at measures of growth versus value on a sector-neutral basis – by removing the sector bias and just looking at growth versus value within each industry – growth has outperformed. Some of this reflects the increased scarcity of growth. As inflation has moderated, fewer companies have been able to enjoy strong sales growth compared with other cycles because sales growth is a function of nominal growth and general prices.
- Since the financial crisis we have seen a relentless fall in bond yields, which form part of the discount rate. The lower the level of bond yields, the greater the benefit for longer-duration companies, particularly if these companies are also seen as 'disruptors' in mature industries.
- The other part of the discount rate is the risk premium. In the post-financial-crisis cycle, the risk premium has generally been higher given greater perceived risks to economic growth, deflation, geopolitical issues and the impact on the competitive environment of technological innovation.

Given the higher risk premium, investors have also increasingly valued the stability or predictability of a company's returns over time. This is also rational. If returns available in less risky assets, such as government bonds or corporate bonds, are very low (because bond yields have fallen to such low levels), then investors are likely to pay more for assets that have higher returns (perhaps a high dividend or free cash flow yields) so long as the expected returns are predictable and relatively safe. This is why in the post-financial-crisis cycle, 'bond-like' equities such as infrastructure companies and government-backed concessions (for example, some toll roads or utilities that have a fixed contract or an inflation-protected return on capital) have also performed strongly.

Taken together, therefore, we can see that there are some relationships between the investment cycle and equity styles. Perhaps the most consistent of these relates to the relative performance of cyclical versus defensive companies.

There has also been some evidence of cycles in their style relationships, such as value versus growth. But these styles are more complicated, because they are affected by a variety of different factors in addition to the economic cycle – in particular, the impact of duration on companies, together with other secular trends relating to industry change and competition.

Other styles or factors within the market, such as large versus small capitalisation or specific stock performance, tend to be even less consistent over time and across cycles, which makes it much harder to make strong and reliable generalisations.

Part II

The Nature and Causes of Bull and Bear Markets: What Triggers Them and What to Look out For

Chapter 6
Bear Necessities: The Nature and Shape of Bear Markets

Bear markets are a natural, or even inevitable, part of an investment cycle. But they can vary enormously in length and severity depending on the triggers and conditions, including the valuations, which precede them. In their worst form, bear markets can be savage, and it can take many months, if not years, to recover the losses incurred. This means that having some understanding of what drives bear markets can be valuable to investors, particularly in the case of those that are long-lasting and structural in nature.

Although avoiding bear markets is an understandable goal, timing is crucial. Selling equities too early in anticipation of a bear market can be as costly as staying fully invested and waiting for one to start. For example, equity investors have, on average, lost about the same amount in the first three months of a bear market as they would have earned in the final months of a bull market. In other words, selling equities too early can place you in the same position as selling after the start of a bear market.

Bear Markets Are Not All the Same

Most investors view both bear and bull markets as a natural consequence of the business cycle. Economic activity tends to generate growth cycles: after years of strong growth, capacity constraints lead to inflationary pressures. Tighter monetary policy then raises the cost of capital and the discount rate while simultaneously reducing the prospects for future growth. Equity prices shift downwards to adjust to a fall in future growth expectations. Just as rising rates tend to trigger a bear market, it often takes a period of interest rate cuts to reverse the process and raise the value of future cash flows. In this way, most bear markets and bull markets are usually, at least in part, a monetary phenomenon.

But investors tend to overgeneralise about bear markets and speak of them as if they were a homogenous group in which experiences have been largely similar. In reality, the triggers, timing and profile of recovery vary significantly, and bear markets come in many shapes and sizes. That said, despite the differences over time, there are some recurring characteristics, as with cycles in general.

Most bear markets are relatively short, lasting about 2 years. However, others are much more drawn out, and the duration from peak to trough may be significantly longer and the decline deeper. The difference often relates to the nature of the economic cycle and the interplay between this cycle and other factors. The variation in length and depth is also because although most bear markets are a consequence of rising interest rates and the onset of recession, not all are. Some are triggered by unexpected shocks and events. Others are associated with recessions but are longer-lasting because they are exacerbated by the impact of either an asset price collapse and/or a major unwinding of economic imbalances.

Another challenge when it comes to defining bear markets is that it can be quite difficult, in real time, to assess when a bear market has actually ended; not all bear markets end in a decisive way with a strong and sustained rebound in prices. It is not uncommon for market volatility to rise towards the end of a bear market and for a sharp recovery to revert to a decline shortly afterwards. Moreover, this can happen several times before a final low in the bear market is decisively reached.

Looking back through history, we can see many examples of deep bear markets that had a volatile and slow recovery. In the UK, for example, a stock market peak was achieved in 1825. A sharp fall of 70% occurred over the following 2 years. Although recoveries and other bear markets followed, the 1825 peak was not surpassed for more than 100 years. Was this just one long bear market or a series of bull and bear markets over a period of long-term structural decline?

Similarly, the S&P composite price index fell by 86% between September 1929 and June 1932. It rose sharply, by 135%, between June 1932 and July 1933. It was not until 1954, however, that the index exceeded its September 1929 levels. Even on a total return basis, it did not recover to its pre-1929 levels until 1945.

Japan's bear market of the 1990s is another example of one that continued to be volatile even after the final low in July 1992. Initially, the Nikkei stock index enjoyed a sharp rebound of close to 40% as evidence of an economic recovery finally emerged, but this did not mark the start of a smooth and steady recovery. Since then, there have been five sharp rallies of 40% or more, but the market continues to languish at roughly half the level of its 1989 high, so even in this case one could argue that the bear market that started in 1989 is ongoing.

Other bear markets are difficult to date precisely because high inflation (or even deflation) has meant that measurements of returns are significantly different in nominal and real (inflation-adjusted) terms. The 1973/1974 bear market is a case in point. A strong initial bounce from a sharp fall is little comfort to an investor who bought close to the top.

Exhibit 6.1 shows some of the prominent triggers for bear markets in the US over the past 50 years. Of the nine bear markets over this period, six were followed by recessions. The others were more a function of political events or other triggers. Two of these bear markets were particularly long and entrenched, and difficult to exit from: the 1973/1974 bear market and the 2007–2009 bear market.

Exhibit 6.1 Bear markets are triggered by different factors each time

Bear market	Factors	Recession?	
1961–1962	'Kennedy Slide': Rising rates from 1959 Cold War tension	No	-
1966	Inflation following Johnson Great Society programme; Fed raised rates by approximately 1.5% in 1 year	No	-
1968–1970	Vietnam war and inflation; Fed raised rates to 9% from 4% 2 years before; between the start of 1968 and mid-1968 rates rose by 3%	Yes	Dec 1969 – Nov 1970
1973–1974	The crash after the collapse of the Bretton Woods system over the previous 2 years, with the associated 'Nixon Shock' and USD devaluation under the Smithsonian Agreement 1973 Oil Crisis: Price of oil rose from $3 per barrel to nearly $12	Yes	Nov 1973 – Mar 1975
1980–1982	'Volcker crash'; the 1979 second oil crisis was followed by strong inflation; the Fed raised its rates from 9% to 19% in six months	Yes	Jan 1980 – July 1980 Jul 1981 – Nov 1982
1987	Black Monday: Flash Crash: computerised 'programme trading' strategies swamped the market; tensions between the US and Germany over currency valuations	No	-
1990	Gulf War: Iraq invasion of Kuwait; oil prices doubled	Yes	July 1990 – Mar 1991
2000–2002	Dotcom bubble; technology companies bankruptcy; Enron scandal; 09/11 attacks	Yes	Mar 2001 – Nov 2001
2007–2009	Housing bubble; sub-prime loan & CDS collapse; US housing market collapse	Yes	Dec 2007 – Jun 2009

SOURCE: Goldman Sachs Global Investment Research.

These were both associated with a recession but in both cases the price declines were larger than average and the falls more persistent. These bear markets were amplified by the unwinding of major imbalances (mainly related to inflation in the case of the 1970s and personal sector deleveraging after the collapse of the US housing market in the case of 2007).

Extending this analysis shows that, on the standard definition (of declines of 20% or more), there have been 27 bear markets in the S&P 500 since 1835 and 10 in the post-war period. There have been significantly more corrections and drawdowns over this period, but these can be ignored either because they resulted in falls below 20% or they were very short-lived.

Over time, most bear markets are a function of one (and sometimes a combination) of three triggers:

- Rising interest rates and/or inflation expectations together with fear of recession.
- An exogenous and unexpected shock that increases uncertainty and pushes down stock prices (as the required risk premium rises).
- The bursting of a major asset price bubble and/or the unwinding of structural imbalances that result in deleveraging and often a banking crisis.

In exhibit 6.2, using these triggers as a starting point, I have applied a classification to each bear market. Although the classification of each event here is somewhat subjective, it nonetheless attempts to group bear markets into different categories based on similar characteristics over the time series history. I have described them in the following way:

- **Cyclical bear.** Typically a function of rising interest rates, impending recessions and expected falls in profits. These markets are a function of a typical economic cycle and are the most common type of bear market.
- **Event-driven bear.** Triggered by a one-off shock that does not necessarily lead to a domestic recession (such as a war, oil price shock, EM crisis or technical market dislocation), but which leads to a short-lived rise in uncertainty and pushes up the equity risk premium (the required rate of return).
- **Structural bear.** Usually triggered by the unwinding of structural imbalances and financial bubbles. Often a price shock, such as deflation, follows. This tends to be the deepest and longest type of bear market.

Exhibit 6.2 US bear markets since the 1800s

S&P 500 – Bear market					Time to recover back to previous level		Volatility	
Type	Start	End	Length (m)	Decline (%)	Nominal (m)	Real (m)	Peak to trough	Trough to recovery
S	May-1835	Mar-1842	82	-56	259	-	13	17
C	Aug-1847	Nov-1848	15	-23	42	-	8	9
C	Dec-1852	Oct-1857	58	-65	67	-	19	25
C	Mar-1858	Jul-1859	16	-23	11	-	21	15
C	Oct-1860	Jul-1861	9	-32	15	-	31	17
C	Apr-1864	Apr-1865	12	-26	48	-	14	8
S	Feb-1873	Jun-1877	52	-47	32	11	11	11
C	Jun-1881	Jan-1885	43	-36	191	17	9	11
C	May-1887	Aug-1893	75	-31	65	49	10	12
C	Sep-1902	Oct-1903	13	-29	17	22	9	10
E	Sep-1906	Nov-1907	14	-38	21	250	15	11
C	Dec-1909	Dec-1914	60	-29	121	159	9	12
C	Nov-1916	Dec-1917	13	-33	85	116	12	12
C	Jul-1919	Aug-1921	25	-32	39	14	15	10
S	Sep-1929	Jun-1932	33	-85	266	284	30	20
S	Mar-1937	Apr-1942	62	-59	49	151	20	10
C	May-1946	Mar-1948	21	-28	27	73	14	12
E	Aug-1956	Oct-1957	15	-22	11	13	9	9
E	Dec-1961	Jun-1962	6	-28	14	18	15	9

(continued)

Exhibit 6.2 *(continued)*

S&P 500 – Bear market					Time to recover back to previous level		Volatility	
Type	Start	End	Length (m)	Decline (%)	Nominal (m)	Real (m)	Peak to trough	Trough to recovery
E	Feb-1966	Oct-1966	8	-22	7	24	10	8
C	Nov-1968	May-1970	18	-36	21	270	9	10
S	Jan-1973	Oct-1974	21	-48	69	154	15	11
C	Nov-1980	Aug-1982	20	-27	3	8	12	20
E	Aug-1987	Dec-1987	3.3	-34	20	49	45	13
C	Jul-1990	Oct-1990	3	-20	4	6	17	14
S	Mar-2000	Oct-2002	30	-49	56	148	19	11
S	Oct-2007	Mar-2009	17	-57	49	55	32	16
Average			**28**	**-38**	**60**	**90**	**16**	**13**
Median			**18**	**-32**	**39**	**49**	**14**	**11**
Average structural			**42**	**-57**	**111**	**134**	**20**	**14**
Average cyclical			**27**	**-31**	**50**	**73**	**14**	**13**
Average event driven			**9**	**-29**	**15**	**71**	**19**	**10**

NOTE: S: structural bear market, E: event-driven bear market, C: cyclical bear market.
SOURCE: Goldman Sachs Global Investment Research.

Cyclical Bear Markets

Bear markets that have been described as cyclical are those that relate to a standard economic downturn triggered by a period of tighter monetary policy. They are also bear markets that have ended, at least in part, as a result of falling interest rates. Defining past bear markets as cyclical is easier than defining them as such at the time. Given that many structural bear markets are also associated with rising interest rates and economic slowdowns, one might assume that there is a risk of a structural factor operating during any bear market. However, one of the key distinctions here is that equity (and bond) prices tend to respond to falling interest rates and leading indicators during a normal cyclical bear market. Although falling interest rates may eventually contribute to a recovery from a structural bear market, the shifts in policy typically need to be more aggressive and take a much longer period of time. Overall, therefore, we can broadly describe cyclical bear markets as a monetary phenomenon that generally reaches a trough in prices 3 to 6 months after the first rate cut.

One of the reasons why most bear markets tend to recover before the end of a recession is that financial prices start to anticipate recovery as a result of falling interest rates. Although there is insufficient data on interest rates to show this for all the cyclical bear markets throughout history, in most cases there is a tendency for equity markets to begin to recover after a period of falling rates. Although this can sometimes take a period of time, because the initial rate falls may not be enough to generate expectations of an imminent economic recovery, an easing of monetary policy is usually an important part of the process of kick-starting growth again and pushing equity prices higher.

Various factors are common to cyclical bear markets. Taking the history of these types of bear markets together shows us that the average cyclical bear market experiences a fall of about 30% and lasts for about 27 months. The level of the market has, on average, not recovered to its previous level until just over 4 years after the decline in nominal terms, and 6 years in real terms (although the averages in real terms are highly variable). Volatility during the bear market is relatively low (see exhibit 6.2). The average volatility of monthly returns from peak to trough has been 14% for cyclical bear markets. For structural bear markets, the figure is significantly higher, at 20%.

Before:

- Strong economic growth.
- Rising interest rates.

After:

- Rate cuts with rapid response.
- Profits recovering quickly.
- Equity market responding to falling interest rates.

In terms of profitability, history suggests that most cyclical bear markets are associated with relatively short-lived declines in profitability. On average, profits start to recover about 10 months after the end of the bear market.

Again, this is partly a response to the decline in interest rates beginning to benefit corporates via lower interest charges, but it is also a result of operational gearing kicking in as volume growth starts to recover. Cyclical bear markets are often global in nature (but they do not have to be) given their dependence on the economic cycle. Economies and interest rates are not always synchronised. Consequently, there are occasions when equity markets decouple, producing a bear market in one country while a bull market runs in another. An example of this is the decoupling of the US equity market from Europe in 1991.

Event-Driven Bear Markets

There are several examples of bear markets that can be described as broadly event-driven. Unlike the more usual cyclical bear markets, these are not triggered by the evolution of the economic cycle, rising interest rates and concerns over future growth. They are, instead, generally the result of an unexpected exogenous event, such as a political issue or an unexpected shock (a sharp rise in oil prices, for example), an event that itself raises the required risk premium sufficiently to require a downward adjustment in prices, even if equity prices were not generally regarded as expensive to begin with. More often than not, such event-driven declines in the market are short-lived and are not associated with a fundamental shift in economic or corporate conditions.

This is not an ideal definition because, on occasion, what starts out as an unexpected event (a political shock, for example) could have been at least partly responsible for triggering a bear market that turns out to be something more sinister. The oil crisis of 1973 can be viewed as such a case. Although not entirely the result of the oil crisis itself, the sharp rise in inflation and interest rates that followed contributed, in no small part, to the collapse in real returns in equity markets over subsequent years.

In this way, it is not always easy to recognise where a particular event-driven crisis ends as the shock often triggers follow-on waves of rising uncertainty, falling investment and, possibly, an economic downturn. Oftentimes, such events, particularly if traumatic, can elicit a powerful policy response that kick-starts a recovery or fuels another problem. For example, the Russian debt default and Asian crises of 1997/1998 resulted in a global easing of monetary policy at a time when domestic demand in the developed economies was strong. The cost of capital fell still further. Import costs fell sharply and boosted already strong corporate margins. Valuations expanded, as a combination of very low interest rates and strong corporate profits raised expectations that this could be sustained into the long term. The scene had been set for the technology boom and eventual bust in 2000.

Despite the shortcomings of definition with respect to event-driven bears, it is at least possible in retrospect to see some sharp falls in equity markets as a consequence of a one-off rise in the required equity risk premium as a result of an event. Because these events in many cases did not result in a shift in the economic cycle or the underlying trend of economic and profits growth, they were generally relatively short-lived.

Looking at past examples, there have been some key differences relative to cyclical bear markets. The average decline in event-driven bear markets of 29% is similar to the average decline of 31% for cyclical bear markets. However, although the cyclical bears lasted an average of 2 years and took 4 years to recover, the event-driven bears lasted an average of just 9 months and had recovered to previous peaks after just over 1 year.

Event-driven bear markets have typically emerged with fairly modest inflation. When there has been deflation, it has also been modest. To some extent, this more stable monetary environment prevented the event from causing the stresses that would have turned the market fall into a more sustained bear market.

Structural Bear Markets

Most structural bear markets are preceded by financial bubbles (which had burst, perhaps as a consequence of rising interest rates or tightening credit conditions) and acute overvaluation, and they are often accompanied by major imbalances in the economy, such as a significant increase in private sector debt, which leaves households (and/or corporates) vulnerable to any shock. Recovery is dictated by the unwinding of imbalances rather than simply by monetary easing. Structural bears are much deeper and sharper than cyclical bears, and recovery typically takes about a decade. High volatility is a prominent feature during the recovery period.

Structural bear markets tend to be much more severe than cyclical or event-driven bear markets. On average, they have been associated with falls of over 50% and have lasted for 4 years. Most worryingly, the structural bears have taken about 8 to 10 years to recoup losses in nominal and real terms. The annualised growth rate of prices in the recovery phase from these bear markets is not materially different from cyclical ones. It just takes a great deal longer for the recovery to occur, and with greater volatility.

Structural bear markets are usually the result of some kind of misallocation of resources. The roots of this are often found in a combination of a new technology cycle and falls in the cost of capital. These are generally also accompanied by a savings and investment imbalance that results in a rising predisposition to economic shocks. For example, structural bear markets often coexist with large current account or budget deficits, coupled with high levels of corporate and/or consumer debt.

This was, for example, the case before the financial crisis of 2008. As exhibit 6.3 shows, private sector debt in the US (and indeed other regions) rose sharply in the decade or so before the financial crisis. At the time, the level of debt in the public sector as a share of GDP was stable, as was the case for central banks' balance sheets. Over the past decade, this pattern has largely reversed. Debt has not disappeared but it has mainly been shifted from the private to the public sector, where it is less vulnerable to shocks. Chapter 9 discusses in more detail how policy and other factors have made the current cycle different from those in the past and have resulted in a more rapid recovery in risk assets.

Exhibit 6.3 US Imbalances have shifted away from the private sector to the public sector and central banks

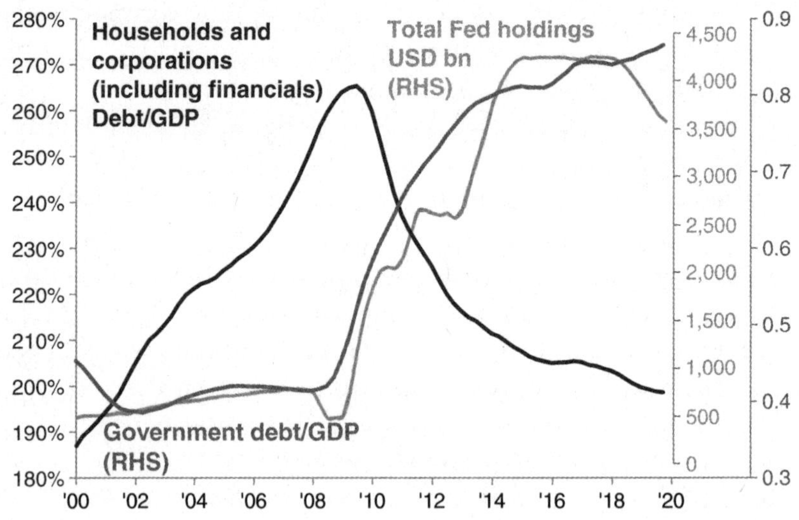

SOURCE: Goldman Sachs Global Investment Research.

Generally speaking, economic imbalances usually take a long time to unwind. Savings rates need to rise as cash flows are used to rebuild balance sheets. This is another reason why structural bear markets tend to last longer than cyclical ones. Very often the only way the process is speeded up is via some kind of sharp economic adjustment that reverses the imbalances faster than would otherwise be the case. For example, the UK had many of the ingredients of a structural bear market in the early 1990s, when the economy had serious imbalances, a deep recession, and there had been a sharp fall in property prices and equities. In this case, the process was speeded up via a collapse in the exchange rate when sterling crashed out of the ERM.[1] This is a more likely option in a relatively small open economy such as the UK (or Sweden, which had a similar experience at the time), but it is harder for a large and relatively closed economy such as the US, where the benefits of devaluation are less clear.

Taken together, then, structural bear markets show the following characteristics:

- They are more savage in terms of magnitude and duration.
- Recovery takes much longer.
- They are associated with ongoing structural economic problems rather than cyclical ones.

Given the severity of these bear markets, it is useful to be aware of any of the common characteristics that occur before they start.

Interest Rate Cuts Have Less Impact on Structural Bear Markets

Unlike the examples of cyclical bear markets, rising interest rates are not usually the trigger for price declines in structural bear markets. Many of the structural bear markets in the past have been preceded by very low interest rates and inflation: a factor that helped the boom in investment and strength in equity prices in the first place. This was true both in the run-up to the 2000 stock market

---

[1] http://news.bbc.co.uk/onthisday/hi/dates/stories/september/16/newsid_2519000/2519013.stm

peak and in the pre-2008 period. Because rising interest rates are not usually the cause of the structural bear, falling interest rates are not usually the cure. Given that the price of money tends to be fairly low when structural bear markets develop, the recovery owes more to the availability and demand for money than the price, although typically interest rates do fall to low levels.

As a consequence, structural bear markets do not typically end until future returns on capital rise sufficiently to boost investment. Admittedly, not all examples are precisely the same. In the early 1970s, the sharp rise in inflation undermined the expected future returns on capital. For many other structural bear markets that I identify, excess capacity is needed to unwind first. This can take longer than it takes for interest rates to fall, which provides one explanation for why cyclical bear markets seem to recover faster than structural ones.

Exhibit 6.4 shows the declines in interest rates in the US that have surrounded structural bear markets. On average, interest rates fell more sharply during structural crises than during cyclical ones,

Exhibit 6.4 Reaction to rate cuts; US structural bear markets

Date		Interest rates cut		Stock market annual return following various points after first interest rates cut			Interest rate cut, as a % of starting level
Peak	Trough	First	Last	3-months	6-months	1-year	
May-1835	Mar-1842	-	-	-	-	-	-
Feb-1873	Jun-1877	-	-	-	-	-	-
Sep-1929	Jun-1932	Nov-1929	May-1931	-8%	-7%	-19%	-67%
Mar-1937	Apr-1942	Apr-1933	Oct-1942	124%	34%	58%	-83%
Jan-1973	Oct-1974	Dec-1974	Nov-1976	-14%	3%	32%	-32%
Mar-2000	Oct-2002	Jan-2001	Jun-2003	-19%	-18%	-15%	-82%
Oct-2007	Mar-2009	Sep-2007	Dec-2008	4%	-6%	-19%	-97%
Average				**18%**	**1%**	**8%**	**-72%**
Median				**-8%**	**-6%**	**-15%**	**-82%**
Standard deviation				**60%**	**20%**	**36%**	**25%**

SOURCE: Goldman Sachs Global Investment Research.

particularly in the US. Although interest rates have fallen on average by about one-third in cyclical bear markets, they have fallen by 70% on average in the structural ones. Also, interest rates tended to continue to fall for a much longer period in the structural cases. Many experienced rate declines that continued for 2 years after the trough in the equity market.

Despite the best efforts of the monetary authorities to generate a recovery in financial markets and, therefore, growth, equity prices were very often still negative a year after the first rate cuts. This marks an important difference between cyclical and structural bears.

The most recent cycle, post the financial crisis, has been particularly unusual in the extent of monetary easing. The collapse in policy rates to zero and the introduction of quantitative easing, largely to deflect the deflationary consequences of the collapse in economic activity and asset prices in the wake of the crisis, has been a particular feature of this crisis (I discuss this in more detail in chapter 9).

Price Shocks: Deflation Is a Common Characteristic

Another key factor that seems to be common during structural bear markets is a price shock, either inflationary or deflationary. More often than not, it is deflation. The deflationary forces, particularly in the corporate sector, are usually a by-product of falls in the cost of capital and overinvestment. Once again, the susceptibility to price shocks is an additional factor that slows the recovery process and lengthens the time it takes for the prospective return on capital to rise sufficiently to generate a recovery.

Belief in a New Era/New Valuations

Many of the great structural bears were preceded by financial bubbles and a belief in a 'new era'. As Alan Greenspan said in testimony before the US Congress on February 26, 1997, 'Regrettably, history is strewn with visions of such "new eras" that, in the end, have proven to be a mirage'. A more detailed account of these surges in sentiment and how they are related to financial bubbles and 'manias' is given in chapter 8.

High Levels of Debt

Investment booms are largely the reason for high levels of debt. But rising corporate debt, as well as personal and government debt, is often associated with structural bear markets. A study by the Bank for International Settlements, which systematically examines the experience of 34 countries over the past 40 years, finds that rapid debt growth is the single best leading indicator of financial crises (see Borio and Lowe 2002).[2]

Equity Market Leadership Becoming Narrow

The 'Nifty Fifty' enthusiasm of the late 1960s revealed another feature of structural bears. This was the time when the top 50 or so companies raced ahead, while the rest of the US market failed to make gains. However, when the bear market of the early 1970s hit, these stocks collapsed more than the market as a whole. The Nifty Fifty constituents underperformed the market for the rest of the 1970s.

The same occurred in Japan in the late 1980s, as banks and property dominated the market. This was also a feature of the late 1990s. Although the S&P, for example, rose at an average annual rate of 25% between 1994 and 1999, more than half of its constituents fell during 1999 itself. Between 1994 and 1996, the prices of two-thirds of stocks rose by 10%, in line with the average annual increase since the end of the Second World War. In 1997, however, the index began to change. By 1999, the five companies whose market value increased the most accounted for about 42% of the

---

[2] See Borio, C., and Lowe, P. (2002). Asset prices, financial and monetary stability: Exploring the nexus. *BIS Working Papers No 114* [online]. Available at https://www.bis.org/publ/work114.html

total increase in the market. The top 100 companies accounted for 139% of the increase, compared with an average of 87% since 1967.

The same kind of concentration occurred in Europe. By the end of 1999, the top 20 companies by market capitalisation accounted for about 30% of the total market.

High Volatility

Not only does the bubble period and subsequent collapse tend to centre on a narrow number of stocks, but also markets overall tend to be highly volatile. One of the key features of structural bear markets is high volatility during the period of price declines and during the recovery. The actual annualised rate of increase in stock prices is not significantly different from cyclical bear market recoveries, but there tend to be a greater number of rallies and false starts.

The Relationship between Bear Markets and Corporate Profits

Exhibit 6.5 shows bear markets since the 1960s and the change in earnings per share (EPS) or corporate profits during and near the bear market. On average, since 1960 earnings per share have actually increased by just 5% during the bear market itself. But this is distorted by two factors:

- EPS does not typically fall (or falls very little) in event-driven bear markets – these markets are all about derisking and hence a decline in valuation; they are not directly cyclically driven.
- The actual period of decline in EPS does not coincide exactly with the dates of the bear market in prices, nor would one expect it to given that equity investors would be expected to try to anticipate the cycle. Also, the decline in earnings (that the market anticipates) often continues after the market reaches a trough.

Exhibit 6.5 EPS of bear markets: EPS falls as much as prices in cyclical and structural bear markets but the timing is different

	Bear market					EPS decline period				
Type	Start	End	Length (m)	Performance	% Change in EPS	Start	End	EPS decline	Length (m)	Lag to start of bear market (m)
E	Dec-1961	Jun-1962	6	-28%	9%	-	-	-	-	-
E	Feb-1966	Oct-1966	8	-22%	5%	Dec-1966	Sep-1967	-4%	9	10
C	Nov-1968	May-1970	18	-36%	-2%	Sep-1969	Dec-1970	-11%	15	9
S	Jan-1973	Oct-1974	21	-48%	51%	Sep-1974	Dec-1975	-11%	15	21
C	Nov-1980	Aug-1982	20	-27%	-4%	Sep-1981	Mar-1983	-14%	18	10
E	Aug-1987	Dec-1987	3	-34%	6%	Mar-1987	Sep-1987	-8%	6	-5
C	Jul-1990	Oct-1990	3	-20%	5%	Jun-1989	Mar-1992	-26%	33	-13
S	Mar-2000	Oct-2002	30	-49%	-3%	Jan-2001	Dec-2001	-15%	11	10
S	Oct-2007	Mar-2009	17	-57%	-23%	Sep-2007	Jan-2010	-34%	28	0
Median			**17**	**-34%**	**5%**			**-13%**	**15**	**10**
Average			**14**	**-36%**	**5%**			**-15%**	**17**	**5**
Average (except event-driven)			**18**	**-40%**	**4%**			**-19%**	**20**	**6**
Average (event-driven only)			**6**	**-28%**	**7%**			**-6%**	**8**	**2**

NOTE: S: structural bear market, E: event-driven bear market, C: cyclical bear market.
SOURCE: Goldman Sachs Global Investment Research.

Removing event-driven bear markets *and* looking at the entire decline of the bear market (taking into account that the precise timing of the EPS decline differs in each cycle) results in an average EPS fall of 19%. This fall is similar to the average price fall in bear markets since the 1960s (excluding event-driven bear markets) of 40%.

This suggests that equity bear markets (excluding event-driven ones) are largely about falls in profits or earnings per share, although valuations typically fall in bear markets. This is because valuations typically start to come down before the actual decline in profitability as investors start to anticipate the event. The experience in a bull market is very much the reverse, where the hope phase is characterised by strong valuation expansion as equity prices start to rise in anticipation of future profit growth in a period when actual profits remain depressed.

On average (excluding event-driven drawdowns), EPS declines lag the start of the bear market by 5 months. Put another way, **prices start to fall 5 months before EPS does. However, the range is wide.** This tendency for the market to rally late in the cycle, even as corporate profits might have peaked, reflects the late-cycle optimism phase, where the market continues to rally contrary to the evidence that earnings have already peaked.

A Summary of Bear Market Characteristics

By splitting bear markets into these groups, I find the following to hold true:

- Cyclical and event-driven bear markets generally see price falls of about 30%, whereas structural ones see much larger falls, of about 50%.
- Event-driven bear markets tend to be the shortest, lasting an average of 7 months; cyclical bear markets last an average of 27 months; and structural bear markets last an average of 4 years.

Exhibit 6.6 Characteristics of a bear market

Pre Bear	Cyclical	Event	Structural
Rising rates	✓	Maybe	✓
Exogenous shock	Maybe	✓	Maybe
Speculative rise in equity prices	✗	✗	✓
Economic imbalances	✗	✗	✓
Rising productivity	Maybe	-	✓
Unusual strength in economy	✗	✗	✓
New era belief	✗	✗	✓
Post peak	**Cyclical**	**Event**	**Structural**
Economic recession/downturn	Usually	Maybe	Usually
Profits collapse	✓	Maybe	✓
Interest rates fall and trigger rise in equity prices/fall in bonds	✓	Usually	✗
Price shock	✗	✗	✓

SOURCE: Goldman Sachs Global Investment Research.

- Event-driven and cyclical bear markets tend to revert to their previous market highs after about 1 year, and structural bear markets take an average of 10 years to return to previous highs.

It is worth noting that these data are in nominal terms, whereas in reality the bear markets of the 1970s were more pronounced given that inflation was extremely high (see exhibit 6.6).

Defining the Financial Crisis: A Structural Bear Market with a Difference

The 2007 financial crisis and bear market could be described as a typical structural bear market but the response to it in terms of policy was unique (perhaps because policymakers were intent on avoiding the mistakes of the past). In many ways, it had the hallmark of a structural bear market, with rising imbalances as an important feature of the cycle that preceded it. But there was less of a speculative bubble in the stock market, or 'new era' belief, than we have seen in the run-up to other bear markets, at least in the equity market. The bubble in this cycle was more evident in the real estate market in the US and parts of southern Europe than it was in equity prices.

What really sets the 2007–2009 bear market apart from other structural bear markets is the policy response. The rapid cuts in interest rates and adoption of QE resulted in a sharper rebound in equity (as well as other financial asset) prices than we have seen in the past. Lower risk-free rates triggered a search for yield in nominal assets such as bonds while also pushing up the present value of future income streams. This unusual backdrop, supported by very low inflation, has paved the way for an extended cycle and a rise in valuations. I look at this particular cycle in more detail in chapter 9.

Finding an Indicator to Flag Bear Market Risk

The damage that bear markets can inflict on investor returns is clear, whatever their type. This raises the obvious question of whether one can identify a set of conditions that would warn of an impending bear market. This poses three main problems:

- **All bear markets are unique.** Although there are similarities in terms of profile and performance when they start, the triggers are often significantly different.
- **There are many false negatives.** The fact that several indicators of data may have moved prior to one or two bear markets in the past does not mean they can be relied on to do so again; there are many occasions when these indicators move in a particular direction and yet no recession follows. The reliability of indicators, therefore, tends to be low, and there are generally many false negatives and necessary, but not sufficient, conditions for a bear market to evolve. In other words, an indicator might be useful in pointing to bear market risk in one cycle but not in another, or a certain variable may need to move in

a particular way prior to a bear market, but just because it has moved in that way does not necessarily mean that a bear market will always follow.

- Most important, because equity prices themselves anticipate the future, it is difficult to find anything that leads equity prices.

The point about bear markets all being different is compounded by the fact that, although some conditions may be the same at the time, such as high valuations and fear of economic downturn, the principal driver varies in each case.

That said, many contributory factors can influence the timing and shape of a bear market. To test the usefulness of factors in predicting or leading a bear market, my team at Goldman Sachs conducted an analysis looking at the consistency of over 40 variables over time. These variables were selected across three categories – macro, market-based and technical – to which a 'rule'-based system is then applied to assess whether each indicator had met a predetermined (although subjective) threshold prior to a bear market. For example, in order to qualify, the Shiller P/E (or P/E based on current prices and average earnings over the past 10 years) needed to be rising from a high level (the 70th percentile) or to have started at a level higher than the 90th percentile (this aims to capture the idea that valuation needs to be either high and rising or very high).

Perhaps unsurprisingly (or it would be too easy for investors), most of the variables could be dismissed because they were unreliable; they either showed no consistent pattern of behaviour prior to a bear market, or they lagged the movements in the equity market itself, or the variables were too volatile to rely on. This boiled down the list of possible indicators to just a few that were reliable signals statistically. Even then, no single bear market had been signalled by all of the indicators moving as expected. Equally, no single indicator has a 100% hit rate of moving in the same way prior to each bear market. The most consistently useful pre-bear market indicators were measures of unemployment and valuation. Most of the 'technical' variables that we looked at (such as positioning and sentiment surveys) were particularly poor because they tended to lag the market itself.[3]

Typical Conditions Prior to Bear Markets

The most common features of bear markets are some combination of deteriorating growth momentum and policy tightening at a time of high valuation.

Although it has been difficult to find variables that consistently turn just prior to a peak in the market, there are a small number of variables that, in combination, tend to move in a particular way in the build-up to a bear market. Although some of these start to exhibit 'risky' levels well in advance, it is the combination that provides a useful indicator of risk. **At the very least, in combination they may provide valuable information after the peak of the market on whether a bear market bounce is genuinely the start of a bigger fall rather than a shorter correction.**

- **Unemployment.** Rising unemployment tends to be a good indicator of recession, particularly in the United States: unemployment has risen prior to every post-war recession in the US. The problem is that rising unemployment (and of course recession) lags the equity market. But very low unemployment does appear to be a consistent feature prior to most bear markets. Combining periods when unemployment has hit a low at a time when equity valuation is particularly high provides quite a useful signal of potential risk in the stock market: the combination of cycle-low unemployment and high valuations does tend to be followed by negative returns.
- **Inflation.** Rising inflation has been an important contributor in past recessions and, by association, bear markets, because rising inflation tends to tighten monetary policy. This indicator is not useful at the precise peak of the market because the peak of inflation typically lags the equity market (and often the

[3] Oppenheimer, P., and Bell, S. (2017). *Bear necessities: Identifying signals for the next bear market.* London, UK: Goldman Sachs Global Investment Research.

economic cycle). But rising inflation has been an important feature of the environment prior to bear markets in the past, particularly before the period of 'great moderation' in the 1990s. By extension, the lack of inflation and inflation expectations in the post-financial-crisis cycle is one of the factors that has supported a much longer economic cycle and less volatility. In the absence of inflation pressures, monetary policy may remain much looser and reduce the risks of recession and, by association, bear markets.

- **The yield curve.** Related to the point about inflation, tighter monetary policy often leads to a flattening, or even inverted, yield curve. Because many, although by no means all, bear markets are preceded by periods of monetary policy tightening, we find that flat yield curves, prior to inversion, are also followed by low returns or bear markets. In recent years the impact of QE and falling inflation expectations (term premia), may have weakened the reliability of this signal.[4] As a consequence, we use the 3-month to 10-year measure, with a focus on the short end of the yield curve (0–6 quarter). The 0–6 quarter forward spread more clearly captures the market's near-term outlook via its funds rate expectations than back-end measures, which are more distorted by term premia. Consistent with Fed research, we find that the near-term 0–6 quarter forward spread has also been a somewhat more significant predictor of recession risk than, for instance, the 3m10y measure. Once again, by combining the signal with valuation, a combination of flat or inverted yield curves together with high valuation can be a useful bear market indicator
- **Growth momentum at a high.** Typically, periods of strong and accelerating economic growth (although a good thing for equity investors in general) tend to be followed by lower equity returns when the pace of growth starts to moderate.

[4] A useful discussion about the value of the yield curve in predicting recessions can be found in Benzoni, L., Chyruk, O., and Kelley, D. (2018). Why does the yield-curve slope predict recessions? *Chicago Fed Letter No. 404.*

Exhibit 6.7 US equity performance during different permutations in ISMs and bond yields (% monthly price return, US manufacturing, ISM, US 10-year BY, data back to 1990)

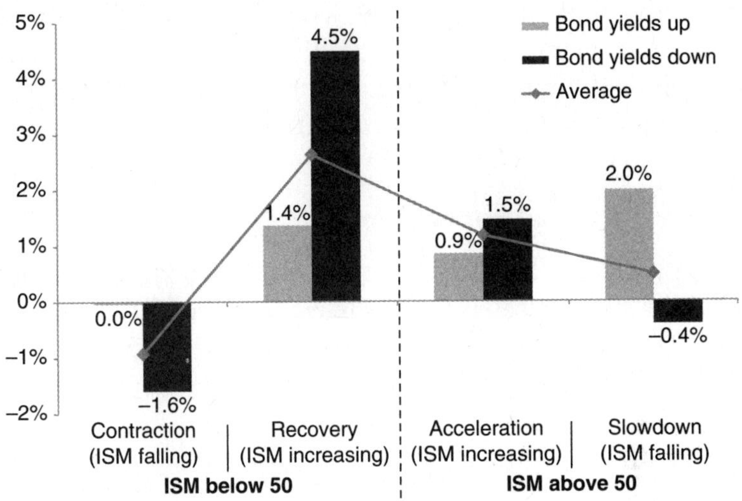

SOURCE: Goldman Sachs Global Investment Research.

Exhibit 6.7 illustrates this for the US. The highest returns are when the ISM is low but recovering, and the lowest are when it is low and deteriorating. On average, the slowdown phase, when momentum indicators are high but deteriorating, tends to be accompanied by lower returns, and so when momentum indicators are very elevated, there is a reasonable chance that they will deteriorate and eventually move below recession levels.

As exhibit 6.7 shows, this fits very much into the phases of the cycle discussed in chapter 3.

The periods when the ISM is in the highest quartile relative to history tend to be followed by lower returns.

- **Valuation.** High valuations are a feature of most bear market periods. Valuation is rarely the trigger for a market fall; often valuations can be high for a long period before a correction or bear market. But when other fundamental factors combine with valuation as a trigger, bear market risks are elevated.

- **Private sector financial balance.** In this measure we calculate the financial balance as total income minus total spending of all households and firms as a measure of financial overheating risk. We select the private sector financial balance, over alternatives such as growth in credit or home prices, because of its empirical track record and its intuitive appeal as a catch-all measure of private sector overspending.[5]

A Framework for Anticipating Bear Markets

Although no single indicator is reliable on its own, the combination of these six seems to provide a reasonable signal for future bear market risk. All of these variables are related. Tight labour markets are typically associated with higher inflation expectations. These,

Exhibit 6.8 The bear market risk indicator hints at low single digit returns for global equities

NOTE: Shaded areas show MSCI world bear markets, S&P 500 bear markets before 1969.

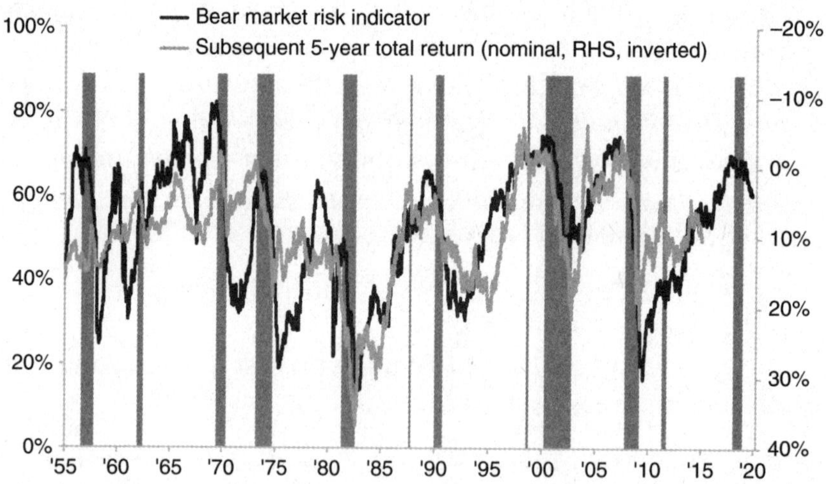

SOURCE: Goldman Sachs Global Investment Research.

[5] A discussion of a broad recession risk indicator and the private sector imbalance can be found in Struyven, D., Choi, D., and Hatzius, J. (2019). *Recession risk: Still moderate.* New York, NY: Goldman Sachs Global Investment Research.

in turn, tend to tighten policy and weaken expectations of future growth. High valuations, at the same time, leave equities vulnerable to derating if growth expectations deteriorate or the discount rate rises, or, worse still, both of these occur together.

Exhibit 6.8 shows the indicator relative to MSCI world equities since 1955. The shaded columns represent falls in the global equity market of 20% and more (standard definition of a bear market). Although the indicator is far from perfect, it does give some kind of indication of risks (when it is close to highs) and opportunities (when it is close to lows).

The indicator also acts as a guide to likely future returns. Exhibit 6.8 shows the indicator alongside the 5-year total return (in other words, returns in the 5 years after any particular reading on the indicator in the past); the returns are inverted and can be read on the right-hand scale. Although the indicator has been reasonably successful in highlighting risks of a turning point (either up or down at extremes), it has also provided some information about prospective returns over the next 5 years.

Chapter 7
Bull's Eye: The Nature and Shape of Bull Markets

Bull markets, like bear markets, can be defined in many different ways. They are made up of the three phases of the cycle that are not associated with sustained drawdowns: the hope, growth and optimism phases discussed in chapter 3.

But just as bear markets can vary in length and strength, so can bull markets. Some are extremely long and strong, exhibiting a sustained secular trend, often with rising valuations. Others can be relatively flat or trendless, where much of the return comes from the dividend or earnings growth.

The 'Super Cycle' Secular Bull Market

Equity investors expect to enjoy a higher return on equities (given their risk and the uncertainty of future returns) than they would expect from a less risky asset such as a government bond (where the return is preknown in nominal terms). But looking at the progression of equity markets over many decades shows that they are not simply composed of a series of cycles near a clear and stable upward trend. Just as within an equity cycle itself, where much of the return comes in a short burst in the hope phase, the longer-term upward trend in equity prices also tends to come in phases.

Taking a log scale of the S&P equity index since 1900, for example (so as to take account of the fact that recent index levels are much higher than those of many decades ago), one can see that equity prices have increased and trended sharply higher over time but that this has not happened in a straight line (Exhibit 7.1). For simplicity, it can be argued that there have been three long 'super cycles', or secular bull markets, since the Second World War. Each of these has been punctuated by occasional sharp drawdowns and 'mini' bear markets (often quite sharp). For example, the secular bull market of 1982–2000 was interrupted by the Savings and Loan crisis in the early 1980s, the crash of 1987, the bond crisis in 1994 (when 30-year US treasury yields rose about 200bp in just 9 months) and the Asia crisis of 1998. But one can still consider these periods 'super cycles' because the powerful returns were driven by some

Exhibit 7.1 US Fat and flat periods between secular bull markets (S&P 500, log scale)

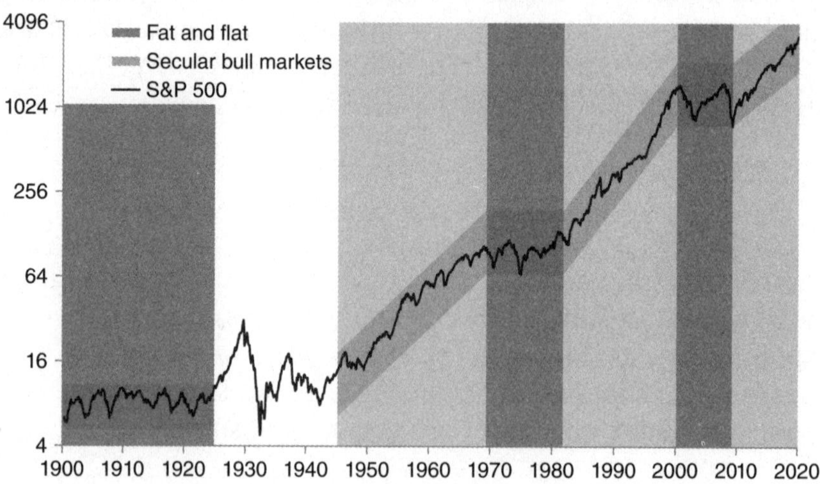

SOURCE: Goldman Sachs Global Investment Research.

very specific structural factors, which remained uninterrupted over long periods of time, even during the corrections.

1945–1968: Post-War Boom

This period was dominated by the powerful post-war economic boom and is often referred to as 'The Golden Age of Capitalism'. It was supported by the United States' initiative to aid Europe economically, known as the Marshall Plan (or the European Recovery Plan), which helped to boost growth and reduce unemployment. Productivity growth was strong, particularly in Europe and East Asia, and the post-war baby boom further strengthened demand.

Although the economic environment was conducive to strong returns in the equity markets in this period, valuations also recovered from their post-war levels aided by a secular decline in the equity risk premium as many of the risks to the global system faded. New international institutions and a rule-based global trading system emerged.[1] The setting up of the International Monetary Fund (IMF) and the World Bank, as part of the new international payments system known as the Bretton Woods monetary system, helped to reduce uncertainty. Meanwhile, global trade was strengthened and expanded by stronger institutional frameworks, such as the General Agreement on Tariffs and Trade (GATT), created in 1948, and the United Nations Conference on Trade and Development (UNCTAD), founded in 1964. In the same year, the sixth round of GATT negotiations started, commonly referred to as the Kennedy Round of multilateral trade negotiations. By 1967, the negotiations had resulted in cuts to trade tariffs by an average of 35%–40% on many items and were widely described at the time as 'the most important trade and tariff negotiation ever held'.[2]

---

[1] Post-war reconstruction and development in the golden age of capitalism. United Nations (2017). *World Economic and Social Survey 2017*.

[2] Norwood, B. (1969). The Kennedy round: A try at linear trade negotiations. *Journal of Law and Economics*, 12(2), 297–319.

Throughout the 1960s, the emergence of fast-growing global companies also spurred confidence in the stock market and in the so-called Nifty Fifty stocks in the United States in particular. The idea behind investing in these stocks was that you need never worry about valuation because these companies either had strong earnings growth or high expectations of strong growth in the future, and many also had strong brands. Although there was no formal index of these companies, there was a generally agreed list of growth stocks that included many technology leaders, such as IBM, Xerox, Texas Instruments and Burroughs, as well as pharmaceutical companies, such as Merck, Pfizer, Eli Lilley and American Home Products. In addition, a variety of retail companies were seen to offer exciting new growth opportunities, such as Avon, McDonald's, Polaroid and Kodak. By 1972, the P/E on Polaroid was 90×, on McDonald's 85× and on Walt Disney 82×. The average P/E for the S&P was 33×, and for the Nifty Fifty companies it averaged about 45× (and for the five biggest in 1973 it was 35.5×; see chapter 9).

As the 1960s progressed, the US dollar, which was fixed in value against gold under the Bretton Woods system of fixed exchange rates, became overvalued. A significant increase in public spending in the US, as a result of President Lyndon Johnson's Great Society programmes and increased military spending to fund the Vietnam War, put further stress on the system. The Gold Standard had come under significant pressure by the late 1960s and was finally dissolved by President Richard Nixon in 1971, when he announced a 'temporary' suspension of the dollar's convertibility into gold.[3] The Nifty Fifty stock bubble burst.

In most equity markets, prices had already reached a plateau about 1966 after an astonishing rise over the previous 15 years (in the US and UK especially). In the US in particular, the peak came in 1968. The bear market that followed was structural in nature and the US market declined in real terms by 75% between 1966 and 1982. But, as in the case of the bear markets of the 1930s and

[3] The end of the Bretton Woods System. IMF [online]. Available at https://www.imf.org/external/about/histend.htm

1940s, it was really at least two bear markets rolled into one. Political and economic shocks were again a key feature. In 1973, the Watergate scandal in the US increased market uncertainty, and by October that year the Arab-Israeli War, together with an OPEC oil embargo and industrial unrest, had fuelled further market instability.

By the end of the 1970s, stock markets had enjoyed some sharp rallies. In the US, Ronald Reagan's defeat of Jimmy Carter in November 1980 and Republican control of the Senate were viewed as market-friendly. For the first time since 1976, the Dow Jones index rose back through 1000. But the enthusiasm did not last. A further sharp round of interest rate hikes (the Fed raised its discount rate to an all-time high of 14%) forced another sharp fall in the stock market and most economies around the world entered another recession. During 1981, inflation, high unemployment and economic stagnation sent stocks throughout the world down to further lows.

1982–2000: The Start of Disinflation

Academics have focused on the fall in inflation as one of the key drivers of this secular bull market post 1982. In particular, some have argued that investors suffered from 'money illusion' after the great inflation of the 1970s. This resulted in two errors: first, investors capitalised future earnings at the then (very high) nominal rate rather than the real rate and, second, they failed to take account of the gains that were generated by depreciating the real value of nominal liabilities.[4] Certainly, sharp rises in inflation in the 1970s had contributed to the collapse of valuations in both bond and equity markets. This inflationary era, which had been so damaging to financial markets, came to a close partly as a result of the so-called Volker credit crunch (a period known for the recession caused by the Fed tightening cycle that started in 1977), which took US Fed

[4] Modigliani, F., and Cohn, R. A. (1979). Inflation, rational valuation and the market. *Financial Analysts Journal*, 35(2), 24–44.

funds rates (policy rates) from about 10% to close to 20%. From that point, inflation started to fall around the world and, coupled with a vigorous recovery in economic activity from a deep recession, confidence – and asset valuations – started to rise. From August 1982 to December 1999, the compound real return on the Dow Jones Industrial Average was 15% per year, well in excess of long-run average returns or indeed the increase in earnings or book value over the period.[5] Much of this secular bull market therefore reflected valuation expansion – a phenomenon that pushed up both equity and fixed income (bond) returns at the same time.

The 1980s also experienced a wide range of deregulation, reform and privatisation under the Reagan and Thatcher administrations in the US and the UK, respectively. In the US, the Economic Recovery Act of 1981 brought in significant tax reform, which resulted in top rate income taxes falling from 70% in 1980 to 28% in 1986. Nondefence spending also fell dramatically and several industries were deregulated, including in the air transport and financial sectors, as the partial repeal of the Glass-Steagall Act of 1933 removed barriers in the financial markets industry that had prevented institutions from combining across banking, securities and insurance businesses. Similar reforms were instituted in the UK, alongside a comprehensive programme of privatisation of a wide array of assets, including utilities. The effect was far-reaching. Companies in public ownership in the UK accounted for 12% of GDP in 1979 but only about 2% by 1997.[6] By the mid-1990s the trend for privatisation had spread to the rest of Europe, even reaching Socialist-led governments such as that of Lionel Jospin in France, which launched a $7.1 billion initial offering of France Telecom in 1997 and made a $10.4 billion secondary offering a year later (as the fervor for telecom companies accelerated around the expanding technology bubble).

[5] Ritter, J., and Warr, R. S. (2002). The decline of inflation and the bull market of 1982–1999. *Journal of Financial and Quantitative Analysis*, 37(01), 29–61.
[6] Privatisation in Europe, coming home to roost. (2002). *The Economist*.

The secular trend was punctuated temporarily by a (sharp but short-lived) crash in 1987 before lower interest rates and a continuation of economic growth pushed equities to all-time highs.

The continuation of the re-rating of equities was spurred by the fall of the Berlin Wall in 1989 and, soon after, the unravelling of the Soviet Bloc. The Dax, the main German stock market index, surged by 30% between October 1989 and July 1990. As a consequence, a more integrated global economy emerged in the 1990s. Throughout this period, equity markets enjoyed a decline in the discount rate; not only did interest rates stay low as a result of the purging of global high inflation but also the end of the Cold War helped push the equity risk premium down further (the required hurdle rate for investing in risky assets compared with low-risk bonds).

This strong secular bull market was buffeted once again by the 1998 Asia crisis, but a decisive policy response resulted in looser money, which helped to propel the technology bubble of the late 1990s. When this bubble eventually burst, it brought to an end the secular uptrend that had started in 1982.

2009 Onwards: The Start of QE and the 'Great Moderation'

Chapter 9 examines some of the specific conditions that have followed the financial crisis in more detail, but this bull market has also been particularly strong and long. Having collapsed by 57% from its 2007 peak, the S&P 500 started a powerful recovery that was to result in the longest bull market in history. Part of the strength of the recovery, as with that from the early 1990s, was a function of the scale of the declines in the economy and market that had preceded it. In the US in particular, the collapse in the housing market had resulted in a huge loss of household wealth. With more than $1 trillion in sub-prime mortgages outstanding, the spread of losses throughout the economy and financial institutions was significant. At the same time, according to then Fed chairman Ben Bernanke, 'too-big-to-fail financial institutions were both a source (though by no means the only source) of the crisis and among the primary impediments to policymakers' efforts to contain it'.[7] Between 2007 and 2010, the median wealth of a household in the United States fell 44%, resulting in levels falling below those of 1969.[8]

But the action put in place to contain the crisis was unprecedented. In March 2009, the Federal Reserve announced plans to spend $1 trillion in newly created dollars on the back of government and mortgage bonds to push interest rates lower through its programme of 'quantitative' easing, which was critical in triggering the rebound in the stock markets.

A second and important contributor to this bull market has been the assent of large technology companies which, in the US equity market in particular, have become the largest sector and have enjoyed spectacular returns (a topic covered in more detail in chapter 11).

Cyclical Bull Markets

Although there are very long trends in the market driven by specific conditions that might result in high annualised returns, cycles still exist within these. But, even when we look at the 'typical' equity cycle, issues of definition emerge. For example, the latest equity bull market that started after the financial crisis in 2009 could be considered ongoing, or could be said to have ended in October 2018, when the market fell by close to 20% (a typical definition of a bear market) before rapidly recovering. Several equity markets did breach the 20% level in this period, although the benchmark US S&P index was down 19% before it rebounded.

Assuming these are two separate bull markets does slightly change the averages. But, as a rule of thumb, and using the US as an example, since 1900 the average bull market has seen prices rise by over 160% (243% in total return terms when dividends are included) in

---

[7] Bernanke, B. (2010, Sept. 2). *Causes of the recent financial and economic crisis*. Testimony before the Financial Crisis Inquiry Commission, Washington, DC.

[8] Phillips, M. (2019). The bull market began 10 years ago. Why aren't more people celebrating? *New York Times* [online]. Available at https://www.nytimes.com/2019/03/09/business/bull-market-anniversary.html

just under 5 years, annualising a return of about 25%. Over the period since 1900, there have been 18 such cycles in the US; alternatively, if we consider the post-war period, there have been 11 (compared with just the three major secular upswings discussed previously).

Exhibit 7.2 shows the last major bull markets (using the US equity market as a guide), together with their annualised returns.

A few key observations follow.

- The average bull market has experienced annualised returns of 25%.
- Annualised returns vary from 17% to 42%. Generally, the highest annualised returns come after the deepest bear markets.
- On average, in past bull markets 75% of the total returns on equities has come from price and 25% from reinvested dividends. The proportion from dividends ranges from 16% to 46% (exhibit 7.2).

Exhibit 7.2 Decomposition of S&P returns during previous bull markets. 75% of the total returns on equities has come from price and 25% from reinvested dividends

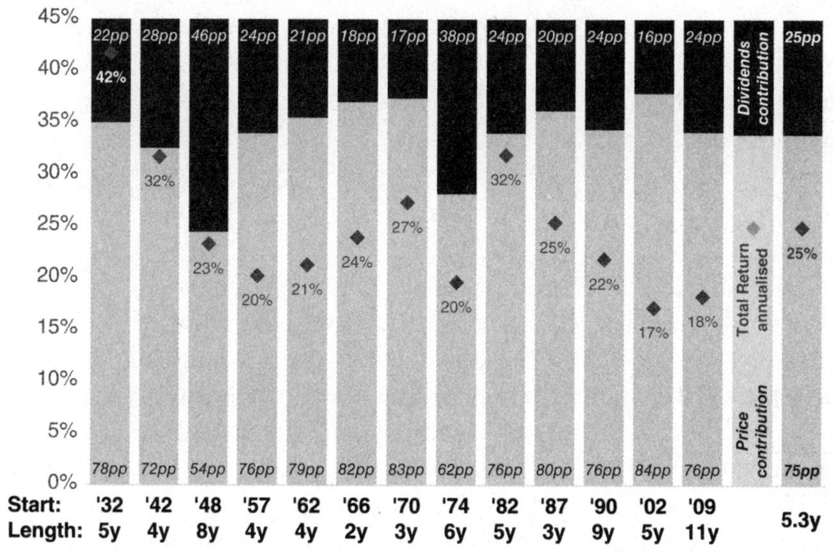

SOURCE: Goldman Sachs Global Investment Research.

Exhibit 7.3 US bull markets

Start	End	Months	Years	Price return	Total return	Annualised total return
Oct-03	Sep-06	34	2.8	60%	-	-
Nov-07	Dec-09	25	2.1	65%	-	-
Dec-14	Nov-16	22	1.8	39%	-	-
Dec-17	Jul-19	19	1.6	40%	-	-
Aug-21	Sep-29	96	8.0	371%	-	-
Jun-32	Mar-37	56	4.7	321%	413%	42%
Apr-42	May-46	49	4.1	150%	208%	32%
Mar-48	Aug-56	100	8.3	259%	477%	23%
Oct-57	Dec-61	49	4.1	86%	114%	20%
Jun-62	Feb-66	43	3.6	80%	101%	21%
Oct-66	Nov-68	25	2.1	48%	58%	24%
May-70	Jan-73	31	2.6	74%	89%	27%
Oct-74	Nov-80	73	6.1	126%	201%	20%
Aug-82	Aug-87	60	5.0	229%	303%	32%
Dec-87	Jul-90	31	2.6	65%	81%	25%
Oct-90	Mar-00	113	9.4	417%	546%	22%
Oct-02	Oct-07	60	5.0	101%	121%	17%
Mar-09	Jan-20	130	10.8	392%	517%	18%
Average		**56**	**5**	**162%**	**248%**	**25%**
Median		**49**	**4**	**94%**	**201%**	**23%**
Min		**19**	**2**	**39%**	**58%**	**17%**
Max		**130**	**11**	**417%**	**546%**	**42%**

SOURCE: Goldman Sachs Global Investment Research.

But, as exhibit 7.3 shows, the variation across these bull markets has been significant.

Variations in the Length of Bull Markets

Exhibit 7.3 also shows that bull markets vary considerably in length, with the shortest being just under 2 years and the longest (the current one) expanding for over 10 years.

The average bull market (in the US) has lasted for 56 months and the median has been 49 months. But the variations are significant (exhibit 7.4).

Exhibit 7.4 S&P bull and bear markets. The average bull market has lasted for 56 months

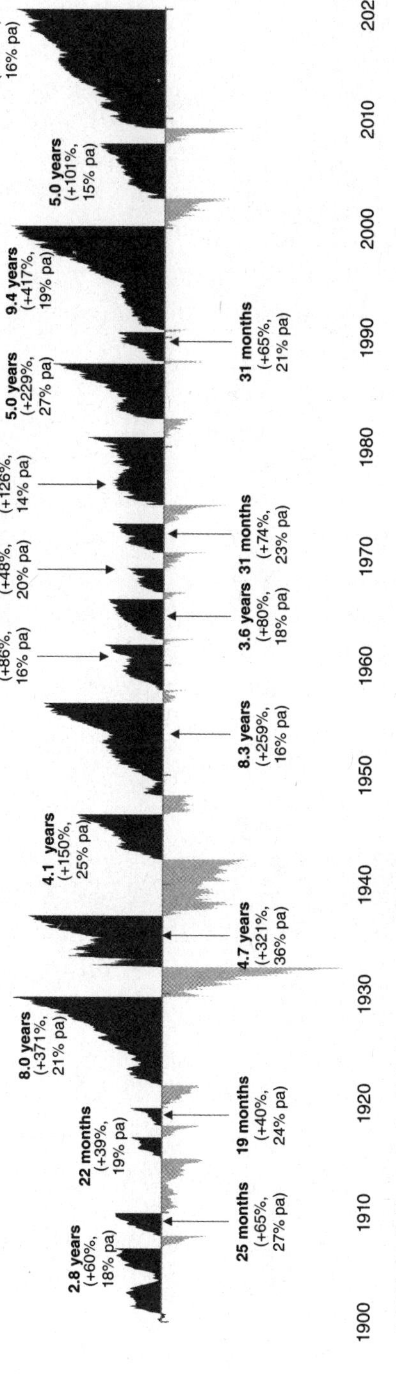

SOURCE: Goldman Sachs Global Investment Research.

Bull markets also vary in terms of their composition – that is to say, what drives them. Returns to equity investors can come from price changes (driven by earnings) and from valuation changes, because the multiple (for example, the P/E ratio) that investors are prepared to pay for expected future earnings can change. When investors are optimistic and/or when the level of interest rates comes down, valuations are likely to rise and generate a higher proportion of the return to investors. Similarly, when investors become worried and/or the level of interest rates rises, valuations will tend to fall.

The variation in the drivers of returns can be seen in exhibit 7.2. The total return (shown in the diamond) is broken down into various percentage compositions. So when we think about bull markets, it is not just the length and strength that is relevant to investors but also the difference between the price return and the total return. Furthermore, the drivers of the price component are important: how much is likely to come from fundamental profit growth and how much from a change in valuations?

In general, we can say the following about bull markets:

- Less volatile and longer economic cycles will mean longer bull markets.
- Lower and more stable interest rates will often result in stronger bull markets, with a higher component coming from valuation.
- Markets that have higher dividend yields (often as a result of more mature industries with a preference for paying out more of the cash flow than retaining it for future investment) will see a higher proportion of their return coming from dividends.

Non-trending Bull Markets

In addition to the long-term structural uptrends, and the more typical cyclical bull markets, there are periods of relatively flat returns. Although they are not very common, these rather trendless periods in markets often come about as a result of high valuations when economies and profits are growing slowly. These can also be split into two categories:

- **Skinny and flat markets (low volatility, low returns).** Flat markets where equity prices are stuck in a narrow trading range and experience low volatility.
- **Fat and flat markets (high volatility, low returns).** Periods (often quite long) when equity indices make very little aggregate progress but experience high volatility with strong rallies and corrections (or even mini bull and bear markets) in between.

Unlike most bull and bear markets, there is no absolute peak/trough on which to pin skinny and flat periods. They are by definition difficult to identify, and it is hard to pinpoint an exact date for when they start and finish. That said, there are several good examples of relatively flat (low return) and relatively skinny (no bear market, no bull market with >25% return over less than 2 years) periods. Since the Second World War there have been seven in the US equity market that broadly fit the criteria. There are more outside the US, given that the US has seen the highest returns globally over this period; once bear markets are excluded, much of the rest of the time is a straightforward bull market.

Exhibit 7.5 shows a list of skinny and flat markets, with approximate start and finish dates.

Although these periods are difficult to identify precisely, and each one has its own set of circumstances, we can nevertheless make a few observations:

- Flat periods in the market with a narrow trading range are not uncommon: the stock market in the US has been in one of these phases about 20% of the time since 1945 (in the case of Europe, over the same period these types of market environment look a bit more common and account for some 30% of the time; the difference is probably explained by the fact that the US equity market has generally had stronger profit growth, which has driven the market higher).

Exhibit 7.5 US skinny and flat periods (S&P 500)

Start	End	Length (y)	Perf (%)	Annualised perf (%)	Max move (%)	Annualised EPS growth (%)	LTM P/E Start (x)	LTM P/E End (x)	Change in LTM P/E (%)	Avg GDP growth (%)	Change in 3M T-Bill (pts)
Sep-46	May-48	1.7	-0.5	-0.3	-14.7	51.1	17.7	8.7	-50.6	-3.7	0.6
Aug-51	Jan-54	2.4	7.7	3.1	19.0	-2.2	8.7	9.9	13.7	5.4	-0.2
Oct-55	Oct-57	2.0	0.4	0.2	-17.7	0.4	12.1	12.0	-0.5	3.4	1.4
Dec-58	Jan-61	2.0	8.5	4.1	-13.9	6.3	18.6	17.8	-4.2	4.9	-0.6
Apr-83	Jan-85	1.7	6.7	3.8	-14.4	15.6	11.7	9.7	-17.1	6.1	-0.4
Jan-92	Dec-94	2.9	5.9	2.0	22.2	9.7	19.4	15.7	-19.1	3.2	1.9
Feb-04	Jul-06	2.4	6.6	2.7	24.7	16.5	22.7	16.7	-26.4	3.6	4.1
Median		**2.0**	**6.6**	**2.7**	**-13.9**	**9.7**	**17.7**	**12.0**	**-17.1**	**3.6**	**0.6**
Average		**2.2**	**5.0**	**2.2**	**0.8**	**13.9**	**15.8**	**12.9**	**-14.9**	**3.3**	**1.0**

SOURCE: Goldman Sachs Global Investment Research.

- They have tended to be relatively short, lasting 1–3 years.
- Often economic growth is strong in these periods, averaging 3%–4%. Hence, earnings are usually strong, causing a 10–15% derating in these low return environments.
- Last, on average, although interest rates are rising during these flattish periods, strong earnings growth helps to buffer the higher rates and falling valuations; hence, the market hovers rather than falls.

Chapter 8
Blowing Bubbles: Signs of Excess

When financial bubbles burst they can be the cause of severe structural bear markets, often with devastating consequences for both broader asset markets and economies. Although bubbles can be concentrated in a single industry or asset class, and do not always spread out to a broader structural bear market, others can be quite broad-based, with an impact across the whole market and beyond. It can therefore be useful for investors to have some understanding of the causes and common characteristics of bubbles, because recovery from them can take a long time.

As with bear markets and bull markets more generally, there is no precise definition of a bubble. The difficulty of satisfactorily detecting bubbles is widely commented on in economic literature.[1] As a former Federal Board vice chairman argued, 'even with the benefit

[1] Gurkaynak, R. (2005). Econometric tests of asset price bubbles: Taking stock. *Finance and Economics Discussion Series*. Washington, DC: Board of Governors of the Federal Reserve System.

of hindsight, statistical tests attempting to confirm the existence of bubbles in historical episodes can remain inconclusive'.[2]

A reasonable working definition might be a rapid acceleration in prices and valuations that makes an unrealistic claim on future growth and returns. The second part of this definition is important because not all strong rises in prices necessarily result in bubbles. The problems start when a rapid price increase creates a seemingly virtuous cycle, attracting new investors and, eventually, excess capital. The commonly held belief that the market offers almost endless profitability often generates a 'fear of missing out': the more a theme is spoken about and the greater the attention it receives, the greater the interest from investors. As confidence in the theme or asset increases, valuations rise to levels that cannot be matched by future returns.

The psychology of the crowd – the belief that one might be missing out on a great opportunity and, at the same time, a sense that there is safety in numbers – is often evident in bubble markets. In his comprehensive study of the early bubbles of the 17th and 18th century, Charles Mackay (1841) asserted that 'men . . . think in herds; it will be seen that they go mad in herds, while they recover their senses slowly, one by one'.

A similar focus on crowd 'contagion', particularly when coupled with a powerful narrative, is also emphasised by Robert Shiller in his book *Irrational Exuberance* (2000). Here Shiller describes a bubble as 'a situation in which news of price increases spurs investor enthusiasm which spreads by psychological contagion from person to person, in the process amplifying stories that might justify the price increase and bring in a larger and larger class of investors, who, despite doubts about the real value of the investment, are drawn to it partly through envy of others' successes and partly through a gambler's excitement'.

The tendency for excitement about a theme to drive investors into a market with little regard for the valuations paid, or the

[2] Ferguson, R. W. (2005). Recessions and recoveries associated with asset-price movements: What do we know? *Stanford Institute for Economic Policy Research*, Stanford, CA.

returns implied by these valuations, is one of the most important hallmarks of a developing bubble. A recent example of this can be found in the US housing market prior to the sub-prime crisis of 2008. Case and Shiller's (2003) work shows that homebuyers had significantly over-optimistic expectations about future housing prices at the time. According to their work, 83%–95% of buyers in 2003 were expecting an annual growth rate for housing prices of about 9%, on average, in the following 10 years, well above long-run averages.[3]

This chapter touches on the issue of bubbles solely in an attempt to identify repeated patterns, characteristics and behaviours that echo across history.

There have been many famous bubbles that have been well documented over a period of more than four centuries. Among the most notable, although by no means the only ones, were the following:

- 1630s: The tulip mania in Holland
- 1720: The South Sea bubble, UK, and the Mississippi bubble, France
- 1790s: The canal mania in UK
- 1840s: The railway bubble in UK
- 1873: The railway bubble in the US
- 1920s: The stock market boom in the US
- 1980s: The land and stock bubble in Japan
- 1990s: The technology bubble, global
- 2007: The housing/banking bubble in the US (and Europe).

When reviewing these bubbles, and their eventual collapse, there are some common threads and characteristics that link them even though they originated in an array of different industries and under very different circumstances. For the sake of simplicity, the following sections bring together some of the similarities and themes that are common to these different

[3] Pasotti, P., and Vercelli, A. (2015). Kindleberger and financial crises. *FESSUD Working Paper Series No 104* [online]. Available at http://fessud.eu/wp-content/uploads/2015/01/Kindleberger-and-Financial-Crises-Fessud-final_Working-Paper-104.pdf

bubble periods in an attempt to draw together a guide to investors who are looking for important warning signs and red flags, but there are many excellent and more in-depth studies of historical bubbles for those seeking more detail, in particular the work of Edward Chancellor.[4]

Spectacular Price Appreciation . . . and Collapse

One of the most important features of bubbles in financial assets is the spectacular and often rapid appreciation of prices and valuations that occurs during the bubble, which generates valuations that ultimately overstate the likely possible future returns. It is the sheer scale of the excitement and speculation, as well as price appreciation, which is really the hallmark of all bubbles. The tulip mania of the 1630s, one of the earliest well-documented bubbles, has become synonymous with the idea of a 'mania' in financial markets. It is intriguing not only because of the staggering price rises during the bubble period itself, but also because the mania appears to have been based purely on greed and speculation, with no fundamental underpinnings to support it.

Although the breadth and impact of the tulip mania has since been questioned (see Thompson 2007) it was, nonetheless, a boom of historic proportions. Between November 1636 and February 1637, the price of some tulip bulbs had increased 20 times and, at the height of the bubble, a single bulb could have the same value as a luxury townhouse.[5]

When the market finally crashed, in February 1637, just as occurred in so many other examples in history, the falls were as spectacular as the rises that preceded them. Also in common with many subsequent bubbles, it is not entirely clear what triggered its ultimate collapse. In this case, there were probably many

[4] A comprehensive account can be found in Chancellor, E. (2000). *Devil take the hindmost: A history of financial speculation*. New York, NY: Plume.

[5] See Thompson, E. (2007). The tulipmania: Fact or artifact? *Public Choice*, 130(1–2), 99–114.

contributory factors. At the height of the boom in 1636 and early 1637, when demand was at its highest, the bulbs themselves were still in the ground and could not be physically delivered until the following spring. Financial innovation played a part in driving prices ever higher. A futures market in bulbs developed that enabled sellers to sell forward tulips at a given price for a particular quality and weight.

The risks compounded when most of these contracts were paid for by credit notes, making the system vulnerable to collapse and, eventually, contagion. Ultimately, the fear that the oncoming spring would force delivery of contracts, many of which might not be deliverable, played a part in its demise. After the fall, the market was slow to recover and, in particular, the lower-quality plain bulbs – which had attracted many smaller speculators at the height of the bubble because the rarer bulbs were too expensive – never recovered from the crash.

The two great bubbles of 1720, nearly a century later, shared some similarities with the tulip mania. The South Sea Company in Great Britain experienced a spectacular ascent in its share price over a very short space of time. In January 1720, the company's shares stood at £128. In June of that year, the British Parliament passed the Bubble Act requiring all shareholder-owned companies to receive a Royal Charter, which the South Sea Company successfully received. This seal of approval gave the company enhanced credibility and investors more comfort, so broadening its appeal. By the end of June 1720, the stock had increased to £1,050. When investors started to lose confidence in early July, prices started to slide and by September of that year the shares had collapsed to £175.[6] The Mississippi Company in France experienced a similar bubble and bust at around the same time. Its stock price increased by a staggering 6,200%, before eventually collapsing by 99%.

---

[6] Evans, R. (2014). How (not) to invest like Sir Isaac Newton. *The Telegraph* [online]. Available at https://www.telegraph.co.uk/finance/personalfinance/investing/10848995/How-not-to-invest-like-Sir-Isaac-Newton.html

Speculation played an important role in the next great bubble, in the mid-19th century in the British railway industry, buoyed by rapid growth and technological changes in the railways. After spectacular stock price rises, by 1850 railway shares had fallen by an average 85% from their peak, and the total value of railway shares was less than half the capital spent on them (Chancellor 2000). Despite the experience of the British railway bubble, a similar pattern was repeated in the US just a couple of decades later. The scale of the collapse in prices and investment in its wake was so devastating that it led to a huge structural bear market and economic downturn that became known as the 'Long Depression' and was the worst economic downturns until the Great Depression of the 1930s. Over the 7 years that followed the 1873 panic, roughly half of the country's factories closed and unemployment rose dramatically. Stock prices plummeted and railway share prices fell 60% between 1873 and 1878. Conditions were exacerbated by significant uncertainty in Europe following the Franco-Prussian War. It took a decade for investment to pick up after the bubble burst, and it was not until the next decade that any investment in railroads picked up again.

A similar pattern was to repeat itself in the stock boom and eventual decline during the stock market crash of 1929, but in this case the impact was broader and more long-lasting. On Black Monday (28 October), the Dow Jones Industrial index fell 13% (having already fallen by 6% since early September) and then by another 12% over the following days. The structural bear market that followed was so severe that the index failed to recover to its previous peak until November 1954 (Ferguson 2005). At its lows, the dividend yield on the Dow Jones index reached 9.5%; companies that had boomed previously became totally unwanted. A seat on the NYSE was sold for $17,000 after the crash, compared with a peak price of $650,000 at the height of the boom in 1929.

Japan's legendary bubble of the 1980s resulted in rises in stock and land prices that were extraordinary by any measure. Fuelled by falling interest rates (the Bank of Japan had cut rates from 5% to 2.5% by early 1987) and the 1985 Plaza Accord (which triggered a depreciation of the dollar against the yen aimed at reducing the US current account deficit by making exports cheaper), asset prices enjoyed a long and steady rise. Japanese companies used their appreciating currency to go on an overseas buying spree that included the purchase of the Rockefeller Center in New York and golf courses in Hawaii and California.

The exuberance was particularly rampant in the property market. The Imperial Palace in Tokyo was reported to be worth more than the entire value of France or California. The value of land in Japan in 1988 theoretically was more than four times that of all the land in the United States, even though the latter was 25 times the size.[7] It was argued that a ¥10,000 note dropped in Tokyo's Ginza district was worth less than the size of the ground that it covered.[8] So large was this bubble that the combined capital gains on stocks and land amounted to 452% of nominal GDP for the 1986–1989 period, and the subsequent losses were 159% of nominal GDP for the 1990–1993 period.[9] The surge in stock prices meant that Japanese companies had become some of the largest in the world. Mitsui & Co, Sumitomo Corp, Mitsubishi Corp and C Itoh all had higher sales than America's largest company, General Motors.[10]

A more recent expression of confidence and, eventually, overvaluation came prior to the collapse of the technology bubble in the late 1990s. Before this bubble had burst, shares in new companies were rising exponentially. When the internet-based company Yahoo! made its initial public offering (IPO) in April 1996, the price of its stock rose from $13 to $33 within a single day, more than doubling the worth of the company. This became a familiar pattern in the period that followed. In 1999, for example, Qualcom shares rose in

---

[7] Cutts, R. L. (1990). Power from the ground up: Japan's land bubble. *The Harvard Business Review* [online]. Available at `https://hbr.org/1990/05/power-from-the-ground-up-japans-land-bubble`

[8] Johnston, E. (2009). Lessons from when the bubble burst. *The Japan Times* [online]. Available at `https://www.japantimes.co.jp/news/2009/01/06/reference/lessons-from-when-the-bubble-burst/`

[9] Okina, K., Shirakawa, M., and Shiratsuka, S. (2001). The asset price bubble and monetary policy: Experience of Japan's economy in the late 1980s and its lessons. *Monetary and Economic Studies*, 19(S1), 395–450.

[10] Turner, G. (2003). *Solutions to a liquidity trap*. London, UK: GFC Economics.

value by 2619%. This scale of price appreciation became commonplace. Thirteen major large cap stocks all increased in value by over 1,000% and another seven large cap stocks each rose by over 900%.[11]

The Nasdaq index increased fivefold between 1995 and 2000, eventually reaching a P/E valuation of 200 times, significantly higher than even the 70 times P/E ratio of the Nikkei during the Japanese stock market bubble (Hayes 2019). By April 2000, just 1 month after peaking, the Nasdaq had lost 34% of its value, and over the next year and a half hundreds of companies saw the value of their stock drop by 80% or more. Priceline, for example, fell 94%. Eventually, by the time it troughed in October 2009, the Nasdaq itself had fallen nearly 80% (see McCullough 2018).

By the end of the stock market downturn of 2002, stocks had lost $5 trillion in market capitalisation since the local peak. At its trough on 9 October 2002, the Nasdaq-100 had dropped to 1,114, down 78% from its peak.

Belief in a 'New Era' . . . This Time Is Different

Of course, noting spectacular price increases and collapses is only of interest if there is a common cause, similar characteristics or recognisable patterns of behaviour that can help investors to spot similarities in the future. Looking at history, one of the most important components and characteristics of bubbles, aside from their price ascent and subsequent decline, is the belief that something has changed, usually a new technology, innovation or growth opportunity. This component of a strong narrative that drives the interest in investment was observed by renowned Austrian economist Joseph Schumpeter, who argued that speculation often occurs at the start of a new industry. More recently, in a testimony before the US Congress on 26 February 1997, then-chairman of the Federal Reserve Alan Greenspan noted that 'regrettably, history is strewn

[11] Norris, F. (2000). The year in the markets; 1999: Extraordinary winners and more losers. *New York Times* [online]. Available at `https://www.nytimes.com/2000/01/03/business/the-year-in-the-markets-1999-extraordinary-winners-and-more-losers.html`

with visions of such "new eras" that, in the end, have proven to be a mirage'.

A recent study by data scientists found that, in a sample of 51 major innovations introduced between 1825 and 2000, bubbles in equity prices were evident in 73% of the cases. They also found that the magnitude of these bubbles increases with the radicalness of innovations, with their potential to generate indirect network effects and with their public visibility at the time of commercialisation.[12]

Although it is not obvious that innovation was a trigger in the case of the tulip mania, it could be argued that it was important in the financial bubbles of the South Sea Company in Great Britain and the Mississippi Company in France in 1720.

Although these bubbles involved frenzied speculation and price rises in the shares of the companies involved, and may appear no more rational than the tulip mania a century earlier, more recent interpretations have suggested that innovations and new technologies did play a part in their development. Furthermore, as is also common in so many bubble periods, a strong narrative helped to justify the increase in expected future returns at the time.[13] Frehen, Goetzmann and Geert Rouwenhorst (2013) argue that 'financial bubbles require a plausible story to justify investor optimism'. In these early bubbles, for example, both companies issued shares in exchange for government debt, an innovation that created an instrument to convert national debt into equity. These companies in return had the exclusive rights to exploit resources (such as tobacco and the slave trade), thereby opening up the possibilities of supernormal profits.

The government-debt-for-equity swap was one innovation (that didn't last). Another, perhaps more important, innovation was the establishment of the first publicly traded insurance companies. These were established in Great Britain as a result of the Bubble Act, which attempted to reduce the risks of speculation.

---

[12] See Sorescu, A., Sorescu, S. M., Armstrong, W. J., and Devoldere, B. (2018). Two centuries of innovations and stock market bubbles. *Marketing Science Journal*, 37(4), 507–684.

[13] See Frehen, R. G. P., Goetzmann, W. N., and Rouwenhorst, K. G. (2013). New evidence on the first financial bubble. *Journal of Financial Economics*, 108(3), 585–607.

The creation of publicly financed, but limited liability, insurance companies changed the nature of risk-sharing, thereby allowing for a significant increase in appetite for funding risky endeavours.

Meanwhile, technological changes (in maritime navigation, for example) made possible the opening up of the Atlantic trade routes, a shift that was game-changing; the new trade routes among Europe, Africa and the Caribbean, which were financed partly as a result of the new risk-sharing instruments, became the dominant trade system through to the early 19th century and resulted in what was arguably one of the first major forms of globalisation. The combination of risk appetite, funding conditions, a vehicle that offered attractive returns and technological advances in navigation that enabled the opportunity to be exploited provided a fertile backdrop for speculation.

Technological advances were also central to the canal boom in Great Britain in the 1770s, because the creation of new and faster means of transportation opened up prospects for cheaper and faster transport routes for coal, textiles and agricultural produce and, as a result, generated huge interest. The first canal, opened in 1767 by the Duke of Bridgewater, ran from the coal mines on his estate northwest of Manchester to the southwest of the city where new textile factories were built. The first canals built generated strong returns on capital, which attracted new investors and entrants to the industry, another familiar pattern of subsequent booms and bubbles. The boom reached a peak in 1793 as a result of the start of the French Revolutionary wars. By the 1800s, the return on capital in canals had fallen from a pre-bubble peak of 50% to just 5%, and a quarter of a century later just 25% of canals were still able to pay a dividend (see Chancellor 2000, p. 124).

The next big wave of technology came with the railway age of the 1840s in the UK and, with it, the next great bubble. The railways captured the public's imagination in an extraordinary way, and the interest in and fascination with the technology was fanned by a proliferation of newspapers and journals dedicated to the railways. These covered developments in the market, often promoting new railways and receiving high compensation through advertising revenues. A similar phenomenon had characterised the canal period a century earlier.

Many high-profile celebrities and politicians became investors in the railway stocks. The Brontë sisters were among them, as were several leading thinkers and politicians such as John Stuart Mill, Charles Darwin and Benjamin Disraeli.[14] They were in good company: King George I was an investor in the South Sea bubble (see Chancellor 2000, p. 73), as was Sir Isaac Newton, who reportedly lost £20,000, equivalent to about £3m in today's terms, when the market collapsed.[15]

This breadth of interest had led more people to believe in the 'sure bet' of the investment. In 1845 an author known as 'successful operator' wrote, 'A short and sure guide to railroad speculation – a few plain rules how to speculate with safety and profit in railway shares'. He argued that 'properly conducted, there are no objects to which capital and intelligence can be more honorably or safely directed, than to investment in railways. [...] The capital of the country [England] has never been more beneficially employed.' This was shortly before the epic collapse of the railway bubble in Great Britain.

Similar to the technology bubble that came about a century and a half later, investors correctly identified the transformational impact of the latest innovations but ultimately overstated the potential returns that such innovations would deliver. There is no doubting that the growth of railways was dramatic, with a rapid rollout of the network and supporting infrastructure. For example, Britain's railway track grew from 98 miles in 1830 to 104,333 miles by 1860. But the eventual financial returns failed to live up to such high expectations.

A similar surge in optimism surrounded the US railway boom in the 1870s. The end of the Civil War saw a period of strong growth in the US and a huge increase in spending and investment in railways.

---

[14] Odlyzko, A. (2010). Collective hallucinations and inefficient markets: The British railway mania of the 1840s. SSRN [online]. Available at `https://ssrn.com/abstract=1537338`

[15] Evans, How (not) to invest like Sir Isaac Newton.

Between 1868 and 1873, the volume of loans by banks, which helped fund the expansion, increased seven times faster than deposits.[16]

The US boom of the 1920s was also underpinned by technological and societal changes. This period bought with it huge interest in and growth of new consumer products. Radio sets, in particular, saw an exponential increase in demand. By the end of the 1920s, radio penetration in the US had ballooned to nearly one-third of US homes. The value of shares in Radio Corporation of America (RCA), for example, rose from $5 to $500 in the 1920s. But when the 1920s crash came, radio stocks plummeted. The majority of radio manufacturers failed. The value of RCA stock, like that of many companies, collapsed by 98% between 1929 and 1932. It did not return to its former high for 30 years.

The telecom sector also fuelled the optimism of technology-led growth at the time. American Telephone and Telegraph (AT&T), the central driver in this fast-growing industry, saw rapid growth and by 1913 had become a government-approved monopoly, in turn allowing independent phone companies to connect to its long-distance network. It employed more than 4,000 scientists, and patents proliferated during this period. In 1915, nearly 40 years after their first telephone call, Dr Bell and Thomas Watson made the first transcontinental call across a 3,400-mile line between New York and San Francisco. Excitement about technology and its potential to grow markets intensified.

In the 1920s era of optimism, confidence in the economy was not only driven by the new technologies but also by the belief that the 'American system' of labour relations could boost productivity and demand. A model of successfully negotiating with unions, in a shift from a confrontational to a cooperative approach to labour, was part of the narrative, and Prohibition was believed to be helpful in reducing alcohol addiction and raising labour productivity. These developments boosted expectations for growth in wages and, in turn, demand. A virtuous cycle developed in which stronger productivity boosted investment in new areas of technology.

[16] Lucibello, A. (2014). Panic of 1873. In D. Leab (Ed.), *Encyclopedia of American recessions and depressions* (pp. 227–276). Santa Barbara, CA: ABC-CLIO.

Many of the features of the 1920s boom in the US were to be found again during 1990s Japan. This bubble was driven by too much easy money, coupled with the belief that productivity had improved.[17] A virtuous cycle emerged, fuelled by easily available finance, low interest rates and strong growth. Between the beginning of 1981 and 1990, the Nikkei's index rose about 20% per year (a fivefold increase). Companies were able to raise vast amounts of money as the cost of capital collapsed, which in turn fuelled an investment and productivity boom. A strong exchange rate (as in the US in the late 1990s) helped reduce inflationary pressures. The Bank of Japan believed that productivity and the growth potential in Japan's economy had increased and that a tightening of policy was not necessary.

Excitement about the ability of innovations and technologies to generate broader gains occurred several times in the second half of the 20th century and was evident in the 1980s in the biotech sector and in the new PC revolution. In 1981 IBM, the leading company in the computer industry, facilitated the widespread commercialisation of the personal computer. PC demand boomed and hundreds of companies began to manufacture PCs in the early 1980s. In 1983, however, several companies such as Atari, Texas Instruments and Coleco, announced losses as a result of failed attempts to market PCs to consumers. In the collapse that followed many PC companies went out of business, including Commodore, Columbia Data Systems and Eagle Computer. The surviving stocks took several years to recover, a pattern that was also seen in the aftermath of the railway booms of the 19th century.

Japan's bubble in the 1980s also reflected a belief in a new era – this time in the potential for Japan to become the biggest economy in the world. At the time, one of the most popular books was *Japan as Number One: Lessons for America* by Ezra F. Vogel, professor emeritus of Harvard University. The book described how Japan had developed into the world's most competitive 'super power' and did

[17] Browne, E. (2001). Does Japan offer any lessons for the United States? *New England Economic Review*, 3, 3–18.

not have many of the problems facing the US and other Western economies. There was a growing focus in the media on Japan's economic ascent. Pushy parents across the West were enrolling their children for Japanese lessons, hoping to keep their skills relevant in the changing world. One of my first job offers was with a leading Japanese bank at the time, and when I told people about the offer most thought my future would be secure working for a Japanese bank, at the cutting edge of global finance.

Interestingly, this has also been a growing phenomenon in the more recent period as the focus has shifted to Chinese dominance. Popular books have captured the zeitgeist of the times; the 2009 bestseller *When China Rules the World: The End of the Western World and the Birth of a New Global Order* by Martin Jacques also reflected the focus of the era and a belief in a changing world with all of its attendant risks and opportunities. Just as the Japanese stock market rose sharply and then collapsed as expectations for these future changes built up and then deflated, a similar pattern occurred in China, albeit to a lesser extent. The Shanghai composite stock price index, reflecting the prevailing optimism, increased by 165% (or 61% annualised) between June 2013 and June 2015. As global growth slowed and concerns about US interest rates intensified, the stock market then collapsed by 48% through to March 2016.

The technology bubble that developed in many countries in the late 1990s became more broad-based and fuelled companies across the technology, telecom and media industries (commonly referred to as TMT).[18] In addition to strong economic growth and low interest rates, the fascination and excitement about technology innovations was key. As with the excitement about the possibilities of faster communications following the first transcontinental calls in 1915, expectations were boosted by dramatic falls in the cost of communication in the 1990s, when the speed of communication accelerated at an even faster rate than before, and with similar consequences.

[18] Stephen King of HSBC wrote a report 'Bubble Trouble' in which he identified significant risks of overvaluations and potential economic consequences before the technology bubble burst in 2000.

The cost of a three-minute telephone call from New York to London fell from $4.37 in 1990 (in 2000 dollars) to $0.40 in 2000.[19]

Deregulation and Financial Innovation

Light touch regulation, or deregulation, is often an ingredient in the buildup of financial bubbles. In the railway boom of the early 19th century in Great Britain, for example, the repeal of the Bubble Act in 1825, introduced after the collapse of the South Sea bubble in 1720, was an important development. Aimed at controlling the formation of new companies, it limited the number of investors in joint stock companies to just five. In rescinding the act, the government made it easier to register, and set up, companies. It also made it much easier for large numbers of an increasingly enthralled public to invest in the new companies. Meanwhile, as noted previously, the financial innovation of new insurance companies allowed for a more conducive environment for risk-taking.

During the railway boom in Great Britain in the mid-19th century, the process of applying for permits to build new railways was relaxed. In order to speed up the process, by 1845 applications were sent directly before select committees in the House of Commons for a decision. But many parliamentarians were involved in the speculation, and so stood to gain. As a result, a huge number of new permits were allowed, further fuelling the speculation. By 1846, 272 Acts of Parliament had passed setting up new railway companies.

Deregulation and greater confidence in institutions also played a role in the boom of the 1920s. The establishment of the Federal Reserve System in 1913 (akin to the wave of independence in central banks in the 1990s) led to greater confidence on the part of investors, and the election of President Calvin Coolidge paved the way for a relaxation of the antitrust laws and a wave of mergers.

---

[19] See Masson, P. (2001). Globalization facts and figures. *IMF Policy Discussion Paper No. 01/4* [online]. Available at `https://www.imf.org/en/Publications/IMF-Policy-Discussion-Papers/Issues/2016/12/30/Globalization-Facts-and-Figures-15469`

The 1980s Japan bubble was also facilitated in part by a process of deregulation. In 1981, for example, the Ministry of Finance gave Japanese companies permission to issue warrants in the Eurobond market in London. These warrants gave an option to purchase shares in a company at a specified price before the expiry date. Because the rapid rise in stock prices increased the value of the warrants, it meant that Japanese companies were able to issue bonds with very low rates of interest. The more companies borrowed at these low rates and issued more warrants, the greater the demand for the stock. A further incentive was afforded because the companies could issue the warrants in dollars. Following the Plaza Accord of 1985, the relentless fall in the value of the dollar meant that investors expected the yen to rise against the dollar over the life of the bond, creating a perceived virtuous cycle.

In 1984, Japan's Ministry of Finance also allowed companies to create special, so-called Tokkin accounts for their shareholdings, which allowed companies to trade securities without having to pay any capital gains tax on their profits. By the mid- to late 1980s, the profits that companies were making in stock market speculation were growing at a rapid pace, which encouraged most industrial companies to become involved. Many companies were deriving more than half of their profits from these Tokkin accounts. Total corporate gains from Tokkin funds rose from ¥240 billion in 1985 to ¥952 billion by 1987 (Chancellor 2000). The rise in debt also reached the household sector. Nearly half of the individuals seeking help from the Japan Credit Counselling Association in Tokyo during 1989 had between 11 and 20 credit cards.[20]

The technology boom of the 1990s was also fuelled by innovation in financial products. The growth of derivative markets was an important driver of this. Between 1994 and 2000 the notional amounts of derivatives in interest rates and currency grew 457%, which is equivalent to the 452% growth from 2001 to 2007.[21]

[20] Johnston, Lessons from when the bubble burst.

[21] Perez, C. (2009). The double bubble at the turn of the century: Technological roots and structural implications. *Cambridge Journal of Economics*, 33(4), 779–805.

Although derivative markets boomed in the 2000s, other forms of innovation were at play in the housing market and were central to the sub-prime boom and subsequent banking and stock market collapse of 2007/2008. This bubble was not really so evident in the stock market valuation more broadly, although its collapse did result in huge falls in stock prices. Light touch regulation of financial institutions, together with financial product innovation, were an important ingredient in the housing boom that preceded the collapse. As Carlota Perez (2009) put it, 'the term "masters of the universe", often quoted to refer to the financial geniuses that were supposed to have engineered the unending prosperity of the mid-2000s, expresses the way in which they were seen as powerful innovators, spreading risk and somehow magically evaporating it in the vast complexity of the financial galaxy'.

During the boom years of the 1990s, banks securitised huge volumes of high-risk mortgage debt in the form of mortgage-backed securities (MBS) and collateralised debt obligations (CDO), which could be sold on to financial markets. This innovation enabled investing institutions to receive the income from mortgage payments, while also exposing them to the underlying credit risk.

The problem was that when the housing market began to fall a vicious cycle developed. Banks collapsed and the credit risk that had spread to institutions around the world resulted in systemic weakness in asset markets. Many of the CDO[22] products were valued on a 'mark to market' basis, which, as prices fell, caused a collapse of the credit markets and, in turn, resulted in market illiquidity. Banks were forced to make dramatic write-downs.[23]

---

[22] A collateralised debt obligation (CDO) is a structured financial product that pools together assets that generate cash, such as mortgages, and then packages this asset pool into different tranches that can be sold to investors. Each varies significantly in risk profile.

[23] Pezzuto, I. (2012). Miraculous financial engineering or toxic finance? The genesis of the U.S. subprime mortgage loans crisis and its consequences on the global financial markets and real economy. *Journal of Governance and Regulation*, 1(3), 113–124.

Easy Credit

Similar to many other bubbles that followed, the rapid growth of new entrants in the 1873 US railway bubble was also facilitated by easy money and new exchange banks that would offer loans against the collateral of railway shares. Railway companies also increasingly allowed private investors to buy on margin, typically requiring only a 10% deposit, with the railway company having the right to call the rest of the capital at any time (an option that was, of course, triggered at a later date, thereby exacerbating the fallout).

The growth in credit financed the expansion of the railways, and between 1865 and 1873 the amount of rail track in the US increased from 35,000 to 70,000 miles, with 18,000 miles laid in 1873 alone. As with many other bubbles, valuations for railways expanded rapidly. Of the 364 operators in 1872, only 194 paid a dividend. As policy tightened, railroad entrepreneurs needed to secure more capital to continue the rapid growth of the railroads. In this bubble, a famous financier, John Crooke and Company, ended up overstretching with his bid to build a second transatlantic railway, the Northern Pacific Railway. Having sourced a huge loan from the government, fears emerged that his company's credit and eventually his company was not good, and he declared bankruptcy in 1873 resulting in the start of the crash. This, in turn, spawned a series of corporate failures. Large numbers of brokerage houses went bankrupt and in 1873 the New York Stock Exchange closed for 12 days to try to curb the collapse.

John Kenneth Galbraith (1955) argued that an explosion in margin borrowing was also significant as a cause of the 1929 crash. Later, it was argued to have been a significant contributor to the 1987 crash, and cheap credit was also central to the Japanese bubble. Very low interest rates and cost of capital enabled the banks to boost their assets. In 1998, the world's 10 largest banks were all Japanese, and they were using their cost of capital advantages to capture global market share. By 1988 Japanese banks had become the world's largest lenders in international banking, with a world share of more than 20%. The spectacular growth of Japanese banks and the rise in market values meant that by the late 1980s the combined market capitalisation of the largest 13 Japanese banks was more than five times greater than the top 50 banks globally.[24] Today, by comparison, the top four banks based on assets are Chinese.

Cheap and available credit was also a hallmark of the dotcom bubble in the late 1990s. Record amounts of capital flowed into the Nasdaq in 1997. By 1999, 39% of all venture capital investments went to internet companies. That year, 295 of the 457 IPOs were related to internet companies, followed by 91 in the first quarter of 2000 alone (see Hayes 2019).

New Valuation Approaches

Many bubbles in history were fuelled by a belief that 'this time is different', and this has encouraged investors to look at, and justify, new ways of valuing companies. During the 1920s, for example, several academics argued that stocks were no riskier than bonds but offered greater potential returns.[25] In addition, a number of studies placed emphasis on compound growth in equities.[26]

Others, such as Charles Dice in his book *New Levels in the Stock Market*,[27] argued that stock prices in the late 1920s were too low. The market, in his view, had not yet priced in the triple revolutions in production, distribution and finance that were raising the value of US industry.

Similar enthusiasm reigned, particularly in the US, during the stock market boom in the 1950s and 1960s. Benjamin Graham in *The Intelligent Investor* (1949)[28] argued that 'old standards of valuation are no longer applicable' as the Fed's attempt to avoid depression through very low interest rates had raised the growth potential of the economy and, therefore, the value of stocks.

---

[24] Cutts, Power from the ground up.

[25] Smith, E. L. (1925). *Common stocks as long-term investments*. New York, NY: Macmillan.

[26] Guild, S. E. (1931). *Stock growth and discount tables*. Boston, MA: Financial Publishing Company.

[27] Dice, C. A. (1931). New levels in the stock market. *Journal of Political Economy*, 39(4), 551–554.

[28] Graham, B. (1949). *The intelligent investor*. New York, NY: HarperBusiness.

Arguments about the justification for higher valuations were also prevalent during the Japanese bubble of the 1990s. A surge in the equity P/E ratio resulted in an increased equity yield spread during the period from the late 1980s to the early 1990s. As reported by Okina, Shirakawa and Shiratsuka (2001), the expected growth rate of nominal GDP computed from the equity yield spread in 1990 was as high as 8 percentage points, with the standard assumption based on the discount factor. This was a growth rate that was highly improbable at the time (or indeed since) given low inflation and demographics. Hence, as with many other bubbles, investors were reflecting an intensification of bullish expectations that were unsustainable in the long run.

The Economist wrote (April 15, 1989): 'What Japanese investors have become aware of is the dramatic way Japan's blue chip companies have changed the sources of their earnings through restructuring. This has made their profits too erratic to give any meaning to rigid measures such as a P/E ratio. Instead, investors have started to assess a company's future stream of earnings by looking at the total value of the firm's assets [. . .] the implication is that shares may be underpriced.'

During bubbles, investors' confidence in the theme has often helped valuations to rise. This occurred during the railway bubble of the 1870s and was repeated in the technology and dotcom bubble of the 1990s. When examining stock pricing during the dotcom bubble, Cooper, Dimitrov and Rau (2001) found that in the late 1990s companies that changed their names to a term related to the internet or to IT (such as appending *.com* to their name) caused an average stock price increase of 53% in the days following the announcement of such a change, even if a company had little activity with or in the IT sector.[29]

[29] Cooper, M., Dimitrov, O., and Rau, P. (2001). A Rose.com by any other name. *The Journal of Finance*, 56(6), 2371–2388.

Accounting Problems and Scandals

Post-bubble realisations of accounting problems have been another regular feature of bubbles throughout history.

Three years after the UK railway bubble had burst (1848), Arthur Smith wrote a book entitled *The Bubble of the Age; or, the Fallacy of Railway Investment, Railway Accounts, and Railway Dividends.*[30] What is interesting about this bubble is that, once it had burst, there was a broad revelation that accounting abuse had taken place. Smith argued that the boom in railway shares that had occurred in the previous few years had resulted in extensive accounting abuse. He argued that 'the dividends of every railway company since the introduction of locomotive power have been paid by charging sums to capital which should be credited to the revenue account. This in effect constitutes paying the dividends out of capital. The railways have invariably required a constant outlay greater than the dividends declared, without reference to the expenditure on branches or extensions.' One such operation was led by a Member of Parliament, George Hudson; it failed because he engaged in the fraudulent practice of paying dividends out of capital (a practice that also occurred in the South Sea bubble).

Graham and Dodd noted in 1934 (in *Security Analysis*) that 'in 1928 and 1929 there occurred a wholesale and disastrous relaxation of the standards of safety previously observed by the exhibit houses of issue. This was shown in the sale of many new offerings of inferior grade, aided in part by questionable methods of presenting the facts to the public. The general collapse in values affected those unsound and unseasoned issues with particular severity, so that the losses suffered by investors in many of these flotations have been little short of appalling.'

---

[30] Smith, A. (1848). *The bubble of the age; or, The fallacies of railway investment, railway accounts, and railway dividends.* London, UK: Sherwood, Gilbert and Piper.

In Japan's bubble of the 1990s, the creation of 'Zaitech', or manufactured accounts, allowed companies to manipulate many assets, which resulted in accounting scandals. Summer 1991 exposed a series of these. One, in particular, involved allegedly involved secret payments of more than $1 billion from the nation's biggest securities firms to a few select clients. These were meant to reimburse clients for trading losses in the market downturns of 1987 and 1990. There were also charges that the world's biggest brokerage firm at the time, Nomura Securities Ltd., worked to manipulate the price of Tokyu Corp. stock.[31]

But the accusations of scandals continued and led to the failure of a number of banks, such as Tokai Bank and Kyowa-Saitama Bank, which were blamed for issuing fictitious certificates of deposit to provide clients with 'collateral' for real estate loans.[32]

Benjamin Graham and David Dodd (1934) wrote that 'instead of judging the market by established standards of value, the new era based its standards of value upon the market price'.

The technology bubble of the 1990s also revealed its fair share of scandals and irregularities. Perhaps the most famous was that of Enron, a company that *Fortune* magazine had named America's most innovative company for 6 years in a row from 1996 to 2001.[33] When Enron filed for bankruptcy on 2 December 2001, it became clear that the audited balance sheet had understated the company's long-term debt by $25 billion. Worldcom was another scandal to emerge from the bubble. It had filed $3.8 billion in expenses that were reported as capital investment, and a further $3.3 billion of irregularities related to the manipulation of reserves, when the company had set aside reserves to cover estimated losses.

---

[31] Sterngold, J. (1991). Nomura gets big penalties. *New York Times*, October 9, Section D, p. 1.

[32] Reid, T. R. (1991). Japan's scandalous summer of '91. *Washington Post* [online]. Available at https://www.washingtonpost.com/archive/politics/1991/08/03/japans-scandalous-summer-of-91/e066bc12-90f2-4ce1-bc05-70298b675340/

[33] Ferguson, N. (2012). *The ascent of money*. London, UK: Penguin.

In sum, although all of the episodes discussed in this chapter were clearly different, the common features of the bubble or mania periods have been as follows:

- A belief in a 'new era' or technology.
- Deregulation and financial innovation.
- Easy availability of credit and financial conditions.
- Justification of new valuation measures.
- The emergence of accounting scandals and irregularities.

These are some of the warning signs that a bull market is turning into a bubble, and that when that bubble bursts it could lead to a severe structural bear market, or at least significant losses in part of the market.

Part III

Lessons for the Future: A Focus on the Post-Financial Crisis Era; What Has Changed and What It Means for Investors

Chapter 9
How the Cycle Has Changed Post the Financial Crisis

Not all cycles are alike, but the environment since the global financial crisis of 2007–2009 has been particularly unusual, given that many of the traditional patterns and relationships between economic and financial markets have changed and, in some cases, appear to have broken down. Understanding these changes is important because it contextualises the market moves that we have seen since the financial crisis and helps us better understand how cycles may evolve in the future.[1]

The financial crisis of 2007–2009 and its aftermath were highly traumatic in terms of both the collapse in the value of risk assets and the global economic fallout. The impact on the global economy has been estimated at over $10 trillion, equivalent to more than one-sixth of the global economy in 2010 alone, and over

[1] There are many useful accounts of the triggers for and consequences of the crisis, and how things have changed since. See, for example, Tooze, A. (2018). *Crashed: How a decade of financial crises changed the world*. London, UK: Allen Lane.

$2 trillion of assets in financial institutions were written down (Oxenford 2018). Some analysts suggest that the impact may have been even greater. One such study estimates that the financial crisis persistently lowered US output by roughly 7 percentage points, representing a lifetime income loss in present-discounted value terms of about $70,000 for every US citizen.[2] The Governor of the Bank of England at the time, Sir Mervyn King, said, 'This is the most serious financial crisis at least since the 1930s, if not ever'.[3]

Unsurprisingly, given the economic impact, the collapse in equity markets was also substantial: US equity markets fell 57% and the world stock market (MSCI World) fell 59%, placing this period firmly in the group of rare structural bear markets, based on the definitions in chapter 6.

In terms of the pattern of market moves going into the crisis and at the start of the bear market, there was a fairly typical (albeit extreme) market cycle near a deep recession. However, the recovery that followed the trough broke with the patterns of the past, because the typical phases of the cycle were knocked off course by a series of shock waves as the second-round effects of the crisis made their way across the world. Although the epicentre had been in the US housing market, with the collapse of sub-prime mortgages and associated credit and banking problems, the stresses extended into European banks (which were very highly levered at the time and also heavily exposed to real estate in southern Europe, which also suffered large losses) and, as a consequence, emerged in the European sovereign debt crisis (2010–2012). A third wave was felt mainly in Asia when, in August 2015, China devalued its currency against the US dollar following a period of weak growth. Commodity prices also collapsed, with Brent prices more than halving in value from nearly $100 per barrel in summer 2014 to $46 in January 2016.

---

[2] Romer, C., and Romer, D. (2017). New evidence on the aftermath of financial crises in advanced countries. *American Economic Review*, 107(10), 3072–3118.

[3] Mason, P. (2011). Thinking outside the 1930s box. BBC [online]. Available at https://www.bbc.co.uk/news/business-15217615

Three Waves of the Financial Crisis

These waves can be described with reference to the causes of stress as they erupted in the different regions.

Wave one in the US started with the housing market collapse and spread into a broader credit crunch, ending with Lehman Brothers filing for bankruptcy and the start of the Troubled Asset Relief Program (TARP) and quantitative easing (QE).[4]

Wave two in Europe began with the exposure of banks to leveraged losses in the US and spread to a sovereign crisis given the lack of a debt-sharing mechanism across the euro area. It peaked with the Greek debt crisis and the insistence that private investors should be 'bailed in' when it came to losses. It ended with the introduction of outright monetary transactions (OMT),[5] the ECB's commitment to do 'whatever it takes' and, finally, the introduction of QE.

Wave three in emerging markets (EM) coincided with the collapse in commodity prices and activity that hit EM equities hard, particularly between June 2013 and the start of 2016.

The impact of the three waves on the US, Europe and EM equity markets is highlighted in exhibit 9.1. The US wave quickly became a global shock as credit markets and banks' balance sheets around the world became impaired. All of the main equity markets fell together and emerging markets (which have a higher beta and are most vulnerable to a collapse in world trade growth) suffered the largest declines. The rebound, triggered by zero interest rate policies and the start of US QE, also had a global impact, and emerging market equities (which had initially suffered most) rebounded strongly.

---

[4] TARP was a programme of the US government that helped to stabilise the financial system through a series of measures that included the TARP bailout programme, authorising $700 billion to bail out banks, AIG, and auto companies. It also helped credit markets and homeowners. Quantitative easing (QE) – or large-scale asset purchases – refers to monetary policy that entails a central bank creating money that is used to buy predetermined amounts of government bonds or other financial assets in order to inject liquidity into the economy.

[5] Outright Monetary Transactions (OMT) is a programme of the European Central Bank under which the Bank makes purchases (outright transactions) in secondary, sovereign bond markets, under certain conditions, of bonds issued by euro area member states.

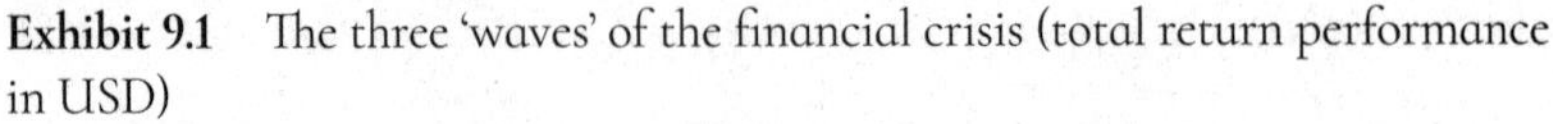

Exhibit 9.1 The three 'waves' of the financial crisis (total return performance in USD)

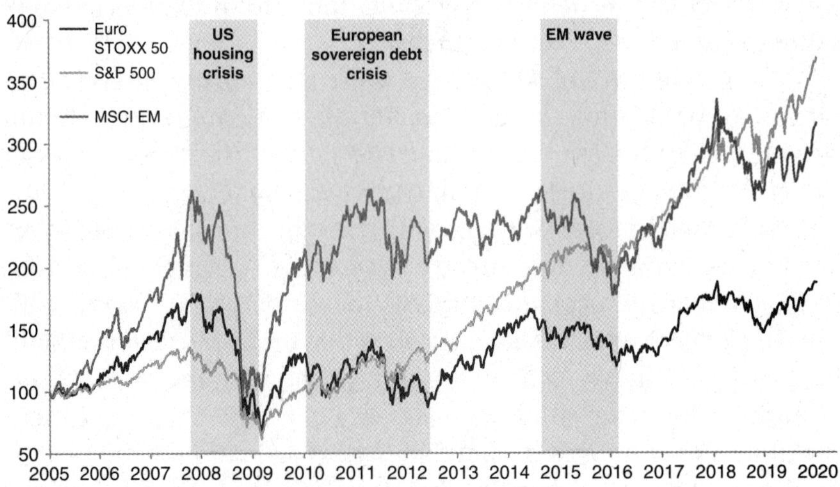

SOURCE: Goldman Sachs Global Investment Research.

But the recovery was then interrupted as the crisis extended to Europe. Here, the combination of highly levered banks and the institutional weaknesses of the euro area fiscal framework led to a sovereign debt crisis and another severe drawdown. For much of this period, however, the US economy and stock market managed to decouple from the rest of the world and continued to make rapid progress.

For Europe, the impact was severe and, by late July 2012, the euro area financial sector was in acute crisis. By summer 2012 Spanish 10-year sovereign yields had reached levels above 7.5% and the 2-year rate was approaching 7%. A flattening of the Spanish government yield curve at levels inconsistent with fiscal and macroeconomic sustainability threatened to cause the sovereign market to seize up. And, given the central role played by that market in the wider functioning of the Spanish financial system (and the deep connectivity between banks and the sovereign), the Spanish banking sector came under threat. Contagion to other peripheral countries became acute as Italian sovereign yields were also climbing towards 7% and existential risks to the euro and to the euro area were widely considered to be high.

Finally, equity markets globally rebounded in mid-2012 as risk premia moderated following aggressive policy intervention by the ECB and verbal assurances that the ECB would do 'whatever it takes' to preserve the euro, demonstrating, once again, the power of central banks to change market expectations. Following his comments, ECB President Draghi announced the ECB's Outright Monetary Transactions (OMT) programme in the September 2012 press meeting. For euro area countries that had accepted the conditionality implicit in a European stability mechanism (ESM) and simultaneously retained market access, the ECB stood ready to purchase shorter-dated government debt in potentially unlimited amounts.

But just as things appeared to be calming down, significant weakness in commodity markets and EM equities triggered a third wave of the downturn, with China at the epicentre. Europe was hit once again, given its large exposure to EM markets, but the US equity market experienced a milder and shorter correction and was once again seen as a relative safe haven.

Since the middle of 2016, equity markets and fixed income (bond and credit) markets have moved higher together, although with significant differences in relative returns. Aggressive monetary easing and quantitative easing have had a strong effect in pushing up valuations in financial markets. Various academic papers have examined the impact of QE on bond prices, particularly following their announcement. Others have shown that it had a meaningful impact on equity markets as well, with some estimates that, in the case of the UK FTSE All-Share index and the US S&P 500, 'unconventional policy measures adopted caused increases in equity prices of at least 30%'.[6]

[6] Balatti, M., Brooks, C., Clements, M. P., and Kappou, K. (2016). Did quantitative easing only inflate stock prices? Macroeconomic evidence from the US and UK. *SSRN* [online]. Available at https://papers.ssrn.com/sol3/papers.cfm?abstract_id=2838128. They argue in this paper that median estimates indicate a peak impact on equities, at the end of the 24-month horizon, of about 30% for the FTSE All-Share and about 50% for the S&P 500.

All equity markets have moved higher together, finally shaking off the impact of the financial crisis. In the context of this rolling crisis, 2016 marked an important turning point as global equity markets rose on the back of strong synchronised growth and receding political/systemic risks. The improvement in growth and profits meant that, for the first time in the cycle, a large share of the ROE markets came from profit growth as opposed to valuation expansion.

Unsurprisingly, this combination propelled global equity markets sharply higher, with the MSCI AC World recording one of its highest returns on a risk-adjusted basis since the mid-1980s.

The Unusual Gap between Financial Markets and Economies

Although the 'typical' phases of the cycle since 2009 have been distorted by the ongoing problems just mentioned, there are some fundamental ways in which the nature and form of the current cycle have also changed since 2008.

In particular, what makes the post-financial-crisis period so unusual is that the economic cycle has been much longer than normal, and much weaker. Taking the US as an example, the economy, at the time of writing, is now in its longest economic expansion for 150 years. But although the US economy has managed to recover more strongly than those in Asia and Europe in recent years, it has still achieved a slower recovery than from most 'normal' recessions. Exhibit 9.2 shows the path of economic growth since the 2009 recession compared with the average recovery from previous recessions over the past 50 years.

The persistence of slow growth post the financial crisis has been even more evident in other parts of the world, in particular in Europe, where the impact of the sovereign debt and banking crises has been even greater.

The slow recovery of activity and the lower inflation profile that followed the Great Recession are, though, consistent with the profile

Exhibit 9.2 A weaker than average economic recovery (US real GDP from trough 10 years onward)

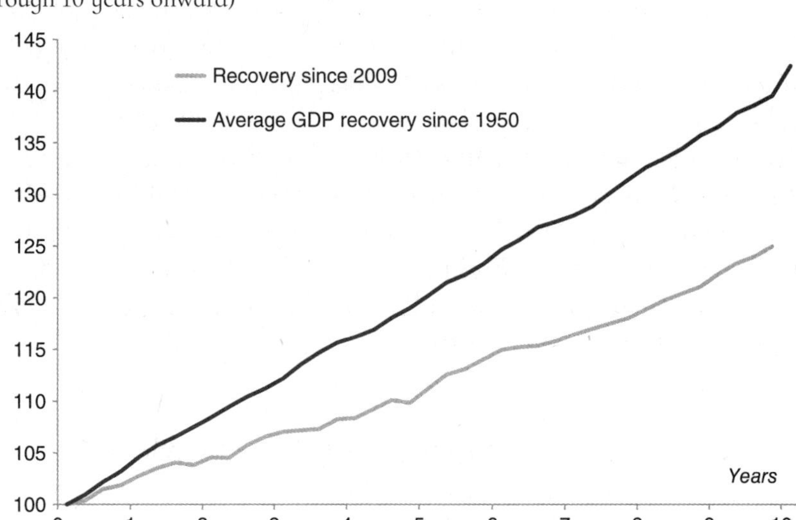

SOURCE: Goldman Sachs Global Investment Research.

of previous economic recoveries from recessions driven by housing or banking sector collapses. Given the leverage that preceded the financial crisis, this should not have been a total surprise. Many studies have shown that business cycles that follow large leverage cycles tend to result in slower and weaker growth recoveries. In a study of roughly 200 recessions since 1850, for example, the Federal Reserve Board of San Francisco[7] found that the profile of the post-recession recovery period is very much dependent on the conditions that preceded it. Specifically, '**a recession and recovery path associated with a financial crisis peak is likely to be much more prolonged and more painful than that found after a normal peak**'. A similar observation has been made in other studies.[8]

[7] Jorda, O., Schularick, M., Taylor, A. M., and Ward, F. (2018). Global financial cycles and risk premiums. *Working Paper Series 2018-5*, Federal Reserve Bank of San Francisco [online]. Available at http://www.frbsf.org/economic-research/publications/working-papers/2018/05/

[8] Terrones, M., Kose, A., and Claessens, S. (2011). Financial cycles: What? How? When? *IMF Working Paper No. 11/76*, [online]. Available at https://www.imf.org/en/Publications/WP/Issues/2016/12/31/Financial-Cycles-What-How-When-24775

Studies of previous episodes of financial stress around the globe point to similarly large and persistent output losses. For instance, Romer and Romer (2017) studied a panel of countries in the Organisation for Economic Co-operation and Development (OECD) and found that gross domestic product is typically about 9 percentage points lower 5 years after an extreme financial crisis.[9]

Interestingly, the pace of recovery from the downturn in 2008 in the US economy was very similar to that achieved by Japan in the early 1990s following the banking and real estate collapse of the late 1980s, although the pace of recovery in Japan fell short of what has been achieved in the US more recently (largely as a function of a more aggressive policy setting).

What is striking about the post-financial-crisis cycle, particularly given the weak economic backdrop, has been the strength of the rebound in equity prices. As exhibit 9.3 shows, despite having experienced a relatively similar profile of economic recovery to

Exhibit 9.3 Weakest but unusually strong financial recovery (S&P 500)

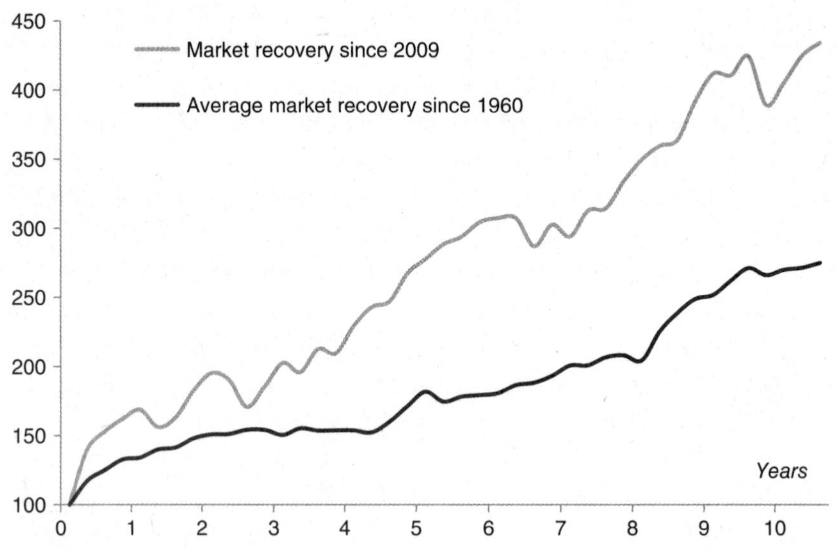

SOURCE: Goldman Sachs Global Investment Research.

[9] Romer and Romer, New evidence on the aftermath of financial crises in advanced countries.

Japan in the 1990s, the equity market (shown here in the US) has been much more powerful than the 'average' recovery from recession and also more powerful than the recovery from the bear market in Japan in the 1990s (exhibit 9.4). The success of this cycle has been its length. The post-financial-crisis equity cycle has (using the S&P 500) recorded its longest rally ever, with over a decade-long boom.

Put another way, despite the rolling waves of the financial crisis, aggregate returns have been strong across the board (albeit from the market lows in 2009). It is difficult to know how much of the recovery in equity markets has been a function of loose financial conditions, zero interest rates and QE, but it is telling that the recovery in equity markets in this cycle has been much sharper than following similarly deep bear markets in the past.

Exhibit 9.5 shows how long it has taken to recoup the losses from major bear markets. The current cycle (at least in the US) has been far quicker than following the collapse in 1929 and in Japan in

Exhibit 9.4 Financial market recovery

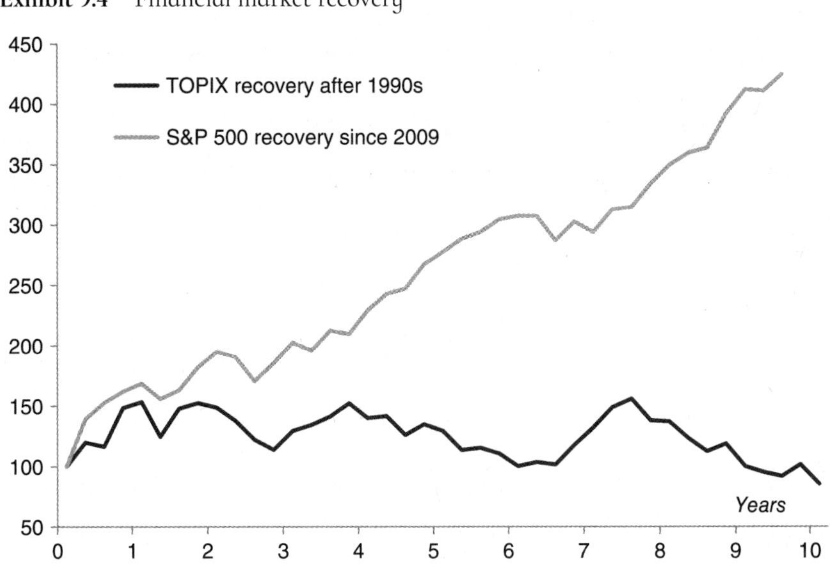

SOURCE: Goldman Sachs Global Investment Research.

Exhibit 9.5 Unlike after the 1930s crisis in the US or the 1990s crisis in Japan, US markets quickly recovered their losses after 2009 (nominal price returns; US: S&P 500; Japan: TOPIX)

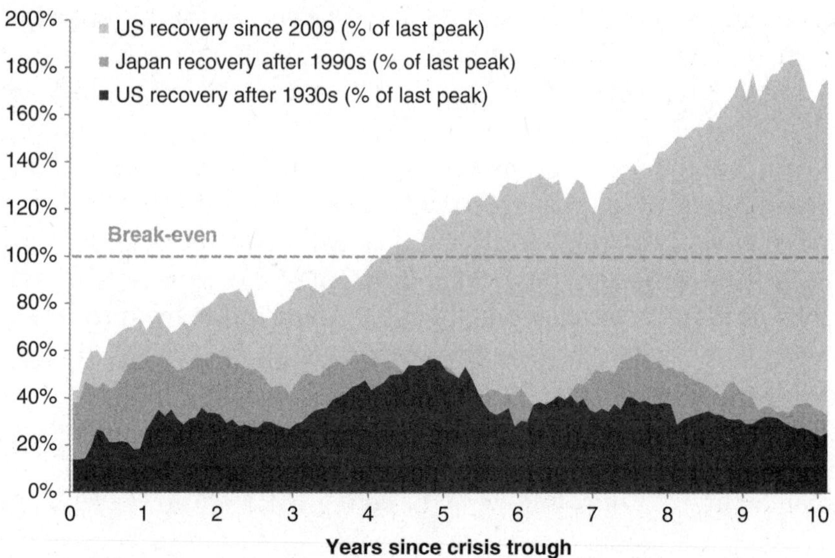

SOURCE: Goldman Sachs Global Investment Research.

1990. Returns recouped 100% of the previous high within 4 years of the crisis in this cycle, while languishing at about 50% of their previous high returns after the 1929 US and 1990 Japan cycles.

All Boats Were Lifted by the Liquidity Wave

Part of the success of financial assets over the past 10 years has been that they have all been driven by a common factor – falling risk-free rates, which have contributed to rising valuations. Although equities have achieved higher returns than bonds, the impact of loose monetary policy has been felt across all asset classes.

The impact of aggressive policy easing (including QE) post the crisis has been meaningful for asset returns. Indeed, the gap between 'inflation' measured in the real economy and that of financial assets has also been notable in this cycle (exhibit 9.6). Financial

Exhibit 9.6 Wide dispersion between asset price inflation and 'real economy' inflation (total return performance in local currency since January 2009)

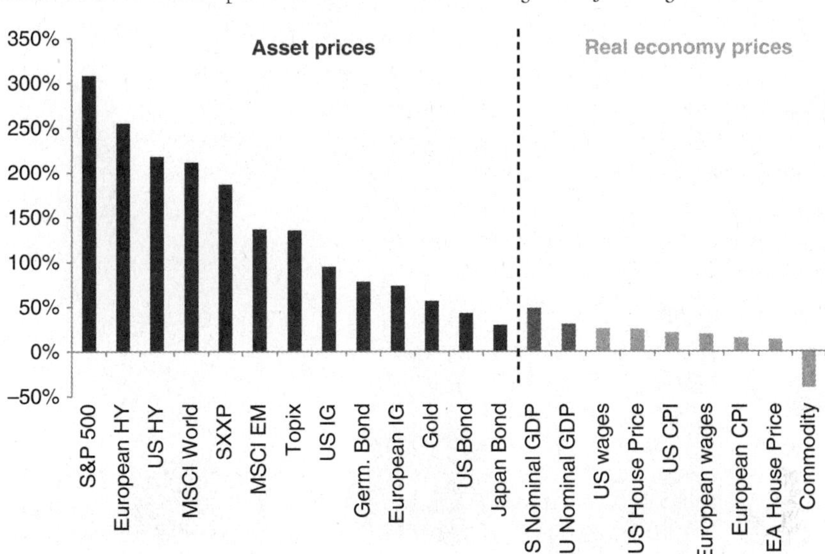

SOURCE: Goldman Sachs Global Investment Research.

assets have seen significant inflation, much of which has reflated rising valuations in markets as interest rates have collapsed.

As a result of this, the post-financial-crisis period has generated the longest and strongest bull market in a standard 'balanced' portfolio (defined here as a benchmark of 60% US equities and 40% US government bonds).

The Unusual Drivers of the Return

The extent to which higher valuations have contributed to returns varies across markets but, as exhibit 9.7 shows, at least relative to the average of past bull markets, valuation has driven a higher proportion of returns in the post-financial-crisis period than on average in the past, particularly in Europe. Even in the US equity market (where profits have been strong), valuation has driven around three times the proportion of market returns compared with average cycles in

Exhibit 9.7 Valuation expansion and rising margins explain more of the rise in markets 10 years after the crisis trough this time (contribution of sales and margins to price returns: S&P 500 except financials, real estate and utilities; current recovery starting March 2009)

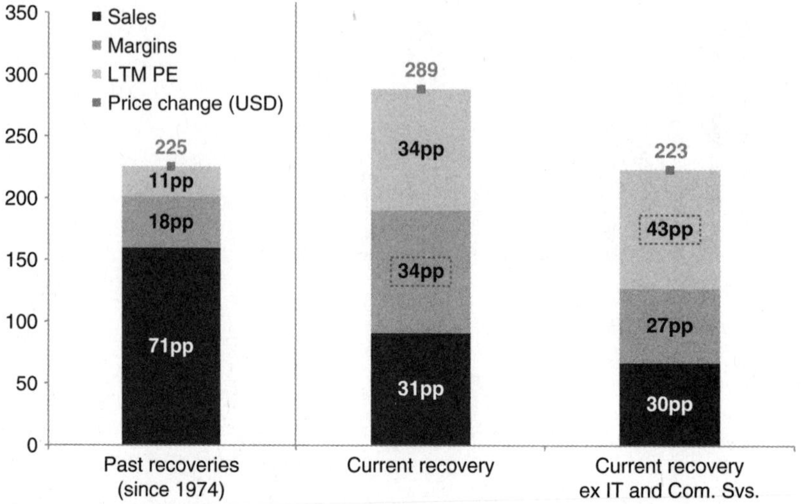

SOURCE: Goldman Sachs Global Investment Research.

the past: roughly one-third of the return compared with an average in previous cycles (over a similar period) of just over 10%. Margins have also contributed to a greater proportion of the returns than typical in previous cycles (partly owing to the sharply rising margins of the technology industry). Meanwhile, revenue growth has been weaker (roughly half of the proportion of returns that it typically accounts for), partly as a result of much lower inflation in general.

Lower Inflation and Interest Rates

The other crucial change since the financial crisis has been in interest rates and bond yields, a topic discussed further in chapter 10.

It is not just nominal interest rates and inflation that have fallen; there has also been a significant shift downwards in real long-term rates (nominal rates minus inflation) (Exhibit 9.8).

Exhibit 9.8 Real bond yields have turned negative (10-year nominal yield minus current inflation)

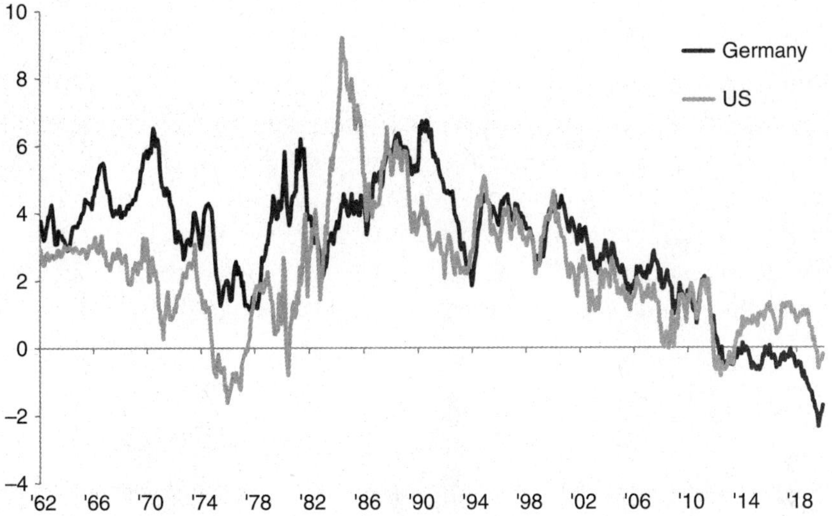

SOURCE: Goldman Sachs Global Investment Research.

There may be many reasons for this. One explanation is that an excess of savings over investment has driven equilibrium real interest rates down. The argument is that changes in monetary policy and fiscal spending have not really been the most important drivers of interest rates. For instance, in his secular stagnation hypothesis, Summers (2015) suggests that chronically weak aggregate demand has, together with ultra-low policy rates, kept desired saving above investment and pushed the natural rate below market rates. The global saving glut (Bernanke 2005) and the shortage of safe assets (Caballero and Farhi 2017)[10] have driven excess savings in emerging market economies, reflected in their current account surpluses, into advanced economies, depressing real rates there. But others point out that slower economic growth and lower inflation (partly reflecting the impact of demographics and partly also the impact of rapid technological disruption) are responsible.

---

[10] Caballero, R. J., and Farhi, E. (2017). The safety trap. *The Review of Economic Studies*, 85(1), 223–274.

Whatever the reasons, forward market measures of inflation have also fallen compared with previous cycles. In the past, labour market tightening often generated substantial and persistent inflationary pressure, causing central banks to raise interest rates sharply, thereby raising the risks of recession. But since the 2000s more effective forward guidance by central banks has contributed to lower and more stable inflation, alongside a flatter Phillips curve (the relationship between unemployment and inflation), resulting in much more stable inflation expectations.[11] To some degree, the impact of QE has also been responsible.[12] I discuss in more detail the impact of inflation expectations and ultra-low bond yields in chapter 10.

A Downtrend in Global Growth Expectations

Although interest rates and inflation expectations have fallen, there has also been a significant fall in long-term growth rates since the financial crisis. This has been reflected both in long-term forecasts for economic activity and in growth of sales and company earnings per share. Exhibit 9.9 shows a 10-year rolling average (to smooth out the data) of sales growth in the stock markets of Europe, the US and the world aggregate. Lower inflation and a weaker recovery in economic activity have resulted in generally weaker sales for companies. The chart also shows that the 10-year annualised growth rate in revenues across the developed world has converged towards the levels that Japan has experienced since the collapse of its asset bubble in the late 1980s.

[11] See Cunliffe, J. (2017). *The Phillips curve: Lower, flatter or in hiding?* Bank of England [online]. Available at `https://www.bankofengland.co.uk/speech/2017/jon-cunliffe-speech-at-oxford-economics-society`

[12] Borio, C., Piti, D., and Juselius, M. (2013). Rethinking potential output: Embedding information about the financial cycle. *BIS Working Papers No 404* [online]. Available at `https://www.bis.org/publ/work404.html` argue that 'to the extent that monetary policy, which sets the price of leverage, can influence the financial cycle, it too may have a persistent impact on the economy's long-run path, and hence also on real interest rates. If the definition of equilibrium also precludes the occurrence of boom-bust cycles, as one would reasonably expect, then it may not be possible to define a natural rate independently of the monetary regime.'

Exhibit 9.9 Top-line growth has been falling along with declining nominal GDP (year-over-year sales growth (10-year rolling average), market except financials)

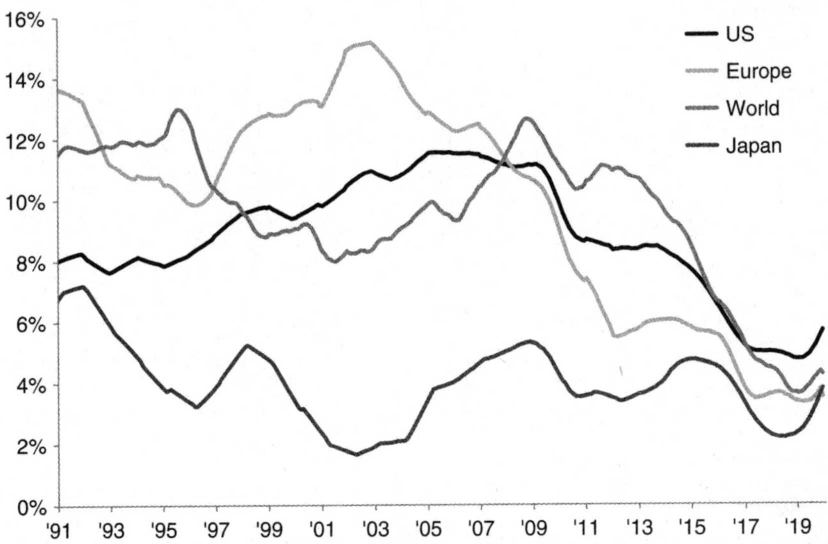

SOURCE: Goldman Sachs Global Investment Research.

The Fall in Unemployment and Rise in Employment

Despite the changes in the Phillips curve relationships and generally slower economic growth, the labour market has been much stronger than most people expected in the aftermath of the financial crisis. The worry was that a period of low growth would result in very high unemployment and, although that was true in some of the most severely crisis-hit economies, particularly in southern Europe, this has not been the rule. In the US, UK, Germany and Japan, unemployment fell to levels unseen for 40 or 50 years.

At the same time, the growth in employment has been impressive by the standards of previous cycles. As exhibit 9.10 shows, at the time of writing US employment has grown for more months without a contraction than ever before. There may be many explanations for this – weaker welfare states and lower taxes have made employment more attractive for many individuals, and there has

Exhibit 9.10 Cumulative months without a negative payrolls print in the US (total NFP)

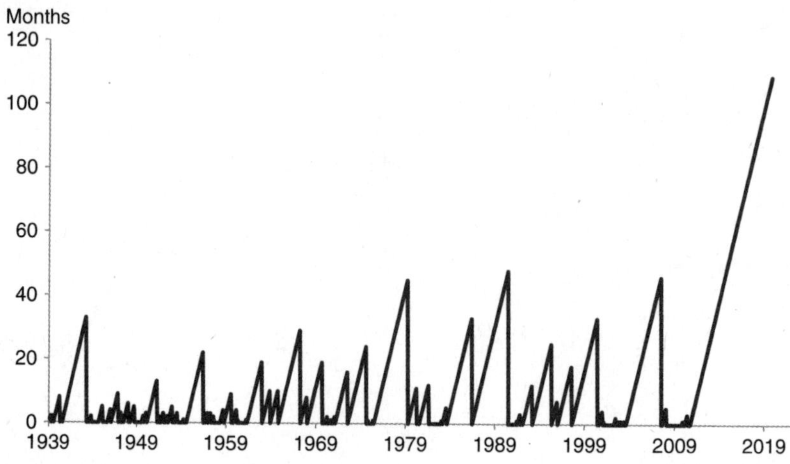

SOURCE: Goldman Sachs Global Investment Research.

also been a significant increase in female labour participation.[13] Less union power and collective bargaining may have also triggered a rise in new entrants to the labour market, and ageing populations are also often given as a reason. Perhaps what is most surprising is that this post-crisis rise in employment has coincided with dramatic changes in technology amid concerns about robots and technology taking away jobs. But in many ways recent technological innovations have helped the labour market to grow and to become more flexible. According to *The Economist*, in the past 10 years the cost of filling a vacancy has fallen by 80%.[14] A recent study showed that people who use the internet to find jobs reduced their time unemployed by up to 25%.[15]

One of the other unusual developments that has emerged since the financial crisis is that, despite rising employment, wages and inflation have remained very low.

[13] See more on female participation in Blau, F. D., and Kahn, L. M. (2013). Female labor supply: Why is the US falling behind? *NBER Working Paper No. 18702* [online]. Available at `https://www.nber.org/papers/w18702`

[14] Across the rich world, an extraordinary jobs boom is under way. (2019, May 23). *The Economist*.

[15] Kuhn, P., and Mansour, H. (2014). Is internet job search still ineffective? *Economic Journal*, 124(581), 1213–1233.

Exhibit 9.11 US labour share of nonfarm business output

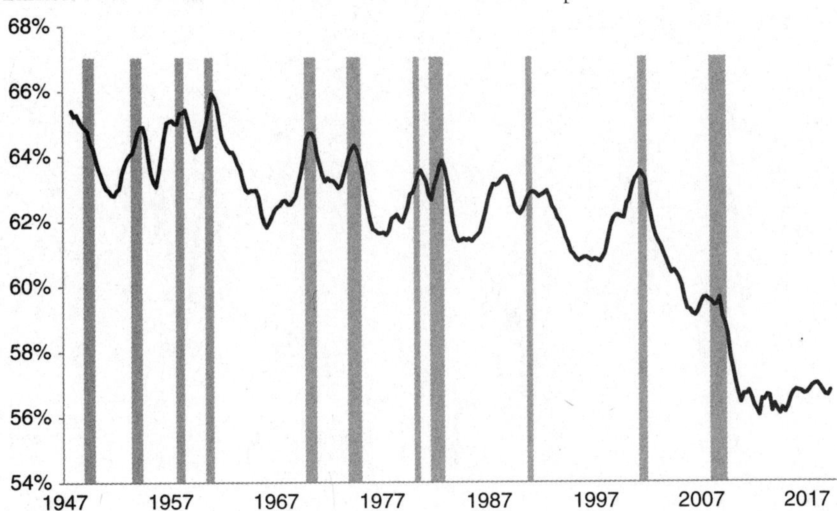

SOURCE: Goldman Sachs Global Investment Research.

Aligned to this, another big change since the financial crisis has been the ongoing fall in the labour share of GDP and the rise in the profit share of GDP (Exhibit 9.11).

The Rise in Profit Margins

The relentless rise in corporate profit margins since the financial crisis has certainly helped to offset what has been a weakening backdrop of sales growth. There are potentially many reasons why corporate margins have increased dramatically. The lack of pricing power in the labour market (reflecting the growing power of technology) and also the rapid rise in margins in the faster-growing technology companies are both partly responsible. In addition, the growing trend of globalisation has been important. German wage inflation has been low in recent years, despite low unemployment, partly because if workers push for higher wages there is a greater chance of these higher-paid jobs shifting to central Europe and elsewhere where the labour market is closely integrated into the German economy.

Exhibit 9.12 The US profit share of GDP has been falling but it has not been reflected in S&P net margins

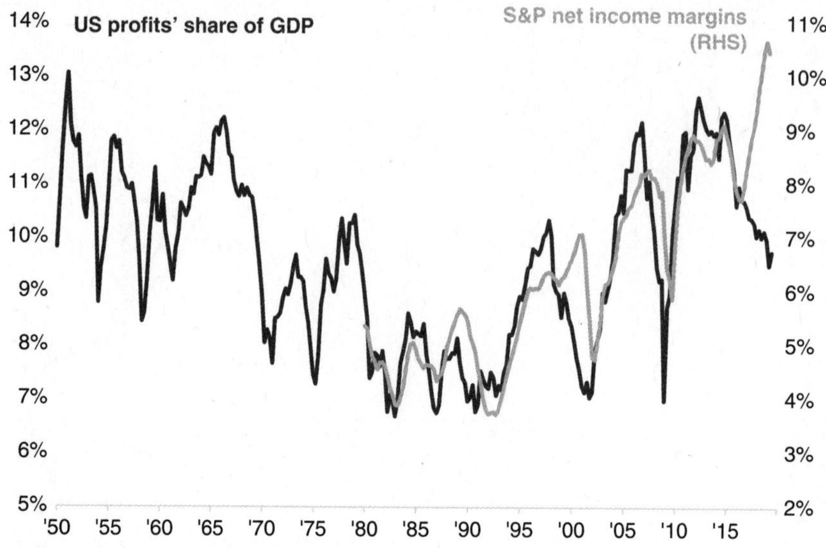

SOURCE: Goldman Sachs Global Investment Research.

That said, there are risks that these margins are not sustainable. In the US at least, there has increasingly been a growing gap between margins in the economy as a whole and those in the stock market specifically (Exhibit 9.12). This is partly explained by the impact of US tax cuts in 2017, which benefited large international companies (represented in the stock market) in particular. It is also partly because of the difference in sector weights: the stock market in the US has a much higher proportion of very large technology companies that have enjoyed a growing market share and higher margins than for typical companies in the broader economy. But there has now been a rise in wages that is starting to wear down profit margins, and this may start to affect the stock market as well. If, moving forward, valuations stop rising and margins peak (which is quite likely in a maturing economic cycle), then lower sales growth will imply lower earnings growth and, with it, lower returns.

Falling Volatility of Macro Variables

But although long-term growth expectations in the economy have fallen, and revenue growth in the corporate sector has slowed, the volatility of growth has also moderated (exhibit 9.13).

Much of this took place with the independence of central banks and the boom in globalisation that followed the collapse of the Soviet Union in the late 1990s. But there has been a renewed fall since the financial crisis. Although the 1990s is often referred to as the period of the 'Great Moderation' because of its stable growth and low inflation, it came to an end largely as a result of the technology bubble in equity markets at the end of the century. But, since then, macro volatility has fallen again. Typical drivers of past recessions, such as industrial shocks, oil shocks and inflationary overheating, have become less of a threat since the financial crisis. Together with this, the current cycle looks likely to be even longer in the absence of significant rises in interest rates, financial bubbles or macro imbalances.

Exhibit 9.13 Volatility of US GDP growth, inflation and unemployment rates has declined, especially since the 1980s (5-year rolling volatility)

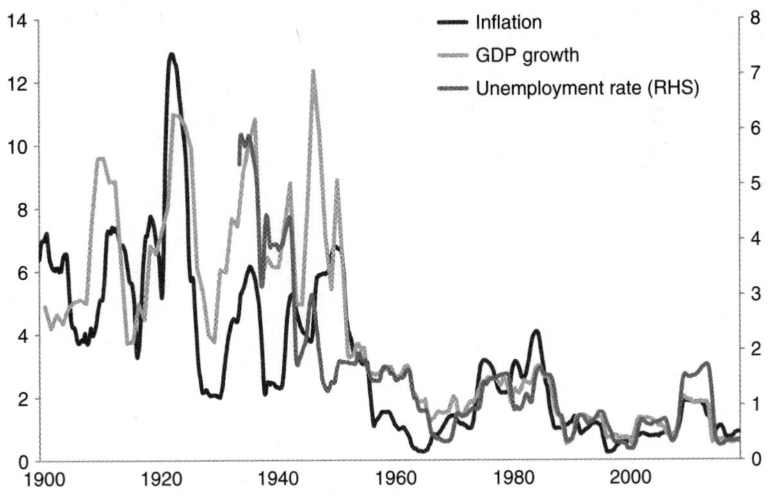

SOURCE: Goldman Sachs Global Investment Research.

It is also striking that, despite the slower pace of revenue growth in the corporate sector, the volatility of company earnings (or EBITDA)[16] has also fallen (Exhibit 9.14).

In historical cycles, profit growth has tended to be very cyclical, rising sharply in periods of economic growth (particularly in the early stages of recovery). Since the financial crisis, profit growth has been relatively low but much more stable (Exhibit 9.15).

The lower volatility of financial assets should make cycles more predictable, as long as this remains the case, but it is plausible that the anchoring of inflation and low rates will make cycles much longer in the future. Another positive factor here is that private sector imbalances are much smaller, helping the private sector to be more resilient to shocks and reducing the risks of private sector deleveraging.

Exhibit 9.14 Median S&P 500 company trailing 10-year EBITDA growth variability

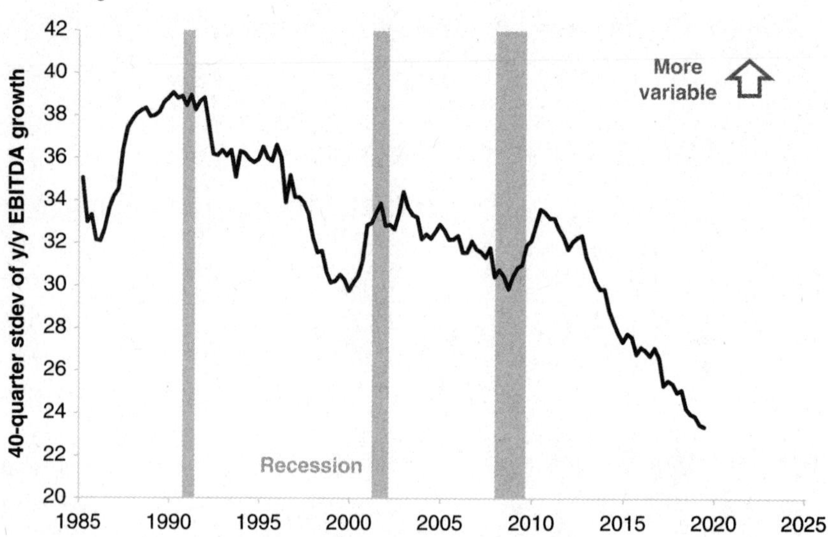

SOURCE: Goldman Sachs Global Investment Research.

[16] Earnings before interest, depreciation and tax.

Exhibit 9.15 EPS rarely falls outside of recessions (MSCI AC World annual realised earnings growth, grey shading indicates recessions [US, Europe, Japan, EM]).

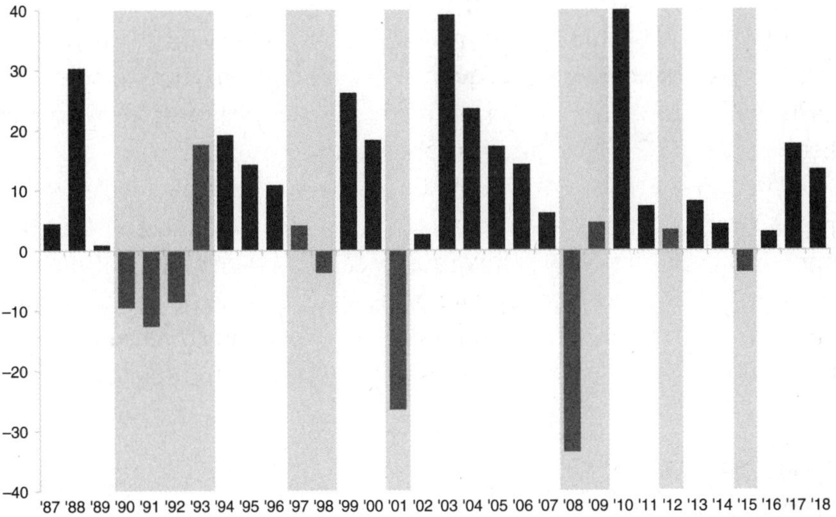

SOURCE: Goldman Sachs Global Investment Research.

The Rising Influence of Technology

Another important change that has influenced the evolution of the equity cycle since the financial crisis has been the impact of technology and its effect on returns. The dramatic growth of some technology companies (or companies that utilise new technologies to disrupt traditional industries, including retail, restaurants, taxis, hotels and banking) has meant that the distribution of profits has diminished even compared with past cycles. As exhibit 9.16 shows, the technology sector has seen a dramatic rise in profits since the crisis. Although the world (excluding technology) saw a strong improvement in earnings as the global economy recovered in 2016, it has only just returned to the levels that prevailed before the financial crisis. The technology sector, meanwhile, has seen a surge in earnings per share over the same period.

Exhibit 9.16 Tech earnings outstripped those of the global market (world LTM earnings [01/01/2009 = 100])

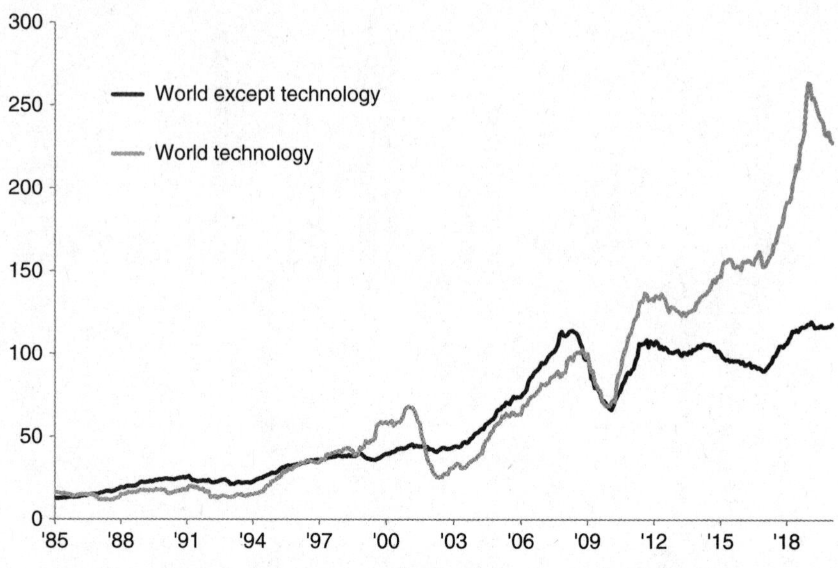

SOURCE: Goldman Sachs Global Investment Research.

This dramatic change, discussed in greater detail in chapter 11, has resulted in a much wider dispersion of returns between relative winners and losers in terms of stock market performance.

The Extraordinary Gap between Growth and Value

I discussed some of the traditional influences in investment styles across the cycle in chapter 5, but the environment post the financial crisis has resulted in a persistent and sustained pattern of relative returns within equity markets that are more pronounced than we have tended to see in the past. In particular, looking at global aggregates, the value segment of stock markets (generally low valuation companies) has significantly underperformed so-called growth companies (those with higher expected future growth) (Exhibit 9.17).

Exhibit 9.17 MSCI World value versus growth

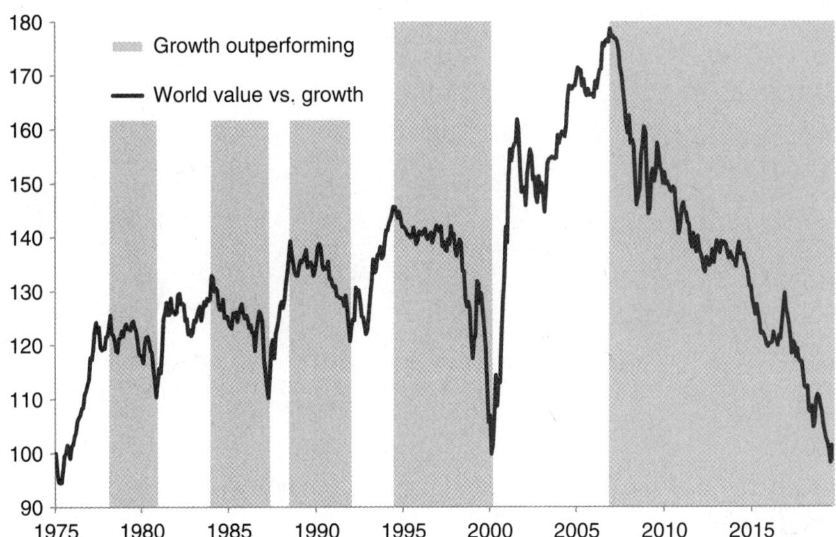

SOURCE: Goldman Sachs Global Investment Research.

There are several reasons for this related to the unique nature of this cycle in particular.

First, growth has been scarce and, therefore, generally highly valued. We have already seen that revenue growth has trended downwards since the financial crisis, but in general the proportion of companies with high growth in most equity markets has also fallen. Exhibit 9.18, for example, shows the share of high-growing versus low-growing companies globally over time. Growth has been defined here as companies expected to grow revenues above 8% annually over the next 3 years, and low growth is defined as those expected to grow at a rate below 4%.

Second, lower bond yields have enhanced the value of growth versus value as a result of the longer 'duration' of growth stocks and, therefore, their sensitivity to lower interest rates. This was a point discussed in more detail in chapter 5. The relationship between bond yields and the relative performance of growth versus value is shown in exhibit 9.19.

Exhibit 9.18 Very few companies have high projected sales growth (MSCI AC World)

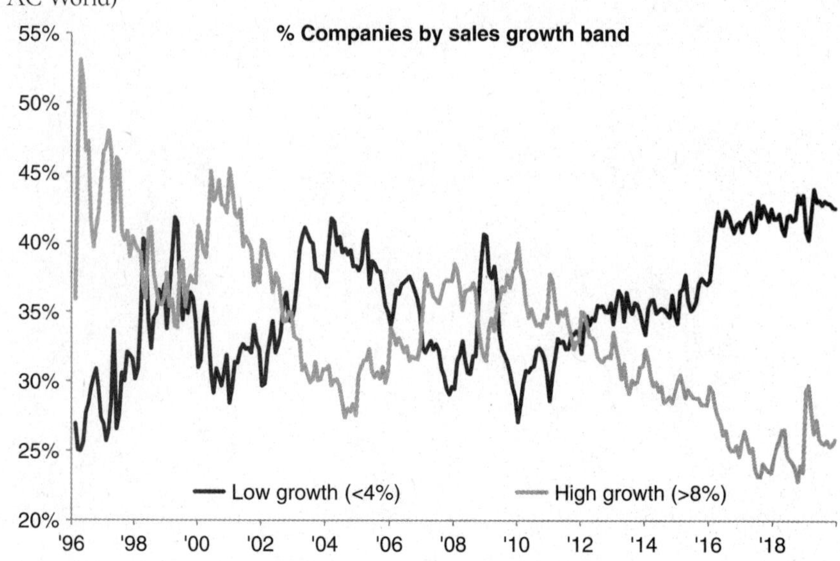

SOURCE: Goldman Sachs Global Investment Research.

Exhibit 9.19 Lower bond yields are likely to weigh on value stocks

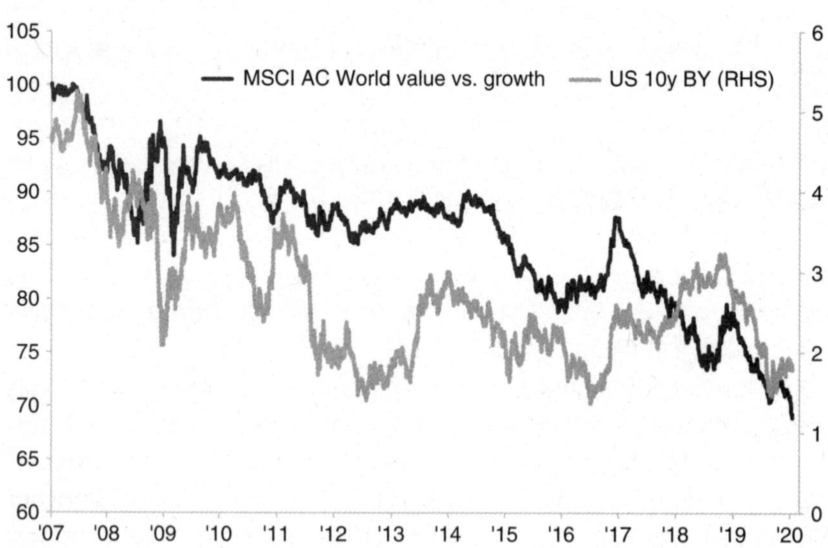

SOURCE: Goldman Sachs Global Investment Research.

Exhibit 9.20 Cyclicals versus defensives have also moved with the bond yield

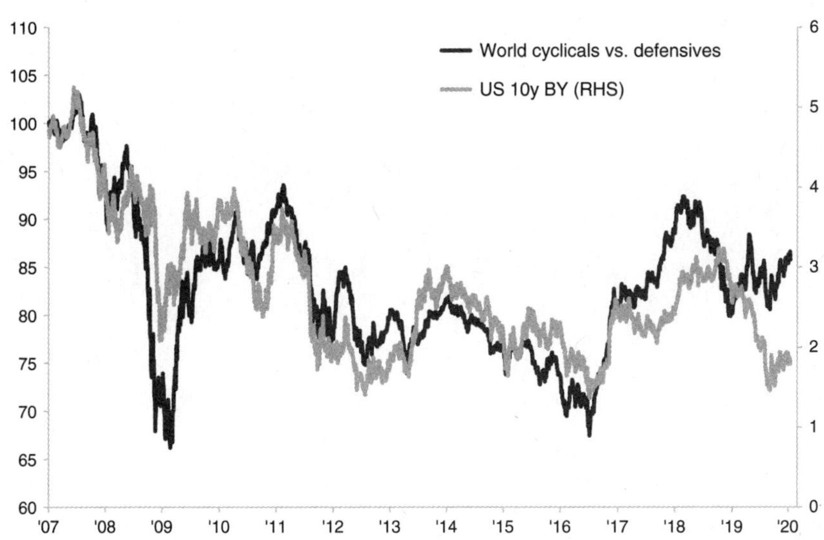

SOURCE: Goldman Sachs Global Investment Research.

Third, lower yields have boosted defensives relative to cyclicals. This is a similar theme to growth versus value. Many of the cyclical sectors are those with a low P/E, whereas most of the defensives are seen to offer better growth or, more important, predictable growth (Exhibit 9.20).

Fourth, lower bond yields have increased the value of companies with low volatility and strong balance sheets, as well as those that are often described as 'quality'. This style of investment has been favoured in what has been an environment of economic and political uncertainty, resulting in a premium for companies that have a high degree of stability or predictability in their future revenue streams (Exhibit 9.21).

Fifth, the shift towards favouring growth relative to value has also had a meaningful impact on the relative performance of different regions of the world. In particular, there has been a persistent trend of outperformance of the US equity market relative to other equity markets since the financial crisis, and this is particularly clear when we compare the performance of the US equity market

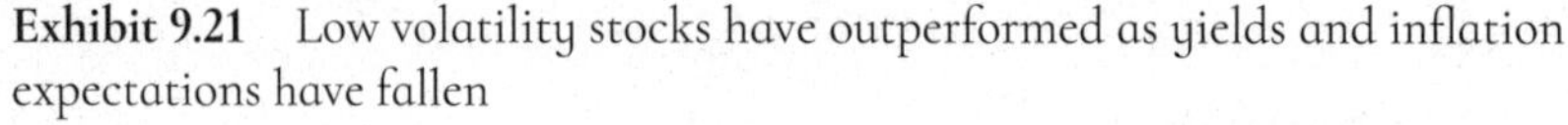
Exhibit 9.21 Low volatility stocks have outperformed as yields and inflation expectations have fallen

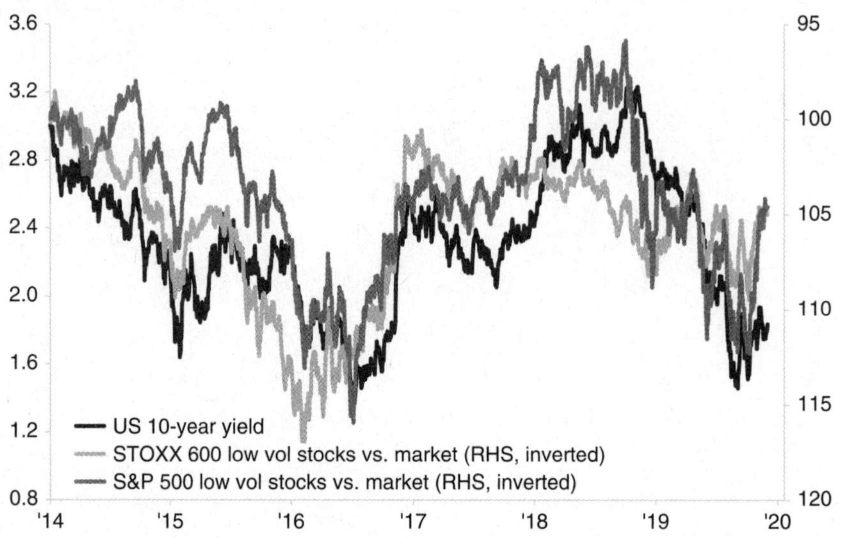

SOURCE: Goldman Sachs Global Investment Research.

with that of Europe. Exhibit 9.22 shows the relative performance of the S&P 500 and the Euro Stoxx index (the main benchmark of equities in the euro area) over time. Between 1990 and 2007 there was no clear trend; the relative performance between these markets was fairly cyclical: sometimes the US outperformed and sometimes Europe outperformed. The period since the financial crisis has seen a repeated trend of outperformance of the US equity market.

What is interesting about this is that this trend of relative performance correlates well with the relative performance of the value versus growth indices. The US is considered to be a growth market with a high concentration of companies that enjoy fast growth, whereas the European market has the opposite: a high proportion of low-growth, 'cheaper' companies in relatively mature industries, and a small proportion of the market made up of high-growing companies.

Exhibit 9.22 The relative performance of Europe over the US has mirrored the relative performance of value over growth

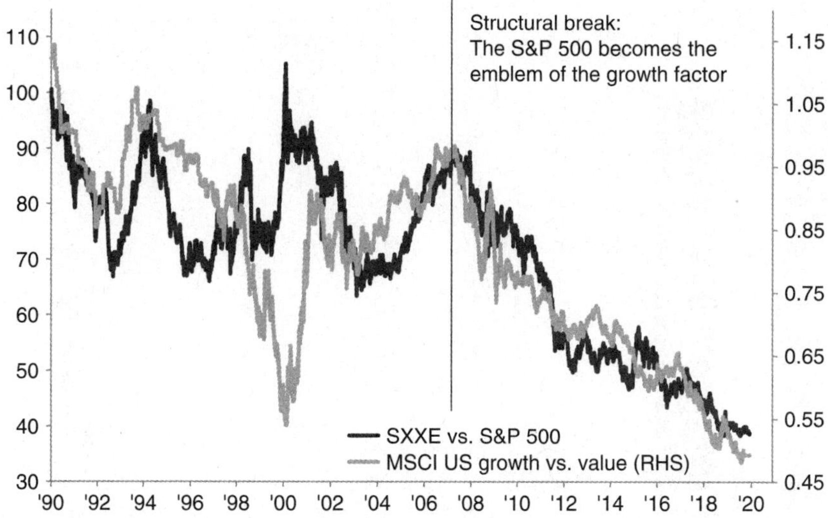

SOURCE: Goldman Sachs Global Investment Research.

The significant differences in regional equity performance that have occurred since the financial crisis also reflect very significant differences between the growth of earnings per share across the different major equity markets. For example, as illustrated in exhibit 9.23, since the last peak in the levels of EPS just before the financial crisis began, the level of US EPS has increased by nearly 90%. A good deal of this has come from the technology sector. In Japan, the equivalent increase has been 12%, and across Europe (shown here as the Stoxx 600 biggest companies), the aggregate rise in EPS has been a meagre 4%. Just as with the US, the weighting of industries within these stock markets matters. In the US, the heavy weight of technology companies has boosted earnings, whereas Europe has a heavy weight in banks (where earnings have largely fallen). When an adjustment is applied to the European numbers to see what EPS growth might have been if Europe had

Exhibit 9.23 The gap between US and Europe EPS roughly halves when adjusting for sector composition (EPS peaked in 2006 for the S&P 500 and TOPIX and 2007 for SXXP and MXAPJ)

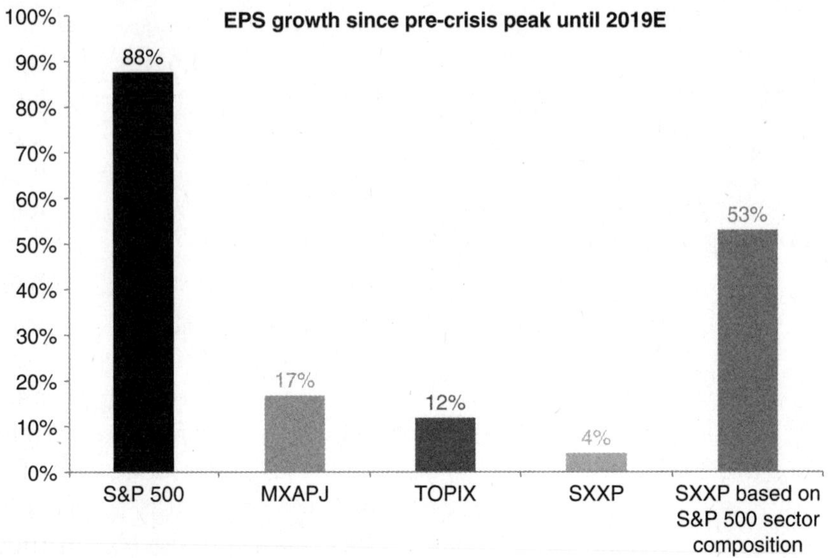

SOURCE: Goldman Sachs Global Investment Research.

the same sector weightings as the US (more tech and less banks, for example), the progression of earnings would have been much stronger, close to 40%.

Lessons from Japan

The shift lower in growth, inflation and interest rates that has become a dominant trend in many economies since the financial crisis does have a precedent. Japan, post its financial crisis in the late 1980s, suffered a similar collapse in its stock market and a boom in bond prices as interest rates embarked on a relentless decline. As a result, the Japanese experience post its financial bubble offers some clues as to the sustainability of some of the trends discussed here in relation to the post-financial-crisis era. To be sure, there are important differences between the financial cycles in Japan since 1990 and the rest of the world post 2008. For one thing, the scale of the bubble in land and property prices in Japan's case was much greater. The surge in land values is discussed in chapter 8. The symbiotic relationship among rising land values, company profits and stock prices meant that the benchmark Nikkei equity index reached a peak P/E valuation of about 60 times (trailing earnings), which is significantly higher than we saw in the run-up to the financial crisis in 2007.

But the issue of growth scarcity has certainly had an impact on the Japanese stock market, as we have seen in the environment post the financial crisis. Although not all growth stocks outperformed value in Japan's case (the broad growth versus value indices show clear underperformance of growth in Japan right up until 2007/2008), there appear to be some specific reasons for this. First, the lack of yield in both the bond and equity markets in Japan made high dividend yield stocks more attractive than they have been in most other markets since 2007 and, second, relatively few companies in Japan were seen as shareholder friendly, so paying a dividend was a good sign of this attribute. Third, the performance of the growth and value factors in Japan in the past 20 to 30 years has been similar to the performance of those factors globally, while value was outperforming in the rest of the world in the early/mid-1990s.

That said, growth scarcity did have a large impact on relative returns in Japan, although it manifested itself in the persistent outperformance of exporters (which enjoyed strong demand in relatively buoyant external markets) particularly relative to banks (Exhibit 9.24). This pattern has also been evident in European markets in the past decade, where weak domestic demand and reasonable growth in other markets have tended to benefit companies with external demand exposure while penalising companies with high domestic exposure on average. What is most notable in Japan is that this has been the case despite (at least initially) the appreciation in the yen.

Exhibit 9.24 Exporters in Japan performed especially well versus banks and this has been persistent (indexed to 100 in 1985)

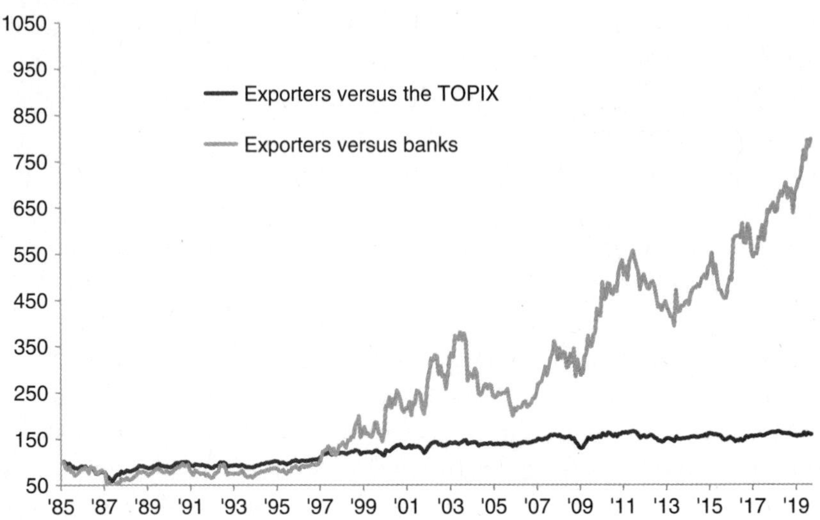

SOURCE: Goldman Sachs Global Investment Research.

Defensive companies that have relatively low sensitivity to the vagaries of economic growth rates have also outperformed in Japan since the 1990s, and the strongest of these were the 'growth defensives' – consumer staples and health care (exhibit 9.25); again, the same has been true in Europe over the past decade. That said, the regulated or higher-yielding defensives had a less clear pattern of outperformance in Japan, whereas in Europe regulation and lack of pricing power has generally meant underperformance for these stocks.

Another similarity between the recent post-crisis market cycle in Europe and that of Japan in the 1990s and beyond has been the underperformance of banks. Indeed, in Italy, where pressures have been most intense, banks have performed even more poorly than in Japan since its bubble burst.

In conclusion, since the financial crisis, several important structural changes have emerged relative to the experience of average cycles in the post-war period:

- There has been an unusual length of the economic cycle (the longest in the US for nearly 150 years).

Exhibit 9.25 'Growth defensives' outperform in Europe and Japan (time 0 = 4Q 1990 Japan, 3Q 2008 Europe)

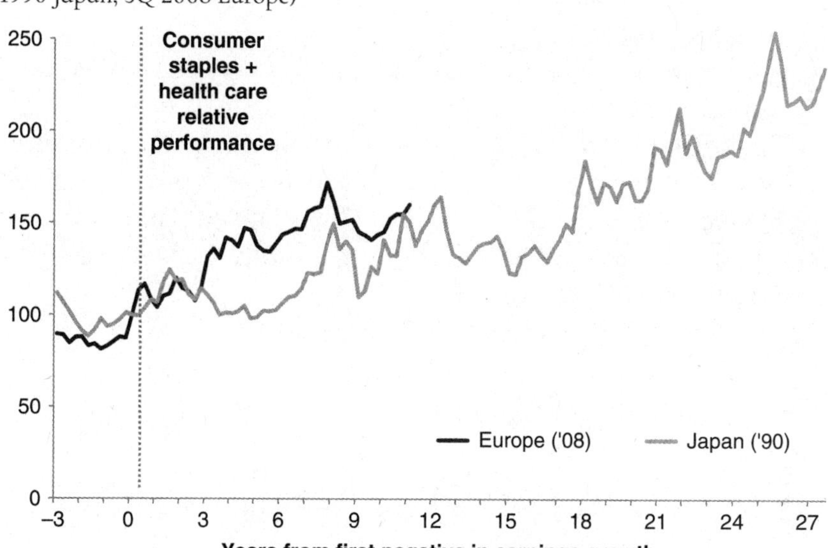

SOURCE: Goldman Sachs Global Investment Research.

- There has been a relatively weak economic cycle in terms of nominal and real GDP growth, resulting in an unusually aggressive period of monetary easing and the advent of QE.
- Despite the cuts in interest rates, long-term growth expectations have moderated and average revenue growth across the corporate sector in the Western economies has slowed.
- Notwithstanding the weaker than average economic and profits growth, financial markets have been unusually strong both in fixed income markets (as policy rates and inflation have moderated) and in equity and credit markets as lower interest rates have pushed up valuations.
- Term premia and inflation expectations have collapsed and bond yields have fallen to record levels, globally and in many individual economies.
- The impact of slow growth and record low interest rates has meant that income and growth have been relatively scarce. The fallout of this has been a secular shift in relative performance

towards low volatility, quality and growth assets within equities and assets that can generate any pickup in yield, such as high yield corporate credit.

- The financial crisis and subsequent recovery have also been overlaid with a huge secular or super-cycle shift in technology. This has resulted in a rapid concentration of revenues and profits in a relatively small number of very large companies, many of which are in the United States. This, coupled with a stronger domestic economy, has helped the US equity market to achieve superior relative returns.

Chapter 10
Below Zero: The Impact of Ultra-Low Bond Yields

Chapter 9 discusses some of the key structural differences that have emerged since the financial crisis compared with previous cycles and, within this, the significant falls in the levels of global interest rates and bond yields.

The collapse in long-term bond yields in both the US and the UK (where there are long-term historical data series) is extraordinary by historical standards, with bond yields in the UK at the lowest levels since 1700 and those in the US the lowest since the 1880s (exhibit 10.1).

The falls in bond yields have become so dramatic in some cases that roughly 25% of government debt globally has a negative yield. In other words, an investor who wishes to buy government debt is actually paying the government to take their money. Even a quarter of investment grade corporate bonds (that is, companies with a very strong balance sheet) have a negative yield. The idea of paying to lend money is an odd concept, but why has it happened and what does it mean for equity returns and the cycle?

There may be many reasons why bond yields have fallen towards, or in some cases below, zero. First, it has been a reflection of central bank policy. The global financial crisis triggered a global effort

Exhibit 10.1 UK bond yield since 1700 – currently close to all-time lows

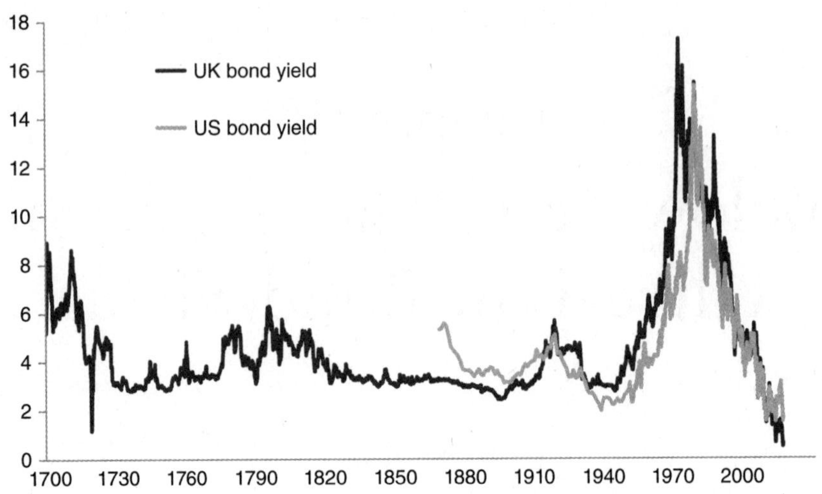

SOURCE: Goldman Sachs Global Investment Research.

to push interest rates down rapidly in the aftermath of the financial crisis in an attempt to soften the blow to economies and avoid the mistakes of much slower action following previous financial collapses (Japan in the late 1980s and the US in the 1930s, in particular). The 'anchoring' of interest rates by central banks was then further cemented in longer-term interest rates and bond yields through the programmes of QE.

Generally, QE is argued to affect yields by pushing down investor expectations about future interest rates through a 'signalling effect' because the buying of government debt by the central bank signals that the target level of interest rates will stay lower than might have otherwise been the case. Another argument is that the central bank purchases of government securities encourages investors to increase their demand for riskier assets in order to achieve an acceptable return, thereby pushing down the yields of other debt securities, such as corporate bonds, more risky bond markets or longer-duration bond markets.[1] Although estimates vary about the

[1] See How quantitative easing affects bond yields: Evidence from Switzerland. Christensen, J., and Krogstrup, S. (2019). Royal Economic Society [online]. Available at `https://www.res.org.uk/resources-page/how-quantitative-easing-affects-bond-yields-evidence-from-switzerland.html`

direct impact of QE on bond yields, most studies have concluded that the Federal Reserve's QE programmes (large-scale asset purchases) had economically and statistically significant effects on the level of Treasury yields and have come to similar conclusions in relation to asset purchases in other countries.[2]

Second, falls in inflation expectations, alongside weaker output since the financial crisis, have also justified lower bond yields. Of course, it is difficult to disaggregate the impact on inflation expectations from QE and growth. Although lower growth, for example, had clearly pushed down Japan's inflation expectations for some time, when the central bank introduced a negative interest rate policy in 2016, market expectations about future inflation over the medium term fell as well.[3]

Inflation expectations have declined materially since the start of the 21st century, in the wake of the technology collapse, and have since remained stable. Exhibit 10.2 shows this for the US.

Exhibit 10.2 Market-implied inflation expectations remain low

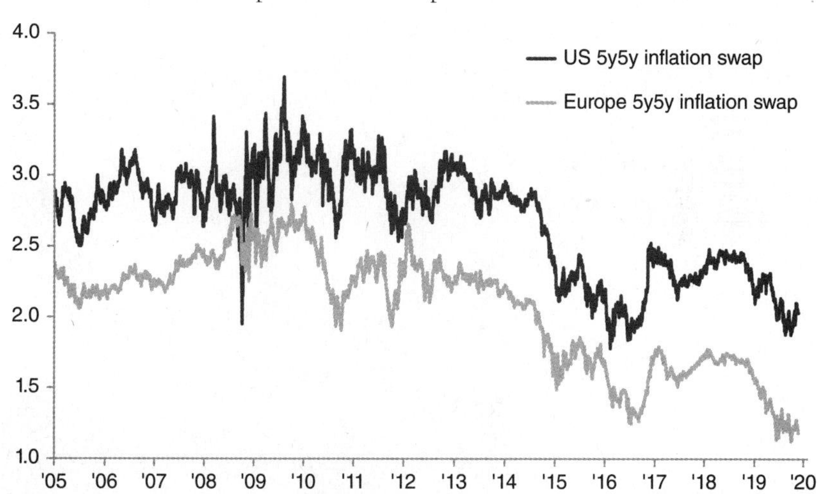

SOURCE: Goldman Sachs Global Investment Research.

[2] See Gilchrist, S., and Zakrajsek, E. (2013). The impact of the Federal Reserve's large-scale asset purchase programmes on corporate credit risk. *NBER Working Paper No. 19337* [online]. Available at `https://www.nber.org/papers/w19337`

[3] See Christensen, J. H. E., and Speigel, M. M. (2019). Negative interest rates and inflation expectations in Japan. *FEBSF Economic Letter*, 22.

Japan and Europe are the two regions where inflation expectations have fallen particularly sharply in recent years, and both have a large proportion of the world's negative-yielding bonds. Similar to Japan, the continuation of negative policy rates in Europe in recent years has had a spillover effect in bond markets elsewhere, including those of the US (exhibit 10.3).

In Europe's case, ECB QE and negative German Bund yields have also had a meaningful impact on sovereign spreads. During the epicentre of the European sovereign debt crisis in 2011, Greek bond yields spiked at over 50% at one point, and again briefly in 2015. Since then, as fears of a breakup of the euro area have faded and QE has strengthened, the spillover effect of negative German yields to other European bond markets has been meaningful, resulting in Greek 10-year yields converging with those of the US (exhibit 10.4).

Third, falling bond yields may also reflect a collapse of the so-called term premium. Theory tells us that the yield on a default-free

Exhibit 10.3 The euro area leads the recent surge in negative-yielding debt (share of global bonds with negative yields, by country)

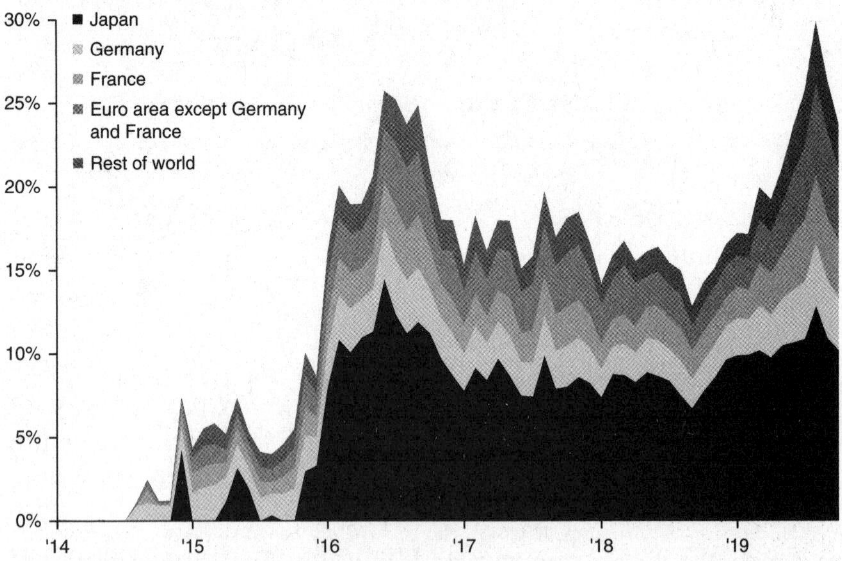

SOURCE: Goldman Sachs Global Investment Research.

Exhibit 10.4 Bond yield convergence (Greece and US 10-year bond yield)

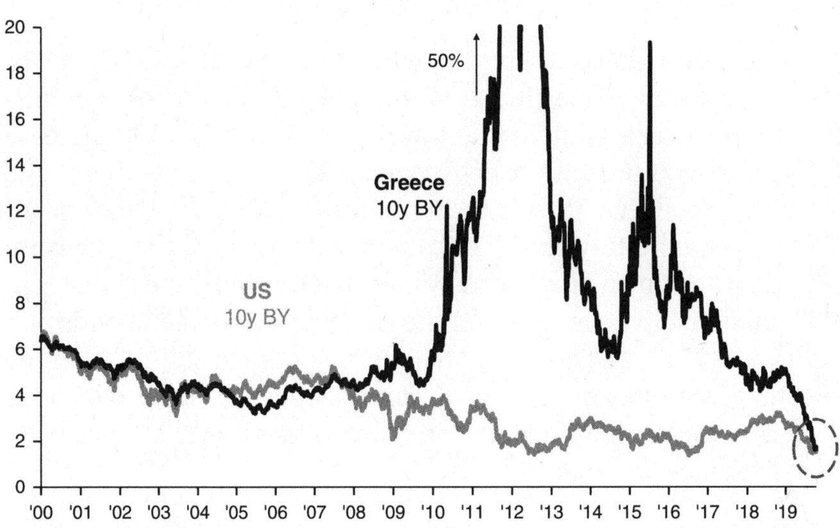

SOURCE: Goldman Sachs Global Investment Research.

government bond is the sum of expected policy rates over the life of the bond plus a term premium. Therefore, bond yield changes usually reflect either a revision in expectations of short-term rates or in the risks associated with duration.

This term premium exists because investors need to be compensated for bearing economic risks (just as with equities and the equity risk premium). For bond holders there are two particularly relevant risks. One is inflation: unexpected inflation erodes the real value of fixed nominal payments, reducing real returns on nominal bonds. This means that bond investors will require a higher term premium when they expect inflation to be high and/or they are more uncertain about its medium-term trajectory. The second is the risk of recession. This is, of course, the primary risk for equity investors. Because recessions imply lower expected wealth and consumption growth, they also result in higher risk aversion, thereby causing investors to demand higher compensation for holding risky assets, and a lower premium for fixed income assets that are safer.

Zero Rates and Equity Valuations

So what does a global environment of negative risk-free rates do for the cycle and for asset valuations and returns? Both theory and history support the argument that lower interest rates should increase the value of equities, all else being equal. The so-called yield gap – the difference between the S&P 500 earnings yield (the inverse of the P/E) and the 10-year US Treasury yield – is one way to measure this relationship and how it has changed. Over time, the changes in this relationship have reflected the correlation between bonds and equities, which, as argued in chapter 4, is not constant. Generally speaking, the prevailing relationship has been positive over very long periods of time over previous investment cycles but has been negative since the financial crisis.

Exhibit 10.5 S&P 500 earnings yield and US Treasury yields (as of 26 July 2019)

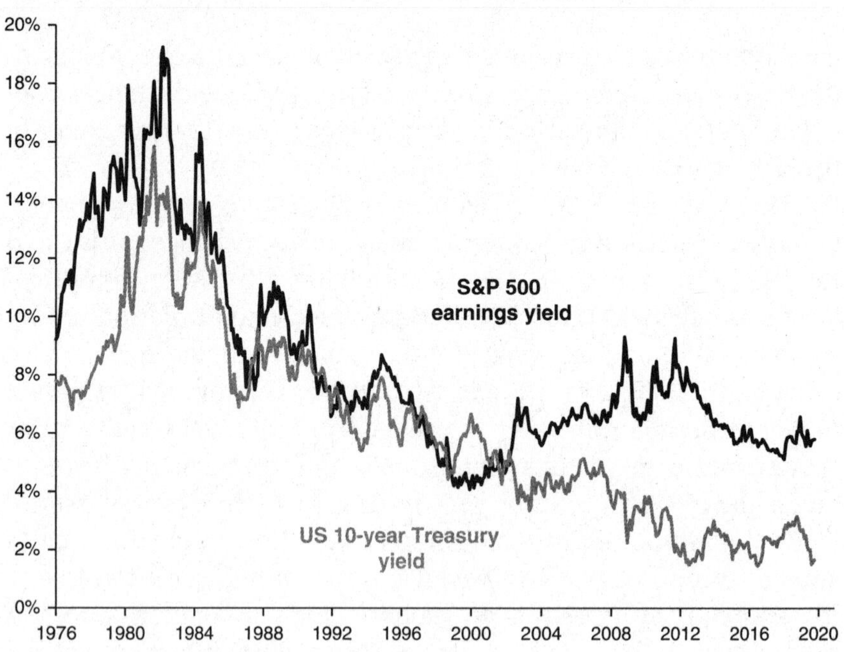

SOURCE: Goldman Sachs Global Investment Research.

Since the financial crisis, as bond yields have fallen relentlessly, the gap between the two has increased. In other words, the equity market P/E valuation is lower (its earnings yield is higher) than might have been expected given the falls in risk-free interest rates, or long-term bond yields, and this effect is even more striking in Europe where government bond yields have turned negative.

When the financial crisis started, the 10-year government bond yield on German bonds (the Bund yield) was about 4.5%, about the same as in the US at the time. But in the period since then, alongside falling inflation expectations and QE, the bond yield has turned negative. A calculation of the yield available to investors in the equity market (the dividend yield plus the yield from companies buying back stock) has seen a steady rise in recent years (exhibit 10.6). The gap between the two is at a record high.

In the US, the gap between the total cash yield in the equity market and the government bond yield is not as wide as it is in Europe, reflecting stronger expectations about the long-term

Exhibit 10.6 Equities have a substantial yield 'cushion' (German 10-year Treasury yield and cash yield [dividend yield and buyback yield])

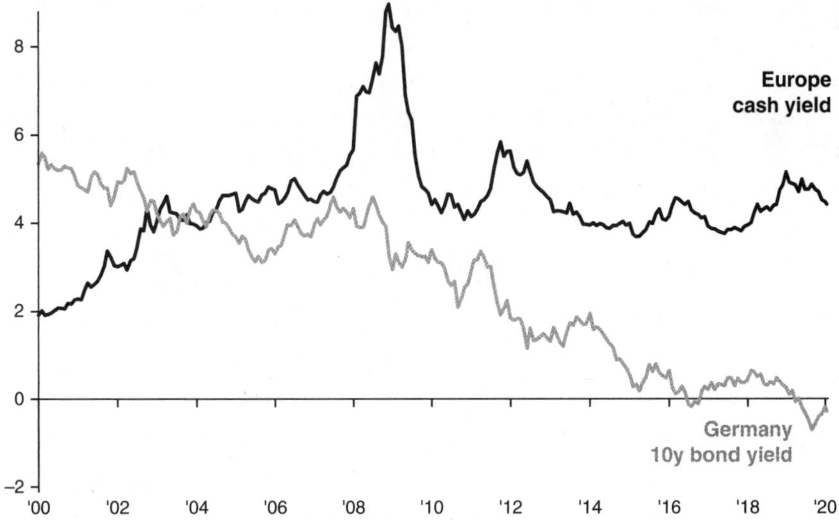

SOURCE: Goldman Sachs Global Investment Research.

Exhibit 10.7 Equities have remained attractively valued over recent years despite falls in bond yields (US 10-year Treasury yield and cash yield [dividend yield and buyback yield])

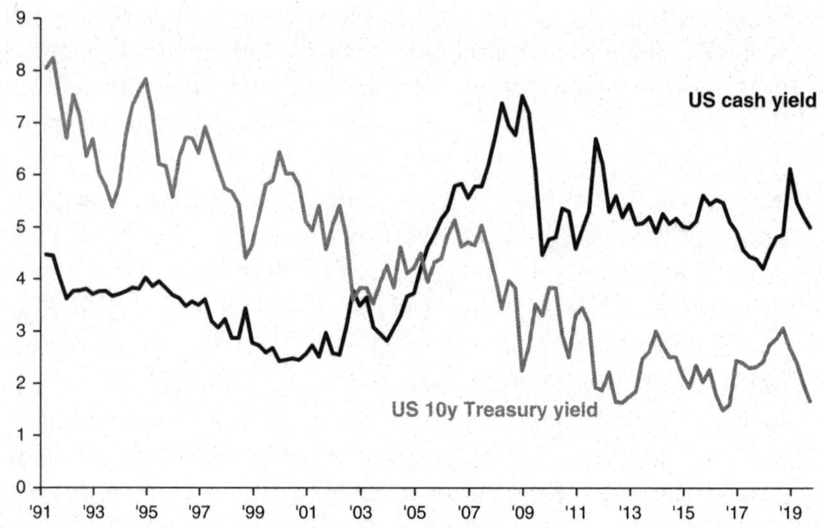

SOURCE: Goldman Sachs Global Investment Research.

growth prospects for company earnings in the US compared with Europe. But the relative relationship with bond yields has, nonetheless, changed a great deal. Back in the early 1990s, for example, an investor was being offered a cash yield in the equity market of about 4% at a time when 10-year government bonds were yielding 8%. Currently, the 10-year bond yield has fallen to below 1.5% but equity investors are being offered a cash yield in the equity market of over 5%. The difference between the two represents a significant decline in long-term growth expectations.

Zero Rates and Growth Expectations

The comparison between the yield on government bonds and equities can approximate for the equity risk premium, or the required return that investors have in equities relative to bonds. This can be affected by uncertainty and by changes in investors' long-term growth expectations, and the zero or negative bond yield environment tends to affect both.

These relationships can be understood in a standard valuation tool used by investors to assess the value today of a future stream of dividends. This approach, a one-stage simple dividend discount model (also referred to as the Gordon Growth model)[4] enables an investor to 'extract', or back out, this risk premium. The formula can be arranged as follows:

$$\text{Bond yield} + \text{ERP} = \text{Dividend yield} + \text{long} - \text{term growth}$$

If the bond yield is zero (or below), this means that the ERP is the same as (or higher than) the sum of long-term expected growth and the dividend yield (referred to as the cost of equity).

Let's take an example for Europe: if we know the dividend yield is, say, 4% (roughly what is available in the European stock markets currently) and long-term earnings growth is equivalent to long-term nominal GDP at, say, 2% (made up of a conservative assumption of 1% real GDP and 1% inflation), then this tells us that the ERP is at least 6% – or higher if the bond yield is negative or if we assume slightly higher long-term inflation (in line with the 2% ECB target).

This suggests that one of the implications of zero bond yields is that investors require a higher future return than would otherwise be the case in equities partly because zero rates increase uncertainty about the future path and partly because they are also associated with lower longer-term growth rates. This is a similar argument to the fall in the term premium for bond yields. Quite how much these factors affect the required future return or ERP is difficult to know. The problem is that in reality there is no definitive observable level for the required risk premium (extra return) that would incentivise investment in equities over a safer asset such as bonds at any point of time and, in any case, whatever that risk premium is, it will likely change over time.

---

[4] See, for example, http://pages.stern.nyu.edu/~adamodar/pdfiles/eqnotes/webcasts/ERP/ImpliedERP.ppt

It is, however, possible to calculate the ex post risk premium – that is, what investors have actually received historically for investing in equities compared with bonds. Assuming that investors were roughly pricing assets correctly in the past (naturally, this may not always have been the case), then this should provide a fairly reasonable estimate of the required ERP through history. Taking 10-year periods for equity performance over bonds, the ex post ERP has been about 3.5% in the post-war period, at least in the US since the 1950s.

Zero Rates: Backing Out Future Growth

If we assume that 3.5% represents a reasonable risk premium through the cycle historically, then it is possible to use this risk premium and combine it with bond yields and the equity market level to back out the implied growth (in dividends or earnings) expected in the future. The results are shown in exhibit 10.8 for Europe (where economic growth has slowed and the equity market is made up of a higher proportion of mature, slower-growing sectors). Exhibit 10.8 shows implied growth using both the 3.5% risk premium and some higher alternatives. Another way to interpret this is to say that, if 3.5% is the correct expected excess return in equities relative to bonds, then the equity market is fairly priced on the basis that investors expect zero earnings and dividend growth into perpetuity. At the other end of the spectrum, the equity risk premium would need to be 8% for the market to be expecting long-term nominal earnings growth of 4.7% (roughly 2.7% real earnings growth and 2% inflation).

Whatever level of ERP one uses, it does appear that implied (or expected) long-term growth has fallen continually in the past decade or so. So, although lower bond yields, and at the extreme case negative yields, might imply a lower discount rate for equities and, as a consequence, higher valuations, the slowdown in long-term growth works to offset this effect. If growth is expected to be lower, so would long-term cash flows or profit growth in the corporate sector.

Exhibit 10.8 Using a 3.5% ERP in a one-stage DDM suggests market is implying <0% per annum DPS growth (implied dividend growth from a one-stage DDM, using alternative ERPs)

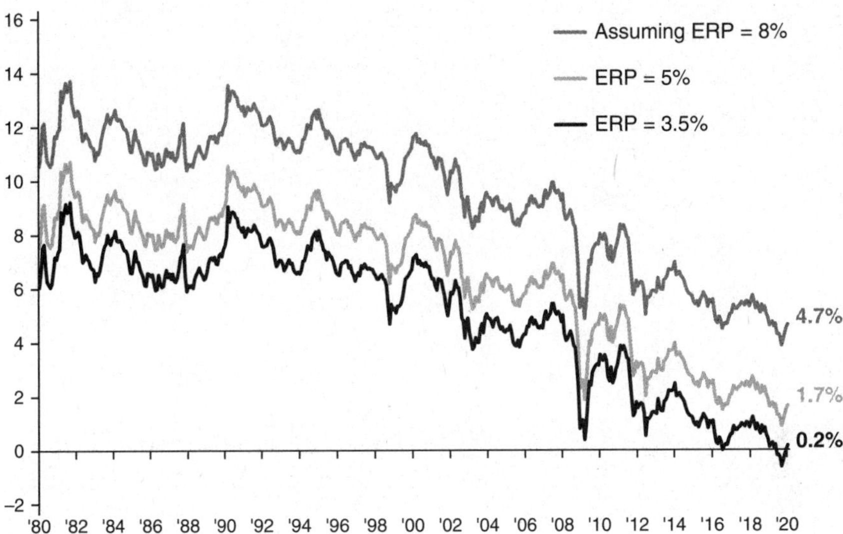

SOURCE: Goldman Sachs Global Investment Research.

Is the downgrading of growth expectations justified? This may not be as extreme as it sounds. After all, Japan has achieved roughly zero nominal GDP over recent decades (and investors worry that the negative bond yield environment in Europe currently suggests that we are likely to see something similar in the future in Europe and possibly elsewhere).

Looking at top-line growth, historical rates of growth have trended downwards in recent years (exhibit 10.9). The rest of the world, including Europe, easily outgrew Japan in the 1990s and 2000s, although the gap is narrowing.

Lower top-line growth is a function of lower inflation and weaker real economic growth over the past decade. Also, consensus expectations for medium-term GDP growth have fallen gradually, from 2.5% in the mid-1990s to closer to 1% for the euro area today.

A look at long-term (6–10 years) forward consensus forecasts from economists shows that, since the financial crisis, long-term real

Exhibit 10.9 Sales growth in Europe slowed and is now close to Japan's level (10-year rolling average sales growth, by region; local currency, world in USD)

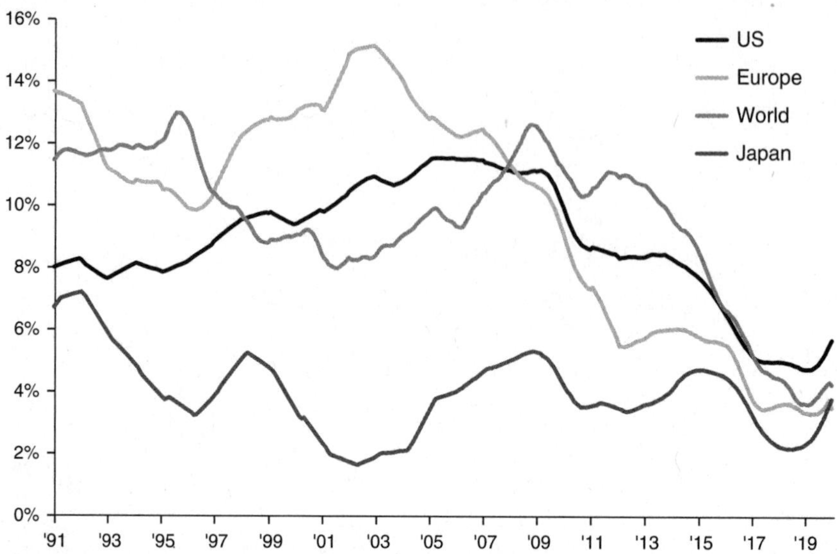

SOURCE: Goldman Sachs Global Investment Research.

GDP growth forecasts have trended downwards, despite the powerful easing of monetary policy and the introduction of QE, and in the case of the US, a large increase in fiscal spending (exhibit 10.10).

Within the broad context of lower growth expectations globally, it is in Europe and Japan where yields have fallen most and where there is the highest share of global negative-yielding bond yields (exhibit 10.11).

Although the theory might have suggested that such big moves downwards in the risk-free rate would have raised the present value of future cash flows and pushed valuations in equities higher, in fact the opposite has been true. P/E ratios in both of these equity markets are at the same level, and both are below that of the US equity market, which has higher bond yields. The explanation for this is that the negative bond yields in both Japan and Germany are associated with lower long-term growth expectations (exhibit 10.12).

Exhibit 10.10 Long-term real global GDP growth forecast is at a historical low (long-term [6y–10y] GDP growth from consensus economics)

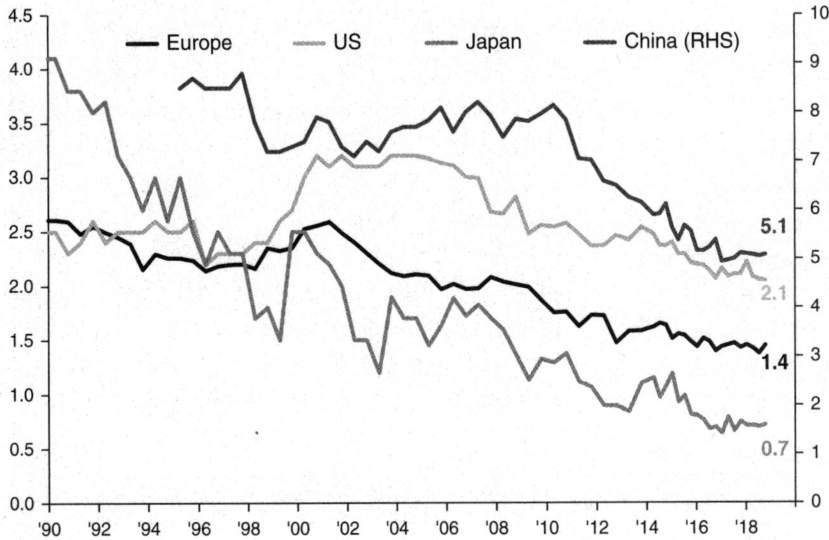

SOURCE: Goldman Sachs Global Investment Research.

Exhibit 10.11 German yields have converged to Japanese levels (and below) (% 10-year government bond yield)

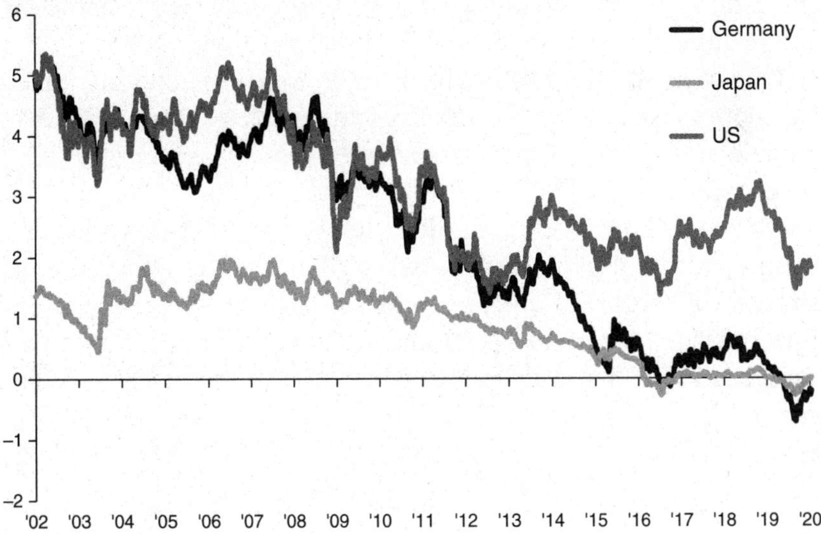

SOURCE: Goldman Sachs Global Investment Research.

Exhibit 10.12 Europe and Japan have similar P/Es (12m forward P/E)

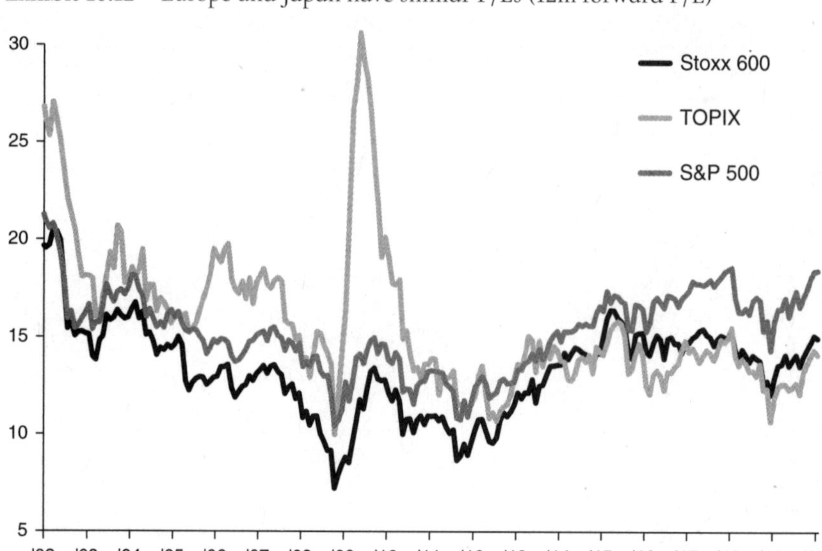

SOURCE: Goldman Sachs Global Investment Research.

The slowing rate of long-term growth in corporate earnings, a development that has been present in Japan for 20 years, is also emerging in Europe as its bond yields, like those of Japan, fall below zero (exhibit 10.13).

One other implication of this is the hit to banks' margins. Faced with both weak loan growth and negative interest rates, there is a strong headwind to performance. For example, in a study of 6,558 banks from 33 OECD countries between 2012 and 2016, research shows that the introduction of zero interest rate policy reduced bank lending.[5] Interestingly, a comparison of the relative performance of banks with their broader equity markets shows that Japanese banks have underperformed fairly consistently since the end of their financial crisis in 1990 and the start of low growth and negative rates.

[5] See Molyneux, P., Reghezza, A., Thornton, J., and Xie, R. (2019). Did negative interest rates improve bank lending? *Journal of Financial Services Research*, July 2019.

Exhibit 10.13 Half of Japan's market has been growing slowly for the last 20 years; in Europe, it is more recent (% of low-growth companies where sales are expected to grow <4% in FY3)

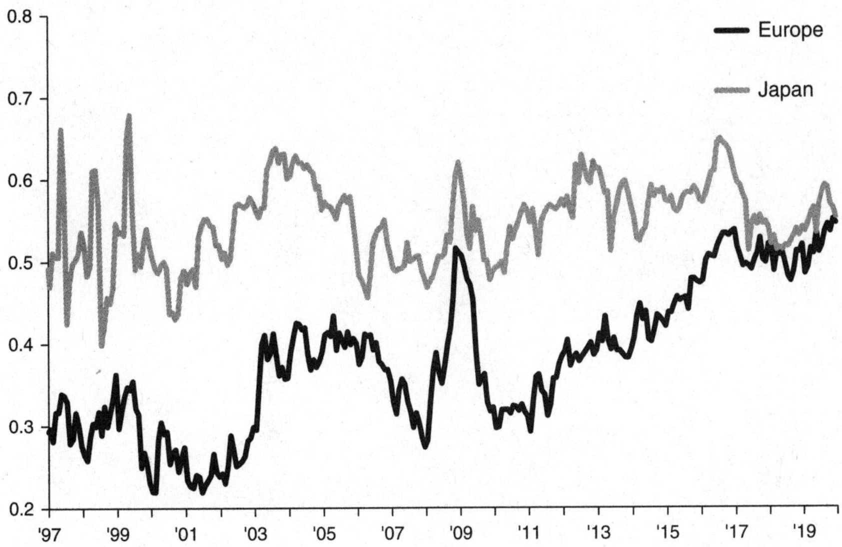

SOURCE: Goldman Sachs Global Investment Research.

A similar pattern has emerged in Europe since the start of the recent financial crisis in 2008 and the weak growth and negative interest rates that have followed.

Zero Rates and Demographics

In both cases, these lower bond yields may be partly a function of other structural factors related to demographics. As exhibit 10.14 shows, the long-term demographic picture in both Europe and Japan, where bond yields are below zero for both, are also where the demographic profile is ageing most rapidly. The life cycle investment hypothesis (Modigliani and Brumberg 1980) argues that people borrow more when they are young and save more when they are old; with a growing proportion of old or middle-aged people, there

Exhibit 10.14 Population declines in both Europe and Japan in the coming decades but faster in Japan

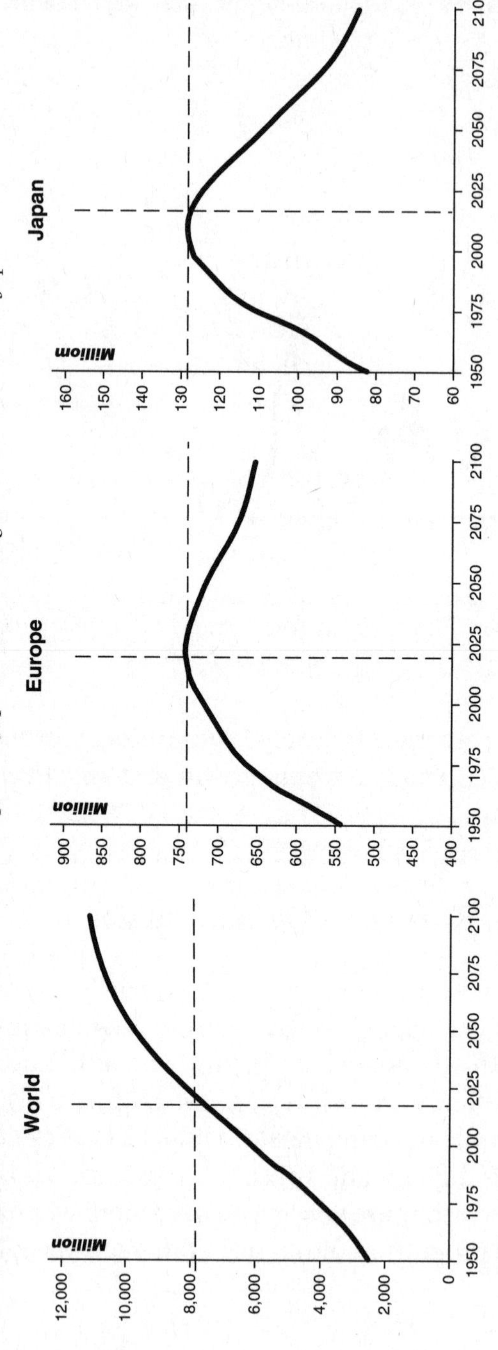

SOURCE: Goldman Sachs Global Investment Research.

should be more demand for income-generating safe assets (such as government bonds), which would push prices up and yields down. Others have argued that the ratio of middle-aged to young people (the so-called MY ratio) helps to explain the level of long-term interest rates.[6]

Zero Rates and the Demand for Risk Assets

One other interesting aspect of zero or negative interest rates is how it has affected the preference for risk assets among long-term investing institutions, such as pension funds and insurance companies.

For these institutions, one of the main impacts is that, as interest rates fall, the net present value of the future liabilities (the discounted value of future cash flows) of a pension plan or an insurance company would increase. For a typical defined-benefit pension plan, a 100-basis-point drop in long-term bond yields could mean, all else being equal, an immediate increase of liabilities in the order of 20%.[7]

A possible result of this is that it forces these institutions to increase their exposure to risk assets in order to meet their long-term return targets. As the OECD put it, 'the main concern for the outlook is the extent to which pension funds and insurance companies have been, or might become, involved in an excessive "search for yield" in an attempt to match the level of returns promised to

---

[6] See Gozluklu, A. (n.d.). *How do demographics affect interest rates?* The University of Warwick [online]. Available at https://warwick.ac.uk/newsandevents/knowledgecentre/business/finance/interestrates/
Others have argued that the overall effect of an ageing population has been to reduce the 'equilibrium' on the dependency ratio, with some estimates suggesting that demographics reduced the equilibrium rate on interest by at least one and a half percentage points between 1990 and 2014 (Carvalho, C., Ferro, A., and Nechio, F. (2016). Demographics and real interest rates: Inspecting the mechanism. *Working Paper Series 2016–5*. Federal Reserve Bank of San Francisco [online]. Available at http://www.frbsf.org/economic-research/publications/working-papers/wp2016-05.pdf).

[7] See Antolin, P., Schich, S., and Yermi, J. (2011). The economic impact of low interest rates on pension funds and insurance companies. *OECD Journal: Financial Market Trends*, 2011(1). See page 15 footnote 2.

beneficiaries or policyholders when financial markets were delivering higher returns, which might heighten insolvency risks'.[8]

There has been some evidence of this effect in the US where, on balance, institutions have taken on more risk as risk-free rates and funding rates have fallen.[9] Others have shown that reaching for yield is not confined to institutions but applies to investors as well.[10]

There are also widespread implications for pension funds. Companies that have large future pension liabilities have been heavily affected by the crisis and the subsequent falls in interest rates (which have increased the net present value of the deficits).[11] For insurance companies, the fall in rates can threaten guaranteed yields of life assurance contracts and make them less resilient in a downturn or locked into structurally lower returns if they increase their weighting in government bonds.[12]

In some regions, and in Europe in particular, the high risk weighting applied to equities for pension and insurance companies for regulatory purposes makes it much harder to increase weightings in risky assets. One possible impact of this is that an increased demand for bonds, through the need to hedge interest rate and liability risks, puts further downward pressure on bond yields. This could, in turn, actually worsen the funding problem for pension

---

[8] For a discussion on the asset/liability mix and the risks of 'searching for yield', see Can pension funds and life insurance companies keep their promises? (2015). *OECD Business and Finance Outlook 2015* [online]. Available at `https://www.oecd.org/finance/oecd-business-and-finance-outlook-2015-9789264234291-en.htm`

[9] Gagnon, J., Raskin, M., Remache, J., and Sack, B. (2011). The financial market effects of the Federal Reserve's large-scale asset purchases. *International Journal of Central Banking*, 7(1), 3–43. These authors also found that US state and municipal sponsors with weak balance sheets have increased their risk exposure as bond yields have fallen. They estimate that up to a third of funds' total risk was related to underfunding and low interest rates between 2002 and 2016. Also see Lu, L., Pritsker, M., Zlate, A., Anadu, K., and Bohn, J. (2019). Reach for yield by U.S. public pension funds. *FRB Boston Risk and Policy Analysis Unit Paper No. RPA 19-2* [online]. Available at `https://www.bostonfed.org/publications/risk-and-policy-analysis/2019/reach-for-yield-by-us-public-pension-funds.aspx`

[10] Lian, C., Ma, Y., and Wang, C. (2018). Low interest rates and risk taking: Evidence from individual investment decisions. *The Review of Financial Studies*, 32(6), 2107–2148.

[11] See Antolin, Schich, and Yermi, (2011). The economic impact of low interest rates on pension funds and insurance companies.

[12] See Belke, A. H. (2013). Impact of a low interest rate environment – Global liquidity spillovers and the search-for-yield. *Ruhr Economic Paper No. 429*.

Exhibit 10.15 Pension and insurance funds continue to focus on debt investments (and largely ignore equity) (EUR bn, quarterly flows into equity and long-term debt by Euro Area pension and insurance funds)

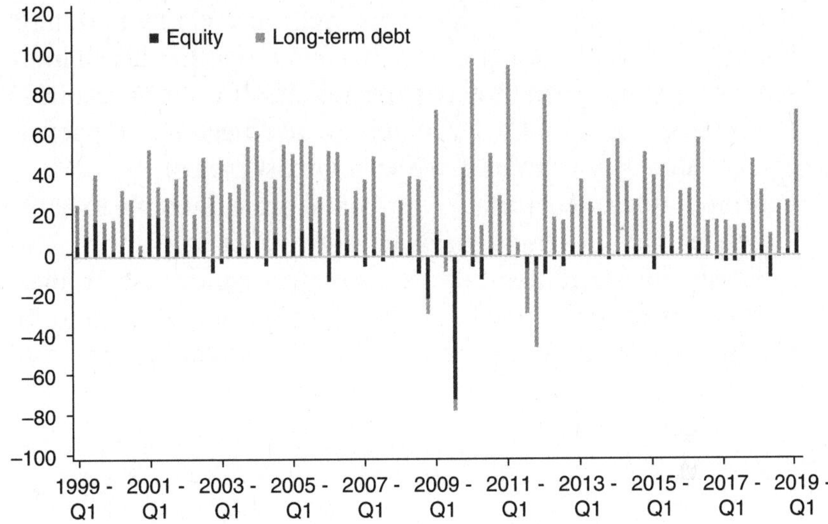

SOURCE: Goldman Sachs Global Investment Research.

funds and insurance companies, as well as putting further downward pressure on bond yields in general. Indeed, as exhibit 10.15 shows, European pensions and insurance companies in aggregate have continued to focus on debt investments such as government bonds in recent years even as bond yields fall below zero.

In conclusion, we can make several observations about zero or negative bond yields:

- The collapse in global bond yields since the financial crisis has been unprecedented and has resulted in about one-quarter of all government bonds having a negative yield. Part of this reflects falling inflation expectations because of lower growth and part reflects that impact on inflation expectations of QE and lower term premia.
- Bond yields at the zero bound do not necessarily benefit equities. In general, the experience from Japan and Europe in particular suggests that lower bond yields have pushed up the

required equity risk premium – the extra return that investors demand for taking risk and buying equities relative to risk-free government bonds.

- Zero or negative bond yields can affect the cycle by making it less volatile but at the same time this leaves equities much more sensitive to long-term growth expectations. If a shock results in a recession, we could see a much greater negative impact on equity valuations than we have seen in past cycles.
- Pension funds and insurance companies are vulnerable to liability mismatching as bond yields fall towards or below zero. This can result in some institutions taking too much risk to meet guaranteed returns, but it can also result in more demand for bonds as the yields fall, resulting in yet lower bond yields.

Chapter 11
The Impact of Technology on the Cycle

In chapter 9, I discussed the changes to the cycle since the Great Recession of 2008 and the financial crisis that followed. This economic cycle has been weaker but longer than usual. Meanwhile, the equity market cycle has been stronger.

The slowdown in nominal GDP relative to previous cycles, combined with lower inflation, has contributed to a more lacklustre progression of corporate earnings. But not all parts of the corporate sector have experienced slow profit growth. The exception has been in technology. The impact of technology on the equity market and its cycle has gained interest over the past decade given the increase in the size and influence of technology companies, particularly in the US. As discussed in chapter 9, technology has been the industry with the strongest profit growth since the financial crisis.

The rapid changes in technology in the digital revolution, sometimes referred to as the third Industrial Revolution, are profound. They have had a large impact on how the equity cycle has evolved since the financial crisis and have contributed to a widening gap between relative winners and losers beneath the surface of the equity market.

Exhibit 11.1 Capital-intensive sectors have underperformed since the financial crisis (World aggregate)

Note: Capital-intensive sectors: forestry and paper, industrial metals and mining, automobiles and parts, leisure goods, construction and materials, oil equipment and services, fixed line telecommunications, mobile telecommunications, electricity, gas, water and multi-utilities non-capital-intensive sectors: beverages, food producers, household goods and home construction, personal goods, tobacco, general retailers, health care equipment and services, pharmaceuticals and biotechnology, software and computer services, technology hardware and equipment

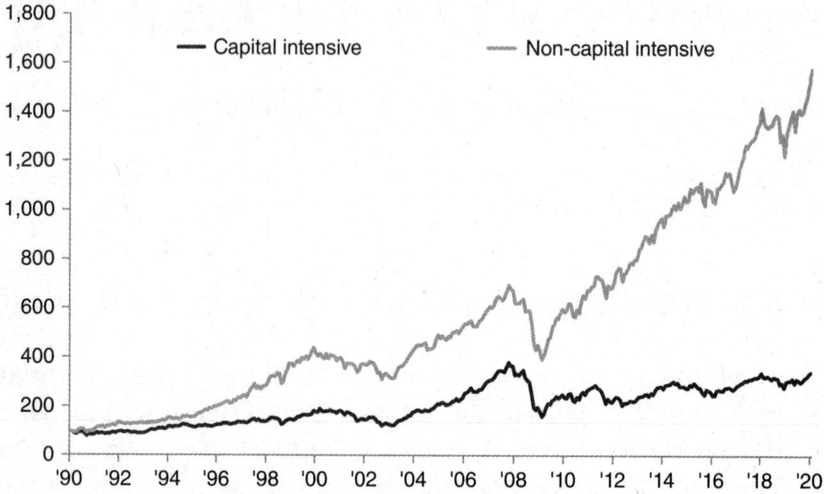

SOURCE: Goldman Sachs Global Investment Research.

The ability of technology companies to leverage their products while employing less capital in their businesses has also had a dramatic impact on the relative performance of sectors and companies in this cycle. For example, a simple split between capital-intensive and less-capital-intensive industries shows how 'lighter' capital sectors of the market have enjoyed stronger returns since the financial crisis (see exhibit 11.1).

The Ascent of Technology and Historical Parallels

Given the success and dominance of the tech sector, today's technology revolution seems unprecedented. According to many estimates (see SINTEF 2013), 90% of the world's data has been generated over the past two years.[1] Over half of the world's population now has access to the internet, and this has grown from virtually nothing in less than 30 years. The explosion of data and cloud storage is transforming not just the companies that facilitate the technology but also those that use it to disrupt traditional businesses.

That said, many of the characteristics of the current digital technology revolution share similarities with historical examples of other periods of rapid technological innovation, which help to contextualise the trends that we are seeing in the current cycle.

The Printing Press and the First Great Data Revolution

One of the earliest and most important waves of technology that revolutionised the way in which the world's economies operated, and how people worked and communicated, was triggered by the invention of the printing press in 1454. This technology fuelled an explosion of information (analogous to the data explosion of recent years), sowing the seeds for the Age of Enlightenment and many other life-changing technologies (or 'killer applications' as they are often referred to in a contemporary setting). Before the printing press, information was handwritten (manuscripts) and its production, and access to it, was tightly controlled by the Church. With the onset of the printing press, the volume of data that became available grew exponentially and, with it, the cost of information collapsed (sound familiar?). According to research by Buring and Van Zanden (2009),[2] the number of books published had increased from none to about 3 million per year by 1550 in Europe – more than the total number of manuscripts (pre-printed books) produced in the entire 14th century (see exhibit 11.2). By 1800, 600 million books had been published. As with all technological innovations, the price of books collapsed as the production costs fell. Massive social and societal changes followed.

---

[1] See Internet World Stats: www.internetworldstats.com.

[2] Buring, E., and van Zanden, J. L. (2009). Charting the "Rise of the West": Manuscripts and printed books in Europe; A long-term perspective from the sixth through eighteenth centuries. *The Journal of Economic History*, 69(2), 409–445.

Exhibit 11.2 The great data revolution – the explosion of book production (invention of printed books resulted in massive data growth and spawned other technologies)

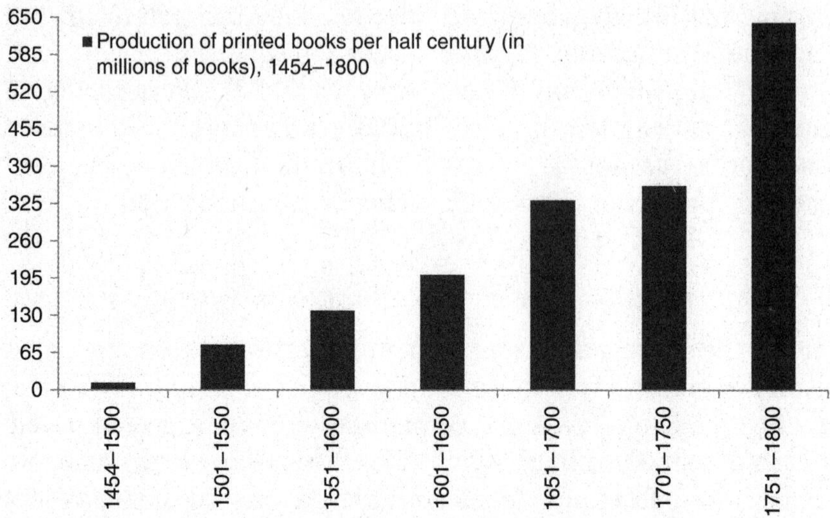

SOURCE: Max Roser (2017) - "Books". Published online at OurWorldInData.org.

The printing press, similar to the internet today, acted as a springboard to generate many other important technologies, which, in turn, spurred new businesses, while at the same time disrupting traditional industries and forcing many to change and evolve.

The Railway Revolution and Connected Infrastructure

Other parallels with the current wave of innovations can be found in the Industrial Revolution, when technology was again at the heart of growth. Many of these technologies developed from each other and even relied on each other, just as smartphones today rely on the internet, and vice versa. The network effect of innovation proved pivotal both following the invention of the printing press and during the railway revolution. During the Industrial Revolution, much of the opportunity was spurred by the extraordinary success and growth of railways. In 1830, England had 98 miles of railway track;

by 1840 this had grown to about 1,500 miles, and by 1849 about 6,000 miles of track linked all of its major cities.[3]

Cheap money and a new (revolutionary) technology attracted a surge in investment, which, in turn, had knock-on effects for the growth in the number of factories, urbanisation and the emergence of new retail markets, all of which was not an obvious consequence at the time. The laying of train tracks helped the growth of telegraph infrastructure in the 1840s. Within 10 years, sending telegrams (previously not possible) had become part of everyday life (a bit like the growth in the internet between the 1990s and 2000s). By the mid-1860s, London was connected to New York and 10 years later messages could be sent between London and Bombay within minutes. Telegram and telegraph companies became very powerful; AT&T was born (1885).

Other technologies have created massive demand and attracted a huge number of new entrants. As broadcast radio took off, demand for radios increased rapidly. Between 1923 and 1930, 60% of US families purchased radios, which resulted in an explosion of radio stations. In 1920, US broadcast radio was dominated by KDKA, but by 1922, 600 radio stations had opened across the United States.

We saw similar patterns in the technology boom of the 1990s as the belief that technology would boost data usage resulted in a surge in value across telecom and media companies, as well as new technology companies. As it turned out, the ultimate winners in the emerging technology spaces were often not those that people expected, or that even existed, in the first wave. Furthermore, many telecom and media companies have been disrupted by the very technological innovations that, 20 years ago, were expected to be so transformative. During the railway boom, the steam engine spawned the development of the railways, and the network effect and connectivity then enabled other technologies to develop. This pattern has also been evident over the past two decades. The development and rapid take-up of the internet has enabled the

---

[3] George Hudson and the 1840s railway mania. (2012). *Yale School of Management Case Studies* [online]. Available at https://som.yale.edu/our-approach/teaching-method/case-research-and-development/cases-directory/george-hudson-and-1840s

development, and rapid penetration, of the smartphone. This has itself spawned an industry of companies based on the apps used on these phones (think of the revolution in taxi and food delivery services, for example) and, in turn, the 'internet of everything' (the world of connected appliances).

Electricity and Oil Fuelled the 20th Century

Another example of extraordinary waves of innovation came with the rapid growth in electricity generation in the early 20th century. In the US in 1900, just 5% of mechanical power was generated by electricity as opposed to steam or water (having risen from just 1% in 1890). By the 1920s, electricity had reached half of all companies and close to half of households. As with other waves of technology that preceded it, prices collapsed. The real price of electricity fell by about 80% between 1900 and 1920,[4] enabling the growth of many other related products (the radio, for example).

Technology: Disruption and Adaption

One other consideration for technological innovation and the impact on industry is that investors often look at the disruptive impact of technology, assuming that it will displace existing industry, but often find that it is additive rather than disruptive. For example, when the railways dominated technology in the 19th century, there were concerns that horses would no longer be required. As it turned out, railways actually created an increased demand for horses because there remained a requirement to transport to the final destination or to the starting destination of a railway station.[5] This 'first mile problem' has interesting parallels with today as mobility and delivery solutions are required for demand as it migrates to the internet.

---

[4] Brookes, M., and Wahhaj, Z. (2000). Is the internet better than electricity? *Goldman Sachs Global Economics Paper No. 49.*

[5] For discussion, see, see Odlyzko, A. (2010). Collective hallucinations and inefficient markets: The British railway mania of the 1840s. SSRN [online]. Available at `https://ssrn.com/abstract=1537338`

For example, food may be bought increasingly through the internet but delivery to the home is often done by motorbikes, bicycles and cars; the same is true for online purchases of products. This, in turn, creates new companies that can use technology platforms to solve these logistical problems more efficiently. A similar trend has become evident in the new solutions in cities to cycle and scooter sharing. So it seems that solving problems that new technologies create also provides the basis for new opportunities to emerge.

In addition to new opportunities, often some forms of adaption by traditional industries are displaced by new technology. For example, when digital watches emerged in the 1970s it was widely expected that mechanical watches would disappear. These fears were misplaced as the traditional watchmakers rebranded themselves and benefitted from the trend for quality and nostalgia. The industry in Switzerland alone generated revenues of CHF 21.8 billion in 2018.[6] The same can be said for cinema. The advent of video technology in the 1980s and then DVDs in 1997 raised expectations that cinemas would shut down given the convenience of being able to watch movies at home. Again, as it turned out, cinema reinvented itself and has become a fast-growing sector in the entertainment industry, with global ticket sales reaching a record $41.7 billion in 2018.[7] Even vinyl records are making a comeback among the younger generation attracted by their retro appeal, with over 4 million chart-eligible albums sold in the UK alone in 2018.[8]

Technology and Growth in the Cycle

One aspect of the current technology boom that has dominated the equity cycle in the past 10 years or so is that economic growth and productivity growth have generally been low. Some have argued

[6] https://www.fhs.swiss/eng/statistics.html

[7] McNary, D. (2019, Jan. 2). 2018 worldwide box office hits record as Disney dominates. *Variety* [online]. Available at https://variety.com/2019/film/news/box-office-record-disney-dominates-1203098075/

[8] https://www.classicfm.com/discover-music/millennials-are-going-nuts-for-vinyl-revival/

that this is a paradox and that it illustrates the limited impact of such technologies and that stock prices must therefore be overvaluing their potential. But there is strong evidence from history that previous waves of technology have also resulted in slower growth in productivity and economic activity than is generally believed. For example, although James Watt marketed a relatively efficient engine in 1774, it took until 1812 for the first commercially successful steam locomotive to appear, and it wasn't until the 1830s that British output per capita clearly accelerated.

Several academic studies have shown that the improvements in productivity in Britain in the late 19th century were small.[9] Productivity growth was slow during the last decades of the 18th century, and it did not improve until 1830. However, this lends itself to the view that initial technological changes often take a long time to feed through to the whole economy.

A similar pattern can be observed in the electrical age in the 1880s. These innovations did not yield substantial productivity gains until the 1920s, when the possibilities of factory redesigns were realised.[10] Indeed, it is possible that a similar effect may be seen after the IT revolution (see David and Wright 2001). In this context, it makes sense that the digital revolution has not yet boosted productivity.[11]

New technologies often have huge potential for productivity growth but can be difficult to adopt efficiently until there is a reorganisation in the manufacturing process and, in many cases, there exists a global standard in the technology. At the same time, the requirement to build out the full network effects can slow the initial penetration and therefore the productivity boost. The use of the steam engine, and coal for smelting, was also subject to these network effects. Coal transport was eventually a major boost to growth

[9] See Antras, P., and Voth, H. (2003). Factor prices and productivity growth during the British Industrial Revolution. *Explorations in Economic History*, 40(1), 52–77; see also Harley, N. F. R., and Harley, C. K. (1992). Output growth and the British Industrial Revolution: A restatement of the Crafts-Harley view. *Economic History Review*, 45(4), 703–730.

[10] Crafts, N. (2004). Productivity growth in the Industrial Revolution: A new growth accounting perspective. *The Journal of Economic History*, 64(2), 521–535.

[11] Mühleisen, M. (2018). The long and short of the digital revolution. *Finance & Development* [online] 55(2). Available at https://www.imf.org/external/pubs/ft/fandd/2018/06/impact-of-digital-technology-on-economic-growth/muhleisen.htm

and productivity but could not be fully adopted until transport networks were in place. Equally, the large fixed costs of investment could be recouped only when enough new users had switched to the new power source. At the same time, the use of steam power required the building of factories and then the building of canals to facilitate the transportation of raw materials and finished products. In the same way, a transfer of transportation away from the internal combustion engine to electrification may be technically possible, but will require an integrated power supply system and refuelling points before it can be fully adopted.

Concerns about the lack of productivity growth and, therefore, the misvaluation of companies associated with technology, were widespread in the 1980s. In 1987, Nobel Laureate Robert Solow argued that 'you can see the computer age everywhere except in the productivity statistics'.[12] These concerns faded when many economies saw a dramatic improvement in productivity in the 1990s. But the weakness in productivity growth in many economies since the Great Recession and the financial crisis has once more stimulated this debate.

Although some argue that the amount of time people work is being underestimated, suggesting that actual productivity could be even weaker, others point to a mismeasurement problem. For example, Goldman Sachs economists[13] analysed the market prices of unused iPhones sold on eBay and found that the 20%–40% price declines in the months near new model rollouts imply significant quality improvements. The inflation gap between secondary-market prices and the telephone hardware CPI implies an annual quality improvement of about 8%. Applying these quality adjustments to the consumption categories for which they are relevant, they estimated a potential understatement of annual consumption growth of between +0.05 percentage points (pp) and +0.15pp over the last decade. Taking these results together, they estimated the combined

---

[12] Roach, S. S. (2015). Why is technology not boosting productivity? *World Economic Forum* [online]. Available at `https://www.weforum.org/agenda/2015/06/why-is-technology-not-boosting-productivity`

[13] Hatzius, J., Phillips, A., Mericle, D., Hill, S., Struyven, D., Choi, D., Taylor, B., and Walker, R. (2019). *Productivity paradox v2.0: The price of free goods*. New York, NY: Goldman Sachs Global Investment Research.

mismeasurement of US GDP growth is currently between ⅔ pp and ¾ pp per year, up from about ¼ pp two decades ago. Although all of these numbers are quite uncertain, their analysis and the recent developments in the literature suggest that the current pace of productivity growth is meaningfully higher than it appears.

This is an important point because it suggests that the weak economic growth encountered post the financial crisis might, at least in small part, be explained by the mismeasurement of the impact of technology on growth and productivity. This may also explain why the growth in technology profits has been so much stronger than the growth of measured GDP over recent years. At any rate, the measurement problem may go some way to explain why the economic and investment cycle has been rather different in the post-financial-crisis period (see chapter 9).

So, although the speed of innovation and the spinoffs that these new technologies create has never seemed faster, history shows that we have experienced similar patterns in the past. The dominant companies that drove the previous waves of technology remained dominant for a very long time. But the networking effect of these companies resulted in the birth of further innovations and new companies. There appear to be three relevant observations in terms of technology opportunities:

- **Companies that invent/innovate (the printing press, radio, TV)**

  Although innovators do tend to be winners, not all innovators or first movers in technology succeed. History is littered with examples of entrants into a new industry but very few succeed. Thirty US manufacturers produced 2,500 motor vehicles in 1899, and 485 companies entered the business in the next decade.[14] Now the market is dominated by three conglomerates. Equally, between 1939 and today, more than 220 manufacturers of television sets have made TVs in and for the US market. Of those, an estimated 23 still make sets today.[15]

[14] Automobile history, History.com, 21 August 2018.
[15] http://www.tvhistory.tv/1960-2000-TVManufacturers.htm

- **Companies that create the infrastructure to support new inventions (railways/oil/power generation/internet search engines)**
  As described, the network companies can end up being highly dominant, but it is difficult to know with certainty at the outset which is likely to survive. For example, AOL was one of the first internet providers but eventually lost out to Google. Myspace was one of the first companies to popularise social media and online profiles and was bought by News Corp, but it ended up losing out to Facebook.
- **Companies that utilise new innovations to disrupt/displace incumbents in existing industries (think of technology platforms/marketplaces)**
  Often in recent years this has reflected the impact of platforms or digital marketplaces that have become successful because they benefit from so-called network effects. As *The Economist* wrote, 'Size begets size: the more sellers Amazon, say, can attract, the more buyers will shop there, which attracts more sellers, and so on'.[16]

But these simple observations do oversimplify to some degree. Ultimately, the winners generally may be a function of a mix of timing (when a product gains general acceptance with the market), good management and financing.

How Long Can Stocks and Sectors Dominate?

Despite the stronger fundamentals of the technology sector today relative to 20 years earlier, the large weight of this sector, particularly in some markets, raises the question of sustainability. What can history tell us about the longevity of sector dominance? How big can a sector or stock get?

Taking the history of the sector composition of the S&P 500 as a benchmark, sector dominance is clearly not a new phenomenon.

[16] How to tame the tech titans. (2018). *The Economist* 18th June 2018, Leaders Section.

Exhibit 11.3 The biggest sector accounts for a smaller share as stock markets become more diversified (share of the biggest sector in the US)

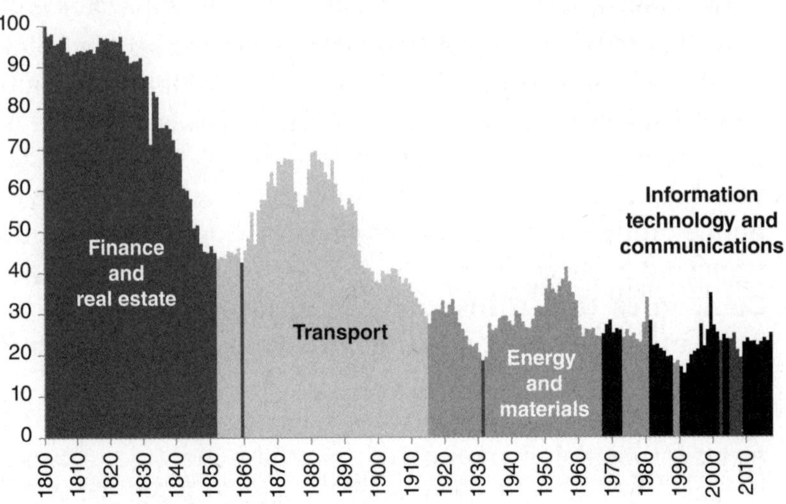

SOURCE: Goldman Sachs Global Investment Research.

Over time, different waves of technology resulted in different phases of sector dominance; as stock markets have become more diversified, the biggest sector has tended to account for a smaller share of the aggregate market.

Industry leadership in the US equity market can be split into three main periods, each reflecting the main driver of the economy at the time.

- **1800–1850s: Financials.** Over this period, banks were the biggest sector. Initially, banks accounted for almost 100% of the equity market, until the stock market developed and broadened out. By the 1850s, the sector's weight had more than halved.
- **1850s–1910s: Transport.** As banks started to finance the rapidly expanding railroad system in the US (and elsewhere for that matter), transport stocks took over as the largest sector in the index. In their boom years, they reached close to 70% of the index in the US before fading to about one-third of the S&P 500's market capitalisation by the end of the First World War.

- **1920s–1970s: Energy.** With the huge growth of industry, powered by oil rather than steam and coal, energy stocks took over as the biggest sector. Energy remained the main sector group until the 1990s, although interspersed with brief periods of leadership from the emerging technology sector (in the first wave, this was led by mainframes and subsequently by software).

How High Do Valuations Go?

Other periods in history have seen growth companies reach higher valuations than we are seeing today. Two previous periods when a group of stocks dominated equity market returns and valuations were the 1960s to early 1970s, the so-called Nifty Fifty era, and the late 1990s, which witnessed the rise of technology. The Nifty Fifty period saw the dominance of a group of 50 companies that, unlike later in the 1990s, were not focused on a particular sector but rather on a concept. There was significant optimism that US economic dominance would allow a new breed of US corporations to become global market leaders and multinationals.

Many of the companies that were favoured did enjoy very high returns (rather different from the tech bubble of the late 1990s, when the market was dominated by new companies with no returns) and a belief that these returns could be maintained into the long-term future. For that reason, they were often referred to as 'one-decision' stocks. Investors commonly were happy to buy and hold them irrespective of the price. There was a popular shift away from value investing towards growth investing. As a result, valuations increased hugely. By 1972, when the S&P 500 had a P/E of 19 times, the average across the Nifty Fifty was over twice this level. Polaroid traded at a P/E of over 90 times, and Walt Disney and McDonald's at over 80 times forward expected earnings. Despite these lofty valuations, Professor Jeremy Siegel (1998) argued that most of the stocks did actually grow into their valuations and achieved very strong returns.

A similar narrative later drove the focus on the 'new economy' of the late 1990s. Then, as in the 1960s, value (or 'old economy')

Exhibit 11.4 Largest companies in tech today, tech 1990s and Nifty Fifty (FAAMG data as of 31 December 2019, tech bubble data as of 24/03/2000, Nifty Fifty data as of 2 January 1973, except 1972 actual for PE)

	Size		Valuation
	Market weight	Market cap ($ Bn)	P/E (FY2)
FAAMG			
Apple	4.6%	1305	18.7
Microsoft	4.5%	1203	25.5
Alphabet	3.0%	993	25.0
Amazon	2.9%	916	65.9
Facebook	1.8%	585	22.1
FAAMG Aggregate	**16.8%**	**5002**	**25.1**
Tech bubble			
Microsoft	4.5%	581	55.1
Cisco Systems	4.2%	543	116.8
Intel	3.6%	465	39.3
Oracle	1.9%	245	103.6
Lucent	1.6%	206	35.9
Tech bubble aggregate	**15.8%**	**2040**	**55.1**
Nifty 50			
IBM	8.3%	48	35.5
Eastman Kodak	4.2%	24	43.5
Sears Roebuck	3.2%	18	29.2
General Electric	2.3%	13	23.4
Xerox	2.1%	12	45.8
Nifty Fifty aggregated	**20.0%**	**116**	**35.5**

SOURCE: Goldman Sachs Global Investment Research.

stocks became unloved. The current rise in technology companies that followed the financial crisis is rather different from the frenzy that drove the bubble in the late 1990s. In the years before the crisis, banks dominated the sector weights in many equity markets (benefitting from a cocktail of strong growth, high leverage and product innovation). With the demise of banks' leadership in markets, technology has quickly become the major leader of market returns and a dominant sector once again. Since 2008, technology has increased its share in the global stock market from 7% to 12%; at the same time, it has nearly doubled its share of the US market, from 13% to 21% in the S&P. In the late 1990s, technology's share of global market capitalisation rose from just 10% of the S&P in 1996 to a peak of 33% in 2000.

Most important, however, the valuation of the companies in the earlier periods was much higher than for those of most technology companies today. As exhibit 11.4 shows, the largest tech stocks during the tech bubble traded at an average P/E of over 50 times (although many stocks were far more expensive than that). **The largest Nifty Fifty stocks traded at an average of 35 times. Today, the largest tech stocks trade on average around 25 times expected earnings, despite the very low level of interest rates (particularly relative to the early 1970s) (see exhibit 11.4).**

How Big Can Companies Get Relative to the Market?

The leading tech companies have become very large in terms of market value in the current cycle, but that reflects the significant growth of technology spending and its ability to displace other more traditional capex spending. Very often the new platforms become virtually the whole market.

But, once again, this is not a new phenomenon. Standard Oil, for example, controlled over 90% of oil production and 85% of sales in the US by 1900. Meanwhile, US Steel, another leading company in a dominant sector, managed to avoid a breakup and became the first 'billion dollar company'.

Yet another wave of technology led to the dominant position of AT&T. AT&T monopolised the US telecommunications market for decades, until one of the most well-known cases of US government antitrust intervention. AT&T maintained more than 70% of sales among publicly listed US telecom companies from 1950 to 1980. A Department of Justice case was first filed against the company in 1974, but the ruling against AT&T did not come until 1982 and a breakup of the company was ultimately ordered for 1 January 1984. The breakup increased the number of companies in the telecom industry as AT&T ('Ma Bell') was divided into eight 'baby bells'. In 1975, AT&T was one of just two companies with more than 5% of sales in the GICS telecom industry. By 1996, there were nine publicly listed US telecom companies with more than 5% of industry sales.[17]

As mainframe computers developed in the 1970s, there was also a significant concentration of market share in the leading companies, particularly in IBM, whose dominance triggered a US Department of Justice antitrust lawsuit in 1969. According to news reports at the time, IBM roughly had a 70% share of the mainframe market during this time. The Department of Justice filed its lawsuit in January 1969, alleging that IBM was suppressing competition through various tactics, such as bundling. The lawsuit lasted 13 years and was eventually dropped in January 1982.

Despite no judgement against IBM, regulatory risk kicked off a steady decline in sales growth and margins. IBM's quarterly year/year sales growth was fairly volatile in the 1960s and 1970s but shifted decidedly lower in the 1980s as the industry moved to new products but regulatory scrutiny persisted.

As software took over as the main driver of technology, there was yet another shift in domination. A raft of litigation surrounding Microsoft's positioning in the industry began in 1992, with heightened focus on the decision to bundle its Internet Explorer with its Windows operating system. *US vs. Microsoft* was filed in May 1998 and a judge ordered that the company be split into two in June 2000. However, the decision was reversed on appeal in June 2001 and led to a settlement that included a consent decree, under which Microsoft changed some of its business practices, such as exclusive agreements. Microsoft's operating system ran on well over 90% of consumer devices in 2000 (see US Department of Justice 2015). However, the provisions outlined in the 2001 settlement

[17] Hammond, R., Kostin, D. J., Snider, B., Menon, A., Hunter, C., and Mulford, N. (2019). *Concentration, competition, and regulation: 'Superstar' firms and the specter of antitrust scrutiny*. New York, NY: Goldman Sachs Global Investment Research.

restricted how Microsoft was allowed to develop and license software. Microsoft's average quarterly year/year sales growth fell from 40% (1988–2000) to 10% (2001–2018), although some of this deceleration can likely be attributed to the changing landscape of technology (for example, the emergence of smartphones and the shift to the 'cloud').

More recently, as mobile computing and internet applications took over, market concentration shifted once again. In internet searches, for example, Google has over a 90% market share, and its next biggest competitor, Bing, has 3.2% (Browser Market Share Worldwide n.d.). So several technology companies have become very large and dominant in the current cycle as well, and questions are being raised about competition and potential legislation and regulation. Again, this is not unique to the current cycle. Just as we found with sectors, the largest companies have remained leaders, often with dominant market positions, for long phases reflecting the economic conditions. The biggest companies in the S&P historically have been as follows:

- **1955–1973: General Motors:** during the 'golden age of capitalism', General Motors' earnings more than 10% of the S&P 500.
- **1974–1988: IBM:** the 'age of mainframes' (peaked at 7.6% of market cap).
- **1989–1992: Exxon:** a spin-off from Standard Oil, which was dominant for a long period nearly a century earlier (peaked at 2.7% of market cap).
- **1993–1997: GE:** (peaked at 3.5% of market cap).
- **1998–2000: Microsoft:** the 'age of software' (peaked at 4.9% of market cap).
- **2000–2005: GE** (again): (peaked 3.5% of market cap).
- **2006–2011: Exxon** (again): (peaked at 5.2% of market cap), although Bank of America and Citigroup were briefly the biggest stocks at points between 2006 and 2007 prior to the financial crisis.
- **2012 to today: Apple (and sometimes Microsoft):** (peaked at 5.0% of market cap).

Dominant companies in previous periods were clearly bigger as a share of the broader market than is the case today. That said, one interesting point is that the biggest companies, particularly those from long ago, were not as large as today's in terms of market weighting or capitalisation. For example, before its breakup, AT&T was worth roughly $47 billion, which is equivalent to $120 billion today. The reach and earnings power of the current dominant companies are much larger than we have seen in the past. The massive size of these dominant companies does make it more difficult for them to grow, but this is not likely to limit the dominant contribution of the technology sector more broadly as newer companies evolve.

Technology and the Widening Gaps between Winners and Losers

Although I argue that the dominance of technology in the current equity market cycle is not a new phenomenon, one way in which technology has changed in this cycle is in terms of how it influences leadership styles in stock markets around the world. Over the past decade, in particular, there are two ways in which the impact of technology has widened the gaps between winners and losers.

The first is through the spread between wages and profits, or the share of output accounted for by the labour market and the share of the corporate sector. Some academic studies have emphasised the role of capital accumulation and capital-augmenting technical change as determinants of the evolution of the labour share (e.g. Bentolila and Saint-Paul 2003; Hutchinson and Persyn 2012).

According to OECD (Multifactor productivity 2012) estimates, total factor productivity (TFP) growth and capital deepening – the key drivers of economic growth – accounted for most of the average within-industry decline in the labour share in OECD countries between 1990 and 2007. This shift is part of a process that has emerged over a long period of time. The labour share of GDP in the US, for example, has been trending downwards since the Second World War, but it has taken a particularly sharp fall since the financial crisis.[18]

Of course, technology is not the only reason for this. The impact of austerity has contributed, as has the influence of quantitative easing. This process has helped to reduce the level of interest rates and boost corporate profits (as well as the trend for corporate buybacks in the United States). Equally, although many tech companies in the US use cheaper labour outside of the US, so do other manufacturers, and these trends predated the internet, the computer and the smartphone. Also, those on a low income in many cases have been beneficiaries of the connectivity that technology provides, particularly in so far as technology platforms have pushed down prices of books, clothes, toys and electrical goods. Technology might, then, have contributed to the boom in consumption.

The second transfer has occurred through the rewarding of growth companies in this cycle relative to value companies. This is another way of saying that companies with high growth (of which there are many in the technology sector) have significantly outperformed companies that look 'cheap' (with low P/E ratios or high dividend yield).

To be clear, the outperformance of growth versus value is the result of many factors and not just a reflection of the success of technology. The ongoing weakness of banks following the financial crisis and the continuing headwind to profits they face as a result of ultra-low, and in many cases negative, interest rates is also partly to blame. Furthermore, the secular fall in bond yields since the financial crisis, alongside inflation, has been an important contributory factor.

Growth companies are seen to have 'long duration' compared with value companies. In other words, the sensitivity of the net

---

[18] The Labour Share in G20 Economies International Labour Organisation for Economic Co-operation and Development with contributions from International Monetary Fund and World Bank Group Report prepared for the G20 Employment Working Group Antalya, Turkey, 26–27 February 2015.

present value of growth companies (where revenues are expected to grow far into the future) to changes in the level of interest rates is higher than for value companies, which tend to be in more mature, slower-growing industries. This means that in a period of falling interest rates, the positive impact on the net present value of technology companies is higher than it is for value companies or those that are particularly sensitive to short-term economic developments. I discuss style drivers in the market in chapter 5 and the ways in which these have changed since the financial crisis in chapter 9.

Summary and Conclusions

Over time, the economic, political and investment landscape undergoes significant changes. Major technological innovations (such as the internet) and challenges (for example, climate change) evolve alongside typical cycles in economic growth rates, inflation and interest rates. That said, despite all of these changes over time, there are patterns in economic activity and financial asset returns that are repeated in cycles.

As a summary, here are a few important takeaways.

What We Can Learn from the Past

- The returns to investors in assets depend on a number of factors but perhaps most important of these are the time horizon of the investment and the starting valuation. The longer an investor is happy to hold the investment, the more likely it is that volatility-adjusted returns will rise.

  For equity investors, these considerations are particularly important. Equities bought at the top of the technology bubble in 2000, for example, achieved among the worst 10-year holding returns in over 100 years because the starting valuations were so high. Similarly, the Japanese stock market (the Nikkei 225) remains roughly 45% below the level at which it peaked in 1989, 30 years ago. The S&P did not return to its 1929 index level until 1955. Although these were extraordinary points in history, much of the explanation for this comes down to valuations. Understandably, great valuation peaks (1929, 1968, 1999) tend to be followed by very poor returns on a risk-adjusted basis, and very low valuations, at market troughs (1930, 1973, 2008), tend to be followed by very strong returns.

- The average annualised total return for US equities since 1860 has been about 10%, over anything from a 1-year to a 20-year time horizon. For 10-year government bonds, the average return has been between 5% and 6% over the same holding periods. Although returns adjusted for volatility (risk) are much lower for equities than for bonds in the short term, over the longer term investors are generally rewarded for taking risk.
- Over long periods of time, equity markets (and other asset classes) tend to move in cycles. Each cycle can generally be further split into phases that reflect the varying drivers as the economic cycle matures: (1) the despair phase, during which the market moves from its peak to its trough, also known as the bear market; (2) the hope phase, typically a short period (on average 10 months in the US and 16 months in Europe), when the market rebounds from its trough through multiple expansions. This phase is critical for investors because it is usually when the highest returns in the cycle are achieved, and it usually starts when the macro data and profit results of the corporate sector remain depressed; (3) the growth phase, usually the longest period (on average 39 months in the US and 29 months in Europe), when earnings growth is generated and drives returns; and (4) the optimism phase, the final part of the cycle, when investors become increasingly confident, or perhaps even complacent, and when valuations tend to rise again and outstrip earnings growth. Typically, this phase has lasted 25 months in the US.

- Bear markets are important to avoid because the returns are heavily concentrated in equity cycles. The variation in returns year by year can be substantial. The worst annual post-war return for the S&P was −26.5% (1974), and the best was +52% (1954). History shows that avoiding the worst months can, over time, be as valuable as investing in the best months. But not all bear markets are the same. We find that, historically, bear markets can be split into three classifications according to severity and longevity: cyclical, event-driven and structural.

  Cyclical and event-driven bear markets generally see price falls of about 30%, whereas structural ones see much larger falls, of about 50%. Event-driven bear markets tend to be the shortest, lasting an average of 7 months; cyclical bear markets last an average of 26 months; and structural bear markets last an average of 3½ years. Event-driven and cyclical bear markets tend to revert to their previous market highs after about 1 year, whereas structural bear markets take an average of 10 years to return to previous highs.

  Bull markets can generate powerful returns. As a rough rule of thumb, and using the US as an example, the average bull market sees prices rise by over 130% over 4 years, annualising a return of about 25%.

  Some bull markets are driven by sustained valuation increases and can be broadly described as secular. The post-war boom in 1945–1968 and the long boom reflecting disinflation and a collapse of the Cold War in 1982–2000 are the best examples. Other bull markets are less clearly trending and tend to be more cyclical. We divide these into the following types:

  - **Skinny and flat markets** (low volatility, low returns). These are flat markets in which equity prices are stuck in a narrow trading range and experience low volatility.
  - **Fat and flat markets** (high volatility, low returns). These are periods (often quite long) when equity indices make little aggregate progress but experience high volatility, with strong rallies and corrections (or even mini bull and bear markets) in between.

What We Can Learn from the Present

- Although markets tend to move in cycles, there are many ways in which the post-financial-crisis cycle has differed from the past. For one thing, the economic cycle is already very long and, in the case of the US, the longest for well over a century. Alongside this, inflation expectations have moderated and bond yields have fallen to record lows. UK long-term bond yields have reached the lowest levels since 1700, and there are more than $14 trillion-worth in government bonds now with negative yields. Technological innovation has also resulted in a widening gap between relative winners and losers in terms of profit growth and returns. The technology sector has been a major source of the margin and profit growth that have been achieved since the financial crisis.
- A backdrop of relatively low economic growth together with very low inflation expectations and bond yields since the financial crisis has meant that investors face a scarcity of income (as policy rates are close to, or even below, zero) and growth: there are fewer high-growing companies than in the pre-financial-crisis period, and the rate of revenue growth for the corporate sector in general has slowed. This combination of factors has resulted in a search for yield within fixed income and credit markets, but has largely been reflected in the outperformance of the growth factor relative to value within equities. In both credit and equity markets, the higher levels of uncertainty about future growth have also increased the premium for quality, that is, stronger balance sheet companies with less sensitivity to the economic cycle. These conditions are likely to last unless, or until, growth and inflation expectations start to revert to the typical levels seen in the cycles prior to the financial crisis.
- As a result of these changes, and the onset of quantitative easing, valuations in financial assets have generally increased, suggesting lower future returns. Bond yields at the zero bound do not necessarily benefit equities. In general, the experience from Japan and Europe in particular suggests that lower bond yields

have pushed up the required equity risk premium – the extra return that investors actually demand for taking risk and buying equities relative to risk free government bonds.

Zero or negative bond yields can affect the cycle by making it less volatile, but, at the same time, this leaves equities much more sensitive to long-term growth expectations. If a shock results in a recession, we could see a much greater negative impact on equity valuations than we have seen in past cycles.

Pension funds and insurance companies are vulnerable to liability mismatching as bond yields fall towards or below zero. This can result in some institutions taking on too much risk to meet guaranteed returns, but it can also result in more demand for bonds as the yields fall, resulting in yet lower bond yields.

- An additional structural shift has occurred as a result of technological innovation. According to many estimates, 90% of the world's data has been generated in the past 2 years.[1] This has resulted in a rapid distributional impact across relative winners and losers. The largest companies have become huge: Amazon, Apple and Microsoft have a combined market capitalisation larger than the annual GDP of Africa (54 countries), and technology is the dominant sector in the US equity market. But history shows that this is not unusual. Over time, different waves of technology have resulted in different phases of sector dominance, starting with financials (from 1800–1850s), transport, reflecting the railway boom (between the 1850s and 1910s), and energy (1920s–1970s). Since then, other than a short period before the financial crisis of 2008, technology has become dominant. This has reflected the evolution of mainframes (IBM became the biggest stock in the S&P 500 in 1974), PCs (Microsoft became the biggest company in 1998) and Apple (which became the biggest company in 2012).

[1] SINTEF. (2013). Big data, for better or worse: 90% of world's data generated over last two years. *ScienceDaily* [online]. Available at https://www.sciencedaily.com/releases/2013/05/130522085217.htm

What We Can Expect in the Future

Future financial cycles have not been the key focus of this book. Nevertheless, we can make some observations about the past and the current cycle that can provide some clues about what to expect in the future.

- One of the most consistent observations that can be made from the history of cycles is that valuations matter. High valuations tend to result in lower future returns, and vice versa. The unusual combination in the post-financial-crisis cycle of relatively low-inflation product markets but high inflation (and strong returns) in financial assets is partly a function of the same common factor: falling interest rates.
- The decline in real levels of interest rates may reflect many factors: ageing populations, excess savings, the impact of technology on pricing, as well as globalisation. It has also, at least in part, reflected largely aggressive policy easing by central banks in the aftermath of the financial crisis.
- This shift lower in real yields, coupled with lower growth rates in general, has helped the economic cycle to be more elongated than we have tended to see in the past but, at the same time, has made economies, companies and investors more dependent on a continuation of these prevailing conditions. This suggests that investors face some unusual challenges in the next few years.
- Although recession in the near term still seems unlikely, the scope to cut interest rates in the face of economic shocks is much more limited today than in the past, making it harder to recover from an economic downturn. Governments may decide that, in the face of historically low funding costs, an increase in borrowing and fiscal expansion is increasingly tempting.
- But if such borrowing results in much stronger economic growth, then it is likely at some point to raise inflation expectations and interest rates from the current historically low levels, with the possible effect of triggering a derating of financial assets as bond yields rise to higher levels.

- One possible outcome is that economic activity recovers back to the pace of growth enjoyed before the financial crisis. This would increase confidence in future growth but, at the same time, would likely drive long-term interest rates much higher, raising the risks of a derating of financial assets and a possibly painful bear market in both equities and bonds. An alternative scenario is that growth, inflation and interest rates remain very subdued, as they have tended to be in Japan over recent decades. Although this may reduce volatility in financial assets, it is likely to be accompanied by low returns. With rising demand for returns given ageing populations and long-run liabilities in the form of health care and pension costs, it will be harder to generate the required returns without taking increased risks.
- Perhaps the greatest challenge will come from climate change and the need to decarbonise economies. Although efforts to do this will be costly, it would also provide significant opportunities for investment and retooling economies so that future growth is more sustainable.
- Technology is beginning to yield results. In the past 8 years, wind power costs have fallen by 65%, solar costs by 85% and battery costs by 70%. Within 15 years, it should be possible not only to deliver renewable electricity at prices that are fully competitive with fossil-fuel-based power but also to provide the low-cost backup and storage required to make it possible to run power systems that are 80%–90% reliant on intermittent renewables.[2]
- Over the long run, even accepting the fluctuations caused by cycles, investing can be extremely profitable. Different assets tend to perform best at different times, and returns will depend on the risk tolerance of the investor. But for equity investors in particular, history suggests that, if they can hold their investments for at least 5 years and, especially, if they can recognise the signs of bubbles and of changes in the cycle, they really can enjoy a 'long good buy'.

[2] Turner, A. (2017). The path to a low-carbon economy. *Climate 2020* [online]. Available at https://www.climate2020.org.uk/path-low-carbon-economy

References

Across the rich world, an extraordinary jobs boom is under way. (2019, May 23). *The Economist*.

Aikman, D., Lehnert, A., Liang, N., and Modugno, M. (2017). Credit, financial conditions, and monetary policy transmission. *Hutchins Center Working Paper #39* [online]. Available at https://www.brookings.edu/research/credit-financial-conditions-and-monetary-policy-transmission

Ainger, J. (2019). 100-year bond yielding just over 1% shows investors' desperation. *Bloomberg* [online]. Available at https://www.bloomberg.com/news/articles/2019-06-25/austria-weighs-another-century-bond-for-yield-starved-investors

Akerlof, G., and Shiller, R. J. (2010). *Animal spirits: How human psychology drives the economy, and why it matters for global capitalism*. Princeton, NJ: Princeton University Press.

An, A., Jalles, J. T., and Loungani, P. (2018). How well do economists forecast recessions? *IMF Working Paper No. 18/39* [online]. Available at https://www.imf.org/en/Publications/WP/Issues/2018/03/05/How-Well-Do-Economists-Forecast-Recessions-45672

Antolin, P., Schich, S., and Yermi, J. (2011). The economic impact of low interest rates on pension funds and insurance companies. *OECD Journal: Financial Market Trends*, 2011(1).

Antras, P., and Voth, H. (2003). Factor prices and productivity growth during the British industrial revolution. *Explorations in Economic History*, 40(1), 52–77.

Baddeley, M. (2010). Herding, social influence and economic decision-making: Socio-psychological and neuroscientific analyses. *Philosophical Traditions of The Royal Society* [online]. Available at https://doi.org/10.1098/rstb.2009.0169

Balatti, M., Brooks, C., Clements, M. P., and Kappou, K. (2016). Did quantitative easing only inflate stock prices? Macroeconomic evidence from the US and UK. *SSRN* [online]. Available at https://papers.ssrn.com/sol3/papers.cfm?abstract_id=2838128

Belke, A. H. (2013). Impact of a low interest rate environment – Global liquidity spillovers and the search-for-yield. *Ruhr Economic Paper No. 429*.

Bentolila, S., and Saint-Paul, G. (2003). Explaining movements in the labor share. *Contributions to Macroeconomics*, 3(1).

Benzoni, L., Chyruk, O., and Kelley, D. (2018). Why does the yield-curve slope predict recessions? *Chicago Fed Letter No. 404*.

Bernanke, B. S. (2005). The global saving glut and the U.S. current account deficit. Board of Governors of the Federal Reserve System speech 77.

Bernanke, B. (2010, Sept. 2). *Causes of the recent financial and economic crisis*. Testimony before the Financial Crisis Inquiry Commission, Washington, DC.

Bernstein, P. L. (1997). What rate of return can you reasonably expect . . . or what can the long run tell us about the short run? *Financial Analysts Journal*, 53(2), 20–28.

Binder, J., Nielsen, A. E. B., and Oppenheimer, P. (2010). Finding fair value in global equities: Part I. *Journal of Portfolio Management*, 36(2), 80–93.

Blau, F. D., and Kahn, L. M. (2013). Female labor supply: Why is the US falling behind? *NBER Working Paper No. 18702* [online]. Available at https://www.nber.org/papers/w18702

Borio, C. (2013). On time, stocks and flows: Understanding the global macroeconomic challenges. *National Institute of Economic and Social Research*, 225(1), 3–13.

Borio, C., Disyatat, P., and Rungcharoenkitkul, P. (2019). What anchors for the natural rate of interest? *BIS Working Papers No 777* [online]. Available at https://www.bis.org/publ/work777.html

Borio, C., and Lowe, P. (2002). Asset prices, financial and monetary stability: Exploring the nexus. *BIS Working Papers No 114* [online]. Available at https://www.bis.org/publ/work114.html

Borio, C., Piti, D., and Juselius, M. (2013). Rethinking potential output: Embedding information about the financial cycle. *BIS Working Papers No 404* [online]. Available at https://www.bis.org/publ/work404.html

Brookes, M., and Wahhaj, Z. (2000). Is the internet better than electricity? *Goldman Sachs Global Economics Paper No. 49*.

Browne, E. (2001). Does Japan offer any lessons for the United States? *New England Economic Review*, 3, 3–18.

Browser market share worldwide. (n.d.). Statcounter Global Stats [online]. Available at https://gs.statcounter.com/search-engine-market-share

Bruno, V., and Shin, H. S. (2015). Cross-border banking and global liquidity. *Review of Economic Studies*, 82(2), 535–564.

Buring, E., and van Zanden, J. L. (2009). Charting the "Rise of the West": Manuscripts and printed books in Europe; A long-term perspective from the sixth through eighteenth centuries. *The Journal of Economic History*, 69(2), 409–445.

Caballero, R. J., and Farhi, E. (2017). The safety trap. *The Review of Economic Studies*, 85(1), 223–274.

Can pension funds and life insurance companies keep their promises? (2015). *OECD Business and Finance Outlook 2015* [online]. Available at https://www.oecd.org/finance/oecd-business-and-finance-outlook-2015-9789264234291-en.htm

Carvalho, C., Ferro, A., and Nechio, F. (2016). Demographics and real interest rates: Inspecting the mechanism. *Working Paper Series 2016-5*. Federal Reserve Bank of San Francisco [online]. Available at http://www.frbsf.org/economic-research/publications/working-papers/wp2016-05.pdf

Case, K., and Shiller, R. (2003). Is there a bubble in the housing market? *Brookings Papers on Economic Activity*, 34(2), 299–362.

Cawley, L. (2015). Ozone layer hole: How its discovery changed our lives. BBC [online]. Available at https://www.bbc.co.uk/news/uk-england-cambridgeshire-31602871

Chancellor, E. (2000). *Devil take the hindmost: A history of financial speculation*. New York, NY: Plume.

Christensen, J. H. E., and Speigel, M. M. (2019). Negative interest rates and inflation expectations in Japan. *FEBSF Economic Letter*, 22.

Cooper, M., Dimitrov, O., and Rau, P. (2001). A Rose.com by any other name. *The Journal of Finance*, 56(6), 2371–2388.

Crafts, N. (2004). Productivity growth in the industrial revolution: A new growth accounting perspective. *The Journal of Economic History*, 64(2), 521–535.

Cunliffe, J. (2017). *The Phillips curve: Lower, flatter or in hiding?* Bank of England [online]. Available at https://www.bankofengland.co.uk/speech/2017/jon-cunliffe-speech-at-oxford-economics-society

Cutts, R. L. (1990). Power from the ground up: Japan's land bubble. *The Harvard Business Review* [online]. Available at https://hbr.org/1990/05/power-from-the-ground-up-japans-land-bubble

David, P. A., and Wright, G. (2001). General purpose technologies and productivity surges: Historical reflections on the future of the ICT revolution. *Economic Challenges of the 21st Century in Historical Perspective*, Oxford, UK. Available at https://www.researchgate.net/publication/23742678_General_Purpose_Technologies_and_Productivity_Surges_Historical_Reflections_on_the_Future_of_the_ICT_Revolution

Dhaoui, A., Bourouis, S., and Boyacioglu, M. A. (2013). The impact of investor psychology on stock markets: Evidence from France. *Journal of Academic Research in Economics*, 5(1), 35–59.

Dice, C. A. (1931). New levels in the stock market. *Journal of Political Economy*, 39(4), 551–554.

Eckstein, O., and Sinai, A. (1986). The mechanisms of the business cycle in the postwar era. In R. Gorden (Ed.), *The American business cycle: Continuity and change* (pp. 39–122). Cambridge, MA: National Bureau of Economic Research.

The end of the Bretton Woods System. IMF [online]. Available at https://www.imf.org/external/about/histend.htm

Evans, R. (2014). How (not) to invest like Sir Isaac Newton. *The Telegraph* [online]. Available at https://www.telegraph.co.uk/finance/personalfinance/investing/10848995/How-not-to-invest-like-Sir-Isaac-Newton.html

Fama, E. F. (1970). Efficient capital markets: A review of theory and empirical work. *The Journal of Finance*, 25(2), 383–417.

Fama, E. F., and French, K. (1998). Value versus growth: The international evidence. *Journal of Finance*, 53(6), 1975–1999.

Ferguson, N. (2012). *The ascent of money*. London, UK: Penguin.

Fama, E. F., and French, K. (2002). The equity premium. *Journal of Finance*, 57(2), 637–659.

Ferguson, R. W. (2005). *Recessions and recoveries associated with asset-price movements: What do we know?* Stanford Institute for Economic Policy Research, Stanford, CA.

Filardo, A., Lombardi, M., and Raczko, M. (2019). Measuring financial cycle time. *Bank of England Staff Working Paper No. 776* [online]. Available at https://www.bankofengland.co.uk/working-paper/2019/measuring-financial-cycle-time

Fisher, I. (1933). The debt-deflation theory of the great depressions. *Econometrica*, 1, 337–357.

Five things you need to know about the Maastricht Treaty. (2017). ECB [online]. *Available at* https://www.ecb.europa.eu/explainers/tell-me-more/html/25_years_maastricht.en.html

Frehen, R. G. P., Goetzmann, W. N., and Rouwenhorst, K. G. (2013). New evidence on the first financial bubble. *Journal of Financial Economics*, 108(3), 585–607.

Fukuyama, F. (1989). The end of history? *The National Interest*, 16, 3–18.

Gagnon, J., Raskin, M., Remache, J., and Sack, B. (2011). The financial market effects of the Federal Reserve's large-scale asset purchases. *International Journal of Central Banking*, 7(1), 3–43.

Galbraith, J. K. (1955). *The great crash, 1929*. Boston: Houghton Mifflin Harcourt.

George Hudson and the 1840s railway mania. (2012). *Yale School of Management Case Studies* [online]. Available at https://som.yale.edu/our-approach/teaching-method/case-research-and-development/cases-directory/george-hudson-and-1840s

Gilchrist, S., and Zakrajsek, E. (2013). The impact of the Federal Reserve's large-scale asset purchase programs on corporate credit risk. *NBER Working Paper No. 19337* [online]. Available at https://www.nber.org/papers/w19337

Goobey, G. H. R. (1956). Speech to the Association of Superannuation and Pension Funds. *The pensions archive [online].* Available at http://www.pensionsarchive.org.uk/27/

Gozluklu, A. (n.d.). *How do demographics affect interest rates?* The University of Warkick [online]. Available at https://warwick.ac.uk/newsandevents/knowledgecentre/business/finance/interestrates/

Graham, B. (1949). *The intelligent investor*. New York, NY: HarperBusiness.

Graham, B., and Dodd, D. L. (1934). *Security analysis*. New York, NY: McGraw-Hill.

Guild, S. E. (1931). *Stock growth and discount tables*. Boston, MA: Financial Publishing Company.

Gurkaynak, R. (2005). Econometric tests of asset price bubbles: Taking stock. *Finance and Economics Discussion Series*. Washington, DC: Board of Governors of the Federal Reserve System.

Hammond, R., Kostin, D. J., Snider, B., Menon, A., Hunter, C., and Mulford, N. (2019). *Concentration, competition, and regulation: 'Superstar' firms and the specter of antitrust scrutiny*. New York, NY: Goldman Sachs Global Investment Research.

Harley, N. F. R., and Harley, C. K. (1992). Output growth and the British Industrial Revolution: A restatement of the Crafts-Harley view. *Economic History Review*, 45(4), 703–730.

Hatzius, J., Phillips, A., Mericle, D., Hill, S., Struyven, D., Choi, D., Taylor, B., and Walker, R. (2019). *Productivity paradox v2.0: The price of free goods*. New York, NY: Goldman Sachs Global Investment Research.

Hayes, A. (2019, April 25). Dotcom bubble. Investopedia.

How quantitative easing affects bond yields: Evidence from Switzerland. (2019). Royal Economic Society [online]. Available at https://www.res.org.uk/resources-page/how-quantitative-easing-affects-bond-yields-evidence-from-switzerland.html

How to tame the tech titans. (2018). *The Economist.*

Hutchinson, J., and Persyn, D. (2012). Globalisation, concentration and footloose firms: In search of the main cause of the declining labour share. *Review of World Economics*, 148(1).

Jacques, M. (2009). *When China rules the world: The end of the western world and the birth of a new global order*. New York, NY: Penguin Press.

Johnston, E. (2009). Lessons from when the bubble burst. *The Japan Times* [online]. Available at https://www.japantimes.co.jp/news/2009/01/06/reference/lessons-from-when-the-bubble-burst/

Jorda, O., Schularick, M., Taylor, A. M., and Ward, F. (2018). Global financial cycles and risk premiums. *Working Paper Series 2018-5*, Federal Reserve Bank of San Francisco [online]. Available at http://www.frbsf.org/economic-research/publications/working-papers/2018/05/

Kahneman, D., and Tversky, A. (1979). Prospect theory: An analysis of decision under risk. *Econometrica*, 47(2), 263–292.

Keynes, J. M. (1930). *A treatise on money*. London, UK: Macmillan.

Kindleberger, C. (1996). *Manias, panics, and crashes* (3rd ed.). New York, NY: Basic Books.

Kuhn, P., and Mansour, H. (2014). Is internet job search still ineffective? *Economic Journal*, 124(581), 1213–1233.

Lian, C., Ma, Y., and Wang, C. (2018). Low interest rates and risk taking: Evidence from individual investment decisions. *The Review of Financial Studies*, 32(6), 2107–2148.

Loewenstein, G., Scott, R., and Cohen J. D. (2008). Neuroeconomics. *Annual Review of Psychology*, 59, 647–672.

Lovell, H. (2013). "Battle of the quants". *The Hedge Fund Journal*, pp. 87.

Lu, L., Pritsker, M., Zlate, A., Anadu, K., and Bohn, J. (2019). Reach for yield by U.S. public pension funds. *FRB Boston Risk and Policy Analysis Unit Paper No. RPA 19-2* [online]. Available at https://www.bostonfed.org/publications/risk-and-policy-analysis/2019/reach-for-yield-by-us-public-pension-funds.aspx

Lucibello, A. (2014). Panic of 1873. In D. Leab (Ed.), *Encyclopedia of American recessions and depressions* (pp. 227–276). Santa Barbara, CA: ABC-CLIO.

Macaulay, F. R. (1938). *Some theoretical problems suggested by the movements of interest rates, bond yields, and stock prices in the United States Since 1856.* Cambridge, MA: National Bureau of Economic Research.

Mackay, C. (1841). *Extraordinary popular delusions and the madness of crowds.* London, UK: Richard Bentley.

Malmendier, U., and Nagel, S. (2016). Learning from inflation experiences. *The Quarterly Journal of Economics*, 131(1), 53–87.

Marks, H. (2018). *Mastering the cycle: Getting the odds on your side* (p. 293). Boston, MA: Houghton Mifflin Harcourt.

Mason, P. (2011). Thinking outside the 1930s box. BBC [online]. Available at https://www.bbc.co.uk/news/business-15217615

Masson, P. (2001). Globalization facts and figures. *IMF Policy Discussion Paper No. 01/4* [online]. Available at https://www.imf.org/en/Publications/IMF-Policy-Discussion-Papers/Issues/2016/12/30/Globalization-Facts-and-Figures-15469

McCullough, B. (2018). An eye-opening look at the dot-com bubble of 2000 – and how it shapes our lives today. IDEAS.TED.COM [online]. Available at https://ideas.ted.com/an-eye-opening-look-at-the-dot-com-bubble-of-2000-and-how-it-shapes-our-lives-today

McNary, D. (2019, Jan. 2). 2018 worldwide box office hits record as Disney dominates. *Variety [online].* Available at https://variety.com/2019/film/news/box-office-record-disney-dominates-1203098075/

Mehra, R., and Prescott, E. C. (1985). The equity premium: A puzzle. *Journal of Monetary Economics*, 15(2), 145–161.

Minsky, H. P. (1975). *John Maynard Keynes*. New York, NY: Springer.

Modigliani, E., and Blumberg, R. (1980). Utility analysis and the aggregate consumption function: An attempt at integration. *The collected papers of Franco Modigliani*. Cambridge, MA: MIT Press.

Modigliani, F., and Cohn, R. A. (1979). Inflation, rational valuation and the market. *Financial Analysts Journal*, 35(2), 24–44.

Molyneux, P., Reghezza, A., Thornton, J., and Xie, R. (2019). Did negative interest rates improve bank lending? *Journal of Financial Services Research*, July 2019.

Mueller-Glissmann, C., Wright, I., Oppenheimer, P., and Rizzi, A. (2016). *Reflation, equity/bond correlation and diversification desperation*. London, UK: Goldman Sachs Global Investment Research.

Mühleisen, M. (2018). The long and short of the digital revolution. *Finance & Development [online]* 55(2). Available at https://www.imf.org/external/pubs/ft/fandd/2018/06/impact-of-digital-technology-on-economic-growth/muhleisen.htm

Multifactor productivity. (2012). OECD Data [online]. Available at https://data.oecd.org/lprdty/multifactor-productivity.htm

Norris, F. (2000). The year in the markets; 1999: Extraordinary winners and more losers. *New York Times* [online]. Available at https://www.nytimes.com/2000/01/03/business/the-year-in-the-markets-1999-extraordinary-winners-and-more-losers.html

Norwood, B. (1969). The Kennedy round: A try at linear trade negotiations. *Journal of Law and Economics*, 12(2), 297–319.

Odlyzko, A. (2010). Collective hallucinations and inefficient markets: The British railway mania of the 1840s. SSRN [online]. Available at https://ssrn.com/abstract=1537338

Okina, K., Shirakawa, M., and Shiratsuka, S. (2001). The asset price bubble and monetary policy: Experience of Japan's economy in the late 1980s and its lessons. *Monetary and Economic Studies*, 19(S1), 395–450.

Oppenheimer, P., and Bell, S. (2017). *Bear necessities: Identifying signals for the next bear market.* London, UK: Goldman Sachs Global Investment Research.

Oxenford, M. (2018). *The lasting effects of the financial crisis have yet to be felt.* London, UK: Chattam House.

Pasotti, P., and Vercelli, A. (2015). Kindleberger and financial crises. *FESSUD Working Paper Series No 104* [online]. Available at http://fessud.eu/wp-content/uploads/2015/01/Kindleberger-and-Financial-Crises-Fessud-final_Working-Paper-104.pdf

Perez, C. (2009). The double bubble at the turn of the century: Technological roots and structural implications. *Cambridge Journal of Economics*, 33(4), 779–805.

Pezzuto, I. (2012). Miraculous financial engineering or toxic finance? The genesis of the U.S. subprime mortgage loans crisis and its consequences on the global financial markets and real economy. *Journal of Governance and Regulation*, 1(3), 113–124.

Phillips, M. (2019). The bull market began 10 years ago. Why aren't more people celebrating? *New York Times* [online]. Available at https://www.nytimes.com/2019/03/09/business/bull-market-anniversary.html

Post-war reconstruction and development in the golden age of capitalism. (2017). *World Economic and Social Survey 2017.*

Privatisation in Europe, coming home to roost. (2002). *The Economist.*

Rajan, R. J. (2005). Financial markets, financial fragility, and central banking. *The Greenspan era: Lessons for the future,* sponsored by the Federal Reserve Bank of Kansas City, Jackson Hole, WY.

Reid, T. R. (1991). Japan's scandalous summer of '91. *Washington Post* [online]. Available at https://www.washingtonpost.com/archive/politics/1991/08/03/japans-scandalous-summer-of-91/e066bc12-90f2-4ce1-bc05-70298b675340/

Ritter, J., and Warr, R. S. (2002). The decline of inflation and the bull market of 1982–1999. *Journal of Financial and Quantitative Analysis*, 37(01), 29–61.

Roach, S. S. (2015). Why is technology not boosting productivity? *World Economic Forum* [online]. Available at https://www.weforum.org/agenda/2015/06/why-is-technology-not-boosting-productivity

Romer, C., and Romer, D. (2017). New evidence on the aftermath of financial crises in advanced countries. *American Economic Review*, 107(10), 3072–3118.

Roubini, N. (2007). *The risk of a U.S. hard landing and implications for the global economy and financial markets.* New York: New York University [online]. Available at https://www.imf.org/External/NP/EXR/Seminars/2007/091307.htm

Shiller, R. J. (1980). Do stock prices move too much to be justified by subsequent changes in dividends?. *NBER Working Paper No. 456* [online]. Available at https://www.nber.org/papers/w0456

Shiller, R. J. (2000). *Irrational exuberance.* Princeton, NJ: Princeton University Press.

Shiller, R. J. (2003). From efficient markets theory to behavioral finance. *Journal of Economic Perspectives*, 17(1), 83–104.

Siegel, J. (1994). *Stocks for the long run* (2nd ed.). New York, NY: Irwin.

Siegel, J. (1998). *Valuing growth stocks: Revisiting the nifty fifty.* The American Association of Individual Investors Journal [online]. Available at https://www.aaii.com/journal/article/valuing-growth-stocks-revisiting-the-nifty-fifty

SINTEF. (2013). Big data, for better or worse: 90% of world's data generated over last two years. *ScienceDaily* [online]. Available at https://www.sciencedaily.com/releases/2013/05/130522085217.htm

Smith, A. (1848). *The bubble of the age; or, The fallacies of railway investment, railway accounts, and railway dividends.* London, UK: Sherwood, Gilbert and Piper.

Smith, B., and Browne, C. A. (2019). *Tools and weapons: The promise and the peril of the digital age.* New York, NY: Penguin Press.

Smith, E. L. (1925). *Common stocks as long-term investments.* New York, NY: Macmillan.

Sorescu, A., Sorescu, S. M., Armstrong, W. J., and Devoldere, B. (2018). Two centuries of innovations and stock market bubbles. *Marketing Science Journal*, 37(4), 507–684.

Sterngold, J. (1991). Nomura gets big penalties. *New York Times*, October 9, Section D, p. 1.

Stone, M. (2015). The trillion fold increase in computing power, visualized. *Gizmodo [online].* Available at https://gizmodo.com/the-trillion-fold-increase-in-computing-power-visualiz-1706676799

Struyven, D., Choi, D., and Hatzius, J. (2019). *Recession risk: Still moderate.* New York, NY: Goldman Sachs Global Investment Research.

Summers, L. H. (2015). Demand side secular stagnation. *American Economic Review*, 105(5), 60–65.

Sunstein, C. R., and Thaler, R. (2016). The two friends who changed how we think about how we think. *The New Yorker* [online]. Available at https://www.newyorker.com/books/page-turner/the-two-friends-who-changed-how-we-think-about-how-we-think

Terrones, M., Kose, A., and Claessens, S. (2011). Financial cycles: What? How? When? *IMF Working Paper No. 11/76*, [online]. Available at https://www.imf.org/en/Publications/WP/Issues/2016/12/31/Financial-Cycles-What-How-When-24775

Thaler, R. H., and Sunstein, C. R. (2008). *Nudge: Improving decisions about health, wealth, and happiness.* New York, NY: Penguin.

Thompson, E. (2007). The tulipmania: Fact or artifact? *Public Choice*, 130(1-2), 99–114.

Tooze, A. (2018). *Crashed: How a decade of financial crises changed the world.* London, UK: Allen Lane.

Turner, A. (2017). The path to a low-carbon economy. *Climate 2020* [online]. Available at https://www.climate2020.org.uk/path-low-carbon-economy

Turner, G. (2003). *Solutions to a liquidity trap.* London, UK: GFC Economics.

US Department of Justice. (2015). U.S. v. Microsoft: Proposed findings of fact. Available at https://www.justice.gov/atr/us-v-microsoft-proposed-findings-fact-0

Vogel, E. (2001). *Japan as number one lessons for America.* Lincoln, NE: iUniverse.com.

Why weather forecasts are so often wrong. (2016). *The Economist explains.*

Suggested Reading

Ahir, H., and Prakash, L. (2014). Fail again? Fail better? Forecasts by economists during the great recession. George Washington University Research Program in Forecasting Seminar.

Balvers, R. J., Cosimano, T. F., and McDonald, B. (1990). Predicting stock returns in an efficient market. *The Journal of Finance*, 45(4), 1109–1128.

Barnichon, R., Matthes, C., and Ziegenbein, A. (2018). *The financial crisis at 10: Will we ever recover?* San Francisco, CA: Federal Reserve Board.

Bell, S., Oppenheimer, P., Mueller-Glissmann, C., and Huang, A. (2015). *Below zero: 10 effects of negative real interest rates on equities*. London, UK: Goldman Sachs Global Investment Research.

Bernanke, B. (2018). The real effects of the financial crisis. *Brookings Papers on Economic Activity*.

Borio, C. (2012). The financial cycle and macroeconomics: What have we learnt? *BIS Working Papers No 395* [online]. Available at `https://www.bis.org/publ/work395.htm`

Burton, M. (1973). *A random walk down Wall Street*. New York, NY: W. W. Norton & Company.

Cagliarini, A., and Price, F. (2017). Exploring the link between the macroeconomic and financial cycles. In J. Hambur and J. Simon (Eds.), *Monetary policy and financial stability in a world of low interest rates (RBA annual conference volume)*. Sydney, Australia: Reserve Bank of Australia.

Campbell, J. (2000, Fall). Strategic asset allocation: Portfolio choice for long-term investors. *NBER Reporter* [online]. Available at https://admin.nber.org/reporter/fall00/campbell.html

Claessens, S., Kose, M. A., and Terrones, M. E. (2011). How do business and financial cycles interact? IMF Working Paper 11/88.

Cribb, J., and Johnson P. (2018). *10 years on – Have we recovered from the financial crisis?* London, UK: Institute of Fiscal Studies.

Crump, R. K., Eusepi, S., and Moench, E. (2016). The term structure of expectations and bond yields. *Federal Reserve Bank of New York Staff Reports No. 775.*

Daly, K., Nielsen, A. E. B., and Oppenheimer, P. (2010). Finding fair value in global equities: Part II—Forecasting returns. *The Journal of Portfolio Management*, 36(3), 56–70.

Diamond, P. A. (1999). What stock market returns to expect for the future? *Social Security Bulletin*, 63(2), 38–52.

Durré, A., and Pill, A. (2010). Non-standard monetary policy measures, monetary financing and the price level. *Monetary and Fiscal Policy Challenges in Times of Financial Stress*, Frankfurt, Germany. Available at https://www.ecb.europa.eu/events/pdf/conferences/ecb_mopo_fipo/Pill.pdf?c87bc7b3966364963b437607ec63d1b8

Fama, E. F., and French, K. (1988). Dividend yields and expected stock returns. *Journal of Financial Economics*, 22(1), 3–25.

Garber, P. M. (2000). *Famous first bubbles*. Cambridge, MA: MIT Press.

Goyal, A. (2004). Demographics, stock market flows, and stock returns. *Journal of Financial and Quantitative Analysis*, 39(1), 115–142.

Howard, M. (2018). *Mastering the market cycle: Getting the odds on your side*. London, UK: Nicholas Brealey Publishing.

Kettell, S. (1990–1992). *A complete disaster or a relative success? Reconsidering Britain's membership of the ERM*. Coventry, UK: University of Warwick.

King, S. D. (2017). *Grave new world: The end of globalization, the return of history*. New Haven, CT: Yale University Press.

Kopp, E., and Williams, P. D. (2018). A macroeconomic approach to the term premium. *IMF Working Paper No. 18/140* [online]. Available at https://www.imf.org/en/Publications/WP/Issues/2018/06/15/A-Macroeconomic-Approach-to-the-Term-Premium-45969

Kuhn, M., Schularitz, M., and Steins, U. (2018). Research: How the financial crisis drastically increased wealth inequality in the U.S. *The Harvard Business Review* [online]. Available at https://hbr.org/2018/09/research-how-the-financial-crisis-drastically-increased-wealth-inequality-in-the-u-s

Lansing, K. J. (2018). Real business cycles, animal spirits, and stock market valuation. *Federal Reserve Bank of San Francisco Working Paper 2018-08* [online]. Available at https://www.frbsf.org/economic-research/publications/working-papers/2018/08/

Lenza, M., Pill, H., and Reichlin, L. (2010). Monetary policy in exceptional times. *ECB Working Paper Series No. 1253* [online]. Available at https://www.ecb.europa.eu/pub/pdf/scpwps/ecbwp1253.pdf

Lincoln, E. J. (2002). *The Japanese economy: What we know, think we know, and don't know.* [online] Washington, DC: Brookings Institution. Available at https://www.brookings.edu/research/the-japanese-economy-what-we-know-think-we-know-and-dont-know/

Loungani, P. (2001). Deciphering the causes for the post-1990 slow output recoveries. *International Journal of Forecasting*, 17(3), 419–432.

Martin, J. (2009). *When China rules the world: The end of the western world and the birth of a new global order*. London, UK: Penguin Books.

Miranda-Agrippino, S., and Rey, H. (2015a). US monetary policy and the global financial cycle. *NBER Working Paper No. 21722.*

Miranda-Agrippino, S., and Rey, H. (2015b). World asset markets and the global financial cycle. *CEPR Discussion Papers 10936.*

Mueller-Glissmann, C., Rizzi, A., Wright, I., and Oppenheimer, P. (2018). *The balanced bear – Part 2: Chasing your tail risk and balancing the bear.* London, UK: Goldman Sachs Global Investment Research.

Mukunda, G. (2018). The social and political costs of the financial crisis, 10 years later. *The Harvard Business Review [online].* Available at https://hbr.org/2018/09/the-social-and-political-costs-of-the-financial-crisis-10-years-later

Musson, A. E. (1959). The Great Depression in Britain, 1873–1896: A reappraisal. *Journal of Economic History*, 19(2), 199–228.

Odlyzko, A. (2012). The railway mania: Fraud, disappointed expectations, and the modern economy. *Journal of the Railway & Canal Historical Society*, 215, 2–12.

Oppenheimer, P. (2004). *Adventures in Wonderland: Through the looking glass; Scenarios for a post-crisis world.* London, UK: Goldman Sachs Global Investment Research.

Oppenheimer, P. (2015). *The third wave: Wave 3 of the crisis and the path to recovery*. London, UK: Goldman Sachs Global Investment Research.

Oppenheimer, P. (2016). *Any happy returns: The evolution of the 'long good buy'*. London, UK: Goldman Sachs Global Investment Research.

Oppenheimer, P., Bell, S., and Jaisson, G. (2018). *Making cents; The cycle & the return of low returns*. London, UK: Goldman Sachs Global Investment Research.

Oppenheimer, P., and Jaisson, G. (2018). *Why technology is not a bubble: Lessons from history*. London, UK: Goldman Sachs Global Investment Research.

Oppenheimer, P., Kerneis, A., Coombs, S., Mejia C., Hickey, J., Ng, C., Pensari, K., and Savina, M. (2002). *Share despair: Anatomy of bear markets and the prospects for recovery*. London, UK: Goldman Sachs Global Investment Research.

Oppenheimer, P., Kerneis, A., Coombs, S., Mejia C., Ng, C., Pensari, K., and Patel, H. (2004). *Bear repair: Anatomy of a bull market*. London, UK: Goldman Sachs Global Investment Research.

Oppenheimer, P., Mueller-Glissmann, C., Moser, G., Nielsen, A., and Bell, S. (2009). *The equity cycle part I: Identifying the phases*. London, UK: Goldman Sachs Global Investment Research.

Oppenheimer, P., Mueller-Glissmann, C., and Rizzi, A. (2017). *Bull market, 8th birthday – Many happy returns?* London, UK: Goldman Sachs Global Investment Research.

Oppenheimer, P., Nielsen, A., Mueller-Glissmann, C., Moser, G., and Bell, S. (2009). *The equity cycle part II: Investing in phases*. London, UK: Goldman Sachs Global Investment Research.

Oppenheimer, P., and Walterspiler, M. (2012). *The long good buy: The case for equities*. London, UK: Goldman Sachs Global Investment Research.

Oppenheimer, P., and Walterspiler, M. (2013). *Long good buy II: 18 months on . . . the case for equities continues*. London, UK: Goldman Sachs Global Investment Research.

Reinhart, C. M., and Rogoff, K. S. (2008). This time is different: Eight centuries of financial folly. *NBER Working Paper No. 13882*.

Reinhart, C. M., and Rogoff, K. S. (2014). Recovery from financial crises: Evidence from 100 episodes. *American Economic Review*, 104(5), 50–55.

Rezneck, S. (1950). Distress, relief, and discontent in the United States during the Depression of 1873–78. *Journal of Political Economy*, 58(6), 494–512.

Schröder, D., and Florian, E. (2012). A new measure of equity duration: The duration-based explanation of the value premium. German Economic Association. *Annual Conference 2012: New Approaches and Challenges for the Labor Market of the 21st Century*, Goettingen, Germany.

Shah, D., Isah, H., and Zulkernine, F. (2019). Stock market analysis: A review and taxonomy of prediction techniques. *International Journal of Financial Studies*, 7(2), 26.

Siegel, J. J. (1992). The equity premium: Stock and bond returns since 1802. *Financial Analysts Journal*, (48)1, 28–38.

Siegel, L. B. (2017). The equity risk premium: A contextual literature review. *CFA Research Foundation Literature Reviews*, 12(1).

Spierdijk, L., Bikker, J., and van der Hoek, P. (2010). Mean reversion in international stock markets: An empirical analysis of the 20th century. *De Nederlandsche Bank Working Paper No. 247* [online]. Available at https://www.dnb.nl/en/news/dnb-publications/dnb-working-papers-series/dnb-working-papers/working-papers-2010/dnb232375.jsp

Vissing-Jorgensen, A., and Krishnamurthy, A. (2011). The effects of quantitative easing on interest rates: Channels and implications for policy. *Brookings Papers on Economic Activity,* pp. 215–265.

Wright, I., Mueller-Glissmann, C., Oppenheimer, P., and Rizzi, A. (2017). *The equity risk premium when growth meets rates.* London, UK: Goldman Sachs Global Investment Research.

Wright, J. H. (2012). What does monetary policy do to long-term interest rates at the zero lower bound? *Economic Journal*, 122(546), F447–F466.

Zhang, W. (2019). Deciphering the causes for the post-1990 slow output recoveries. *Economics Letters,* 176(C), 28–34.

Index